MAGDA AND ANDRÉ TROCMÉ

MAGDA AND ANDRÉ TROCMÉ

Resistance Figures

EDITED BY PIERRE BOISMORAND

TRANSLATED BY JO-ANNE ELDER

INTRODUCTION BY MICHAEL D. BESS

McGill-Queen's University Press

Montreal & Kingston • London • Ithaca

English translation of *Magda et André Trocmé: Figures de résistances*

ISBN 978-0-7735-4352-2 (cloth)
ISBN 978-0-7735-9190-5 (ePDF)
ISBN 978-0-7735-9191-2 (ePUB)

Legal deposit second quarter 2014
Bibliothèque nationale du Québec

Printed in Canada on acid-free paper that is 100% ancient forest free (100% post-consumer recycled), processed chlorine free

This book has been supported by funding from the Jewish Community Foundation. Funding was also received from the French Ministry of Foreign and European Affairs, as part of the translation grant program. Cet ouvrage a bénéficié du soutien des Programmes d'aide à la publication de Culturesfrance/Ministère français des Affaires étrangères et européennes.

Funds have also been donated by Charles Malécot.

McGill-Queen's University Press acknowledges the support of the Canada Council for the Arts for our publishing program. We also acknowledge the financial support of the Government of Canada through the Canada Book Fund for our publishing activities.

Library and Archives Canada Cataloguing in Publication

Trocmé, Magda, 1901–1996
[Magda et André Trocmé. English]
Magda and André Trocmé : resistance figures / edited by Pierre Boismorand ; translated by Jo-Anne Elder ; introduction by Michael D. Bess.

Translation of: Magda et André Trocmé.
Includes translations of sermons, letters, published articles, diaries, and speeches from the war years and from the 1920s to the 1970s.
Includes bibliographical references and index.
Issued in print and electronic formats.
ISBN 978-0-7735-4352-2 (bound).–ISBN 978-0-7735-9190-5 (ePDF).–
ISBN 978-0-7735-9191-2 (ePUB)

1. Trocmé, Magda, 1901–1996. 2. Trocmé, André, 1901–1971. 3. Righteous Gentiles in the Holocaust – France – Le Chambon-sur-Lignon – Biography. 4. Jews – France – Le Chambon-sur-Lignon – History. 5. World War, 1939–1945 – Jews – Rescue – France – Le Chambon-sur-Lignon. I. Trocmé, André, 1901–1971, author II. Boismorand, Pierre, editor III. Elder, Jo-Anne, translator IV. Bess, Michael, writer of introduction V. Title. VI. Title: Magda et André Trocmé. English.

D804.66.T76T7713 2014 940.53'180922 C2014-900655-1
C2014-900656-X

This book was designed and typeset by studio oneonone in Sabon 10.5/14

Contents

Introduction Michael D. Bess

Between 1940 and 1944, the villagers of a remote mountain region in south-central France quietly defied their own government and the occupying forces of Nazi Germany, saving the lives of some 5,000 refugees, including about 3,500 Jews. While the rest of the world seethed with the organized violence of all-out war, this group of people created a clandestine safe haven of activist Christian love, opening their homes to strangers from all over Europe. They knew full well that they and their families risked deportation or execution if they were caught by the Gestapo. But they had reached the conclusion that true adherence to the teachings of Jesus left them with only one path to follow. Amid these dire circumstances, under the yoke of Hitler's Reich, the parable of the Good Samaritan became, for them, not just an abstract ideal but a call to direct and purposeful daily action.

This book explores the lives and ideas of two key figures in this remarkable story, skillfully pieced together from their own letters, essays, sermons, and diaries. André Trocmé was the Protestant pastor of the community of Le Chambon-sur-Lignon, one of the principal villages along the Plateau Vivarais-Lignon that undertook the rescue of Jews during the war; his Italian wife, Magda, was his spiritual and practical partner in this endeavor. After the war, both of them received the title of Righteous Among the Nations, bestowed by Israel's Yad Vashem foundation, in honor of those non-Jews who risked their lives to save Jews during the Holocaust. More broadly, Magda and

André Trocmé are increasingly recognized today as major personages in the history of twentieth-century pacifism and non-violent activism. This book shows us, in their own words, how they came to be the extraordinary people they were – their inner struggles, doubts, and misgivings as well as their faith and ideals. It traces a long journey of self-discovery by two moral pioneers as they gradually unearthed within themselves the strength and the clarity to achieve what they did.

▲▼▲

André Trocmé was born in 1901 in the northern French town of Saint-Quentin, in Picardy, near the Belgian border. His father owned a textile factory, and through his second wife, who was German, the family had numerous close relatives in Germany, whom young André got to know quite well as he grew up. His memories of the German occupation of his town during the First World War are poignant, therefore, because he was forced at this early age to experience the contradictory emotions brought about by the military occupation of his home by people from a culture that was not at all foreign to him. André was in his mid-teens when he experienced what he was later to describe as his religious calling. He became intensely involved in Christian youth groups, many of whose members came from working-class backgrounds; these friendships helped him to understand and empathize more vividly with the plight of the poor and the labouring classes. His academic studies came to be increasingly oriented toward a career in the Protestant clergy.

But his relationship with the Protestant church of France proved to be a tempestuous one. By the time he had reached his early twenties, he had gradually come round to a theological and philosophical position of social Christianity, as well as of uncompromising pacifism and non-violence – and this put him at odds with the church hierarchy, which continued to uphold a doctrine that affirmed the right (and duty) to bear arms on behalf of one's nation in times of war. With typical forthrightness, the young clergyman André Trocmé informed his superiors in the church that his conscience would allow him to do no such thing – and that he would not be shy in letting his parishioners know about his beliefs. The leaders of the church responded by obstructing or delaying his parish assignments, and only reluctantly accepted his service in small, marginal parishes where his dissenting voice would not be widely heard. It was in this fashion that, in 1934, he came to a position as the pastor of a village lost amid the forested highlands of south-central France, Le Chambon-sur-Lignon.

He was accompanied by his wife, Magda, whom he had met during a year-long stay in New York in 1926, where he had come to study at the Union Theological Seminary. Magda had been born in Florence in 1901, the daughter of an officer in the Italian Army and a mother who was descended from Russian Decembrist émigrés who had rebelled against the Czar in the early 1800s. She was exactly the same age as André, but a very different kind of person. Where André was rather shy, contemplative, and introverted, Magda was fiery, talkative, and outgoing. Where he preferred solitude and reading, she made friends easily. Where he tended to be a dreamer, she was stubbornly practical, down-to-earth, plain-spoken. But this basic difference in their characters should not mislead us: both were fiercely intelligent persons who thought for themselves and possessed keen critical minds. Both of them felt a passionate need to live their daily lives in consonance with their moral values, and both were strong-willed individualists, willing to buck the trends of the mainstream society and culture if their conscience called for it. Both were richly endowed with humour and a zest for life. Their marriage offers an unusually strong example of spiritual and intellectual partnership.

By 1934, when they moved to Le Chambon, the Trocmés had four children. André worried that his meagre salary as the pastor of this tiny parish would prove insufficient to his family's needs; but Magda's resourcefulness and tireless work around the household allowed them to make ends meet. André ended up working very closely with his assistant pastor, Édouard Theis, who shared his deep belief in non-violence and Christian witness. The two men became lifelong friends. In 1938 they founded a new school in the village, the École Nouvelle Cévenole (later renamed Collège Cévenol), dedicated to fostering the values of international cooperation and brotherhood. (The word "Cévenol" refers to the nearby mountain range of the Cévennes.)

Unfortunately, the timing was not good, for Europe was sinking rapidly into war. After the French surrender in June 1940, Hitler divided France into two halves. The northern part of the nation was under direct German occupation; the southern half would be administered from the small town of Vichy by a new puppet government, under the leadership of the old war hero, Marshal Philippe Pétain. Pétain's worldview was resolutely authoritarian, traditionalist – and anti-Semitic. The policies of his Vichy regime therefore meshed closely with the social and racial policies of the Third Reich. During the Second World War, more than 75,000 Jews were deported from France into the German network of slave-labour camps and extermination camps – with the active collaboration of the French police and government. Most of those deported did not survive the war.

From their pulpit in Le Chambon, Trocmé and Theis unflinchingly advocated noncompliance with any new laws that contravened the Christian conscience of their parishioners. But this, they believed, was not enough. In grim times like these, the duty of a Christian was not merely to engage in meek noncompliance, but to cross over the line into proactive resistance. It would be a rigorously non-violent form of resistance, however, animated not by hate but by an adamant insistence on Christ's teachings of justice, peace, and brotherly love. Unlike the armed antifascist resistance – which was also gradually being organized in the surrounding countryside by some opponents of Vichy and the Germans – this antifascist movement would be waged by means of what Trocmé called "the weapons of the spirit."

The villagers, many of whom were descended from Huguenots who had been persecuted centuries before for their religious beliefs, were in an unusually good position to empathize with the desperate refugees knocking at their doors. What followed, in the village of Le Chambon and the surrounding hamlets and countryside of the Plateau Vivarais-Lignon, was one of the more extraordinary episodes of militant goodness in modern history: hundreds of persons, quietly breaking the laws of a notoriously ruthless and efficient police state, over a period of four years of foreign occupation and war. Although not everyone in Le Chambon and the other villages participated actively in the ongoing rescue operation, not a single person ever ratted out his neighbors. Working together, villagers and farmers gradually built up – *invented, improvised*, it would be more accurate to say – a system for harbouring the Jews and other refugees who came to the remote mountain plateau seeking safety. They housed them temporarily in barns or vacant summer rental rooms in their farms, but also in their own homes when necessary. They fed them, out of the meagre provender of a rationed wartime economy. They found persons who could equip them with false identities and forged documents. Then they sent them, by means of secret routes and safe houses – a sort of underground railroad – across the Rhone Valley to neutral Switzerland. From there, the fleeing Jews could make their way eventually out of Europe, into the safety of the Americas. Some 3,500 Jewish men, women, and children thereby escaped deportation and the Holocaust.

It was dangerous work. Trocmé and Theis were arrested at one point by the Vichy police, along with one of their close co-workers, Roger Darcissac, and placed in an internment camp; but they did not give up their non-violent struggle, and resumed the rescue work as soon as they were released a month later. In June 1943 André's nephew, Daniel Trocmé, was arrested by the German police; the young man had been taking care of Jewish children and university-age youths in a pair of foster homes in Le Chambon, and refused to be separated from his wards when the soldiers came to take the older youths away. Daniel Trocmé was therefore deported along with a number of them, and died in 1944 in the German concentration camp of Majdanek. André Trocmé was arrested again in 1944 by German soldiers in Lyon, but improvised a way to escape (the jaw-dropping account of how he managed this reads like a thriller by John le Carré). Shortly afterwards, he and Édouard Theis were informed by a contact in the antifascist resistance that their names were on a list of persons targeted for assassination by the Gestapo. They therefore went into hiding for the final months of the war, until the liberation of France in June 1944. But even then, with their two pastors gone, in those final months of increasingly brutal German Occupation, the villagers and farmers of Le Chambon and the Plateau Vivarais-Lignon continued their rescue operation as before.

One might expect that, in the years after 1945, as the emergency of war receded and the long task of rebuilding unfolded, the new French government of the Fourth Republic would have proudly held up the story of the Trocmés and the Plateau Vivarais-Lignon as a shining example of national achievement and moral leadership. But this is not what happened. In order for the French government to have officially recognized this remarkable story, it would also have been necessary to acknowledge what all those Jews were fleeing from – and this would inevitably have raised difficult questions about the broad support that the collaborationist Vichy regime had received among the French population. Official commemoration of the wartime resistance therefore focused on less complicated sites of memory, such as the village of Oradour-sur-Glane, in which French villagers had been straightforwardly the victims of Nazi brutality. The story of Le Chambon went untold and unsung.

I myself spent a splendid year in Le Chambon in 1973–74, as an American student at the Collège Cévenol that Trocmé and Theis had founded back in 1938. Three grandchildren of the Trocmés were among my classmates. Yet no one told me anything about what had transpired in this village during the war. In the eyes of the Chambonnais, what they had done during the wartime years had been simply their duty as Christian believers. To have made a fuss over it in the aftermath, showcasing their deeds, would have amounted to a deplorable form of pride and self-promotion. So the story went largely unrevealed and unexplored until historians began gradually piecing it together, decades later. I only discovered what had happened in "my village" many years later, in graduate school, when I came across Philip Hallie's wonderful account, *Lest Innocent Blood Be Shed*.

But the remarkable life-trajectory of André and Magda Trocmé does not end with their achievements during the Second World War. Within a few years, they had thrown themselves wholeheartedly into working for the International Fellowship of Reconciliation (IFOR), a pacifist organization that had formed in the aftermath of the First

World War. By 1947, they had left Le Chambon and moved to Versailles, where they served as co-directors of the Mouvement International de la Réconciliation, the French branch of the IFOR. From this new post, they helped launch an international campaign against nuclear weaponry, traveling far and wide to disarmament conferences and peace rallies. In 1958 they organized one of the first non-violent protests in France against the civilian uses of nuclear energy, staging a sit-in demonstration at one of France's nuclear reactors in the Rhone Valley at Marcoule. A little later, as the Algerian uprising precipitated a crisis in the French government, they emerged as prominent and outspoken opponents of the "dirty war" being waged by the French army in its efforts to hold on to the Algerian colony. Even after André accepted an invitation in 1960 from the Church of Saint-Gervais in Geneva, Switzerland, to become its new pastor, their tireless activism continued unabated. By the time André's health began deteriorating, leading ultimately to his death in 1971, they had logged together another full decade of writing, travel, and advocacy on behalf of non-violence and international peace.

Their personal papers, public writings, and other biographical documents have been assembled and archived at the Swarthmore College Peace Collection in Pennsylvania.

▲▼▲

As we stand back and survey the lives of these two figures, reflected in detail through the first-hand materials assembled in this volume, two key features stand out. First and foremost, it becomes clear that what they achieved did not happen by chance: people like André and Magda Trocmé are not just born that way, with a goodness that emerges effortlessly on its own. They struggled at it, and worked at it, animated by a combination of deep humility and a seemingly unquenchable desire to bring their character and deeds into greater consonance with their moral values. What they were able to accomplish during the war in Le Chambon was the result of a sustained effort of painstaking moral preparation that had begun decades before – and it was an effort that continued unabated, long after the war had ended in 1945. The goodness that they brought into the world was not just a miracle that appeared out of nowhere. It was more like a garden that you have to nurture over many years before you begin to harvest its fruits.

This is what makes their story particularly compelling – and morally challenging. For the Trocmés do not emerge from this volume as shining, saintly figures far removed from the grit, struggle, and moral ambiguity that characterizes ordinary people. Their letters, sermons, and diaries reveal them in the full richness and depth of their humanity – as persons who wrestled again and again with spiritual doubt, moral failings, and character flaws, as much as any of us. These first-hand testimonials therefore bring their goodness within the reach of other ordinary people like you and me. It suggests that this kind of goodness is something that any of us can aspire to cultivate within ourselves. We may not succeed at achieving the remarkable things that the Trocmés did, but such an accomplishment does not lie utterly beyond our reach. Therein lies the challenge that their example presents to each of us.

André and Magda Trocmé actively sought, throughout their lives, ever-renewed ways to embody their non-violence in concrete action. Theirs is not just a Second World War story, but a story of entire lifetimes lived in an active search for a deeper and more resonant brotherly love. In this sense, the way they lived their lives seems to beckon to us, saying: whatever your life-circumstances, whatever the particular trials of injustice, violence, or inhumanity that history brings to you, the ultimate challenge always remains the same. It is to seek each day anew, as they did, a greater degree of consonance between our values and our deeds.

Chronology

	ANDRÉ TROCMÉ	MAGDA TROCMÉ AND THE TROCMÉ FAMILY
1901	Easter Sunday, April 7: André Pascal Trocmé is born in Saint-Quentin, an ancient city in northern France, to Paul Trocmé, a French industrialist, and Paula Schwerdtmann, a teacher and the daughter of a German pastor. André has nine half-brothers and half-sisters from his father's first marriage, as well as a brother, Pierre, born in 1899. The Trocqmé / Trocmé family is thought to have converted to Protestantism in the 17th century.	November 2: Magda Grilli di Cortona is born in Florence, Italy, to Oscar Grilli di Cortona and Elena Nelly Wissotzky Poggio. The Grilli di Corona family is an old, aristocratic family from Tuscany; the Wissotzky family are Russian exiles. Magda's mother dies a month after her birth, and she is raised by Italian nursemaids, then German and English governesses.

	ANDRÉ TROCMÉ	MAGDA TROCMÉ AND THE TROCMÉ FAMILY
1910		Magda's father remarries. She is not invited to the wedding and is distanced from her family by her stepmother. Magda has a stepbrother and two stepsisters from this marriage.
1911	June 24: André's mother dies in a car accident. He is raised by German governesses after this time. September: He begins studies at the Lycée Henri-Martin in Saint-Quentin.	Magda enters the Mantellate convent school in Florence. Under pressure she is re-baptized as a Catholic, but she later rejects this baptism and refuses to go to confession.
1914	August 28: Saint-Quentin is occupied by the German army. The Trocmé family is forced to provide lodging to German officers.	Magda visits Russia with her grandmother, Varia Wissotzky, to see her grandfather, now a senior Russian officer. During this visit, Magda witnesses the catastrophic beginnings of the Great War.
1916	After a year of religious instruction, André is confirmed in the Saint-Quentin church. He joins the Union chrétienne des jeunes gens, or UCJG, a Protestant youth movement.	

	ANDRÉ TROCMÉ	MAGDA TROCMÉ AND THE TROCMÉ FAMILY
1917	February: Civilians in Saint-Quentin are evacuated. The Trocmé family leaves for Belgium.	
1918	December: André moves to Paris and enrols in Lycée Buffon, where he becomes active in the Protestant student movement.	
1919	September: The Trocmé family moves to Rue Jacob, in Paris. André finishes his baccalaureate and begins his theological studies at the Faculté libre de théologie protestante de Paris, and in the religious studies program of the Sorbonne.	Magda passes her matriculation exams with honours. Her stepmother prevents her from going on to university, and instead places her in a girls' finishing school.
1920–23	André's studies are interrupted by his military service from 1921 to 1923. His liberal beliefs and his refusal to carry a rifle result in his being consigned to a "discipline company" and then a geographical unit. After his military service, André continues his studies in Paris.	1921: Magda passes the entrance exams for teachers' college with outstanding marks. In the next several years, she achieves excellent results in Italian literature, with a thesis on Dante. Because of her frail health, she is sent to a sanatorium for rest on two occasions.

	ANDRÉ TROCMÉ	MAGDA TROCMÉ AND THE TROCMÉ FAMILY
1924	André writes his thesis on prohibition and churches in the USA. He joins a pacifist organization (Conseil européen pour la réconciliation) and attends its congress in Germany.	Magda continues her studies and becomes active in the Young Women's Christian Association, where she works with young girls and single mothers rejected by their families.
1925	Spring: André finishes his studies in Paris. September: leaves for New York with a scholarship to Union Theological Seminary. October: hired as a French tutor for Winthrop and David Rockefeller.	Spring: Magda leaves for the US with a scholarship to the New York School of Social Work. She works as an intern with Italian immigrant families arriving in the US, and gives private lessons to make ends meet.
1926	During the summer, André spends time with the Rockefellers in Florida, New York, and Maine. He writes a thesis on a Swiss theologian, Alexandre Vinet.	Early spring: Magda meets André at International House, where she is living. They travel to Washington together. April 18: They become engaged.

	ANDRÉ TROCMÉ	MAGDA TROCMÉ AND THE TROCMÉ FAMILY
1926	He plans to travel around the world with Magda, but his father refuses to allow this. Paul Trocmé also refuses to allow his son to marry in the USA, as the couple had hoped. October: Under pressure from his father, André abandons the idea of doing his doctorate at Union Theological Seminary.	After her engagement, Magda spends two months resting in a sanatorium; her stay is a gift of the Rockefellers. Afterwards, Magda and André, complying with his father's wishes, go to France. November: André and Magda are married in Saint-Quentin and go to Switzerland and Italy on their honeymoon.
1927	André is hired as a pastoral assistant in the town of Maubeuge, not far from the Belgian border.	Magda and André move to Sous-le-Bois, near Maubeuge. Magda works with women in her husband's parish and with Italian miners' wives. August: Their daughter Nelly is born.
1928	September: André is called to Sin-le-Noble, in the industrial north of France, as a minister. He also serves the city of Douai and nearby villages. He and Magda attend several pacifist congresses in Italy and England.	Magda and André move to Sin-le-Noble. Magda is asked to teach Italian to immigrant children, but refuses because of the pro-Mussolini content of the curriculum.

	ANDRÉ TROCMÉ	MAGDA TROCMÉ AND THE TROCMÉ FAMILY
1930		Their son Jean-Pierre is born.
1931		Magda gains a diploma allowing her to teach Italian in French lycées. Their son Jacques is born.
1933		Their son Daniel is born.
1934	Spring: André applies for a job as a minister in first one French town, then another, but the church authorities refuse his applications because of his pacifist views. September: He is given a one-year appointment as interim minister in the small town of Le Chambon-sur-Lignon in south-central France.	 September: André, Magda and their four children move to Le Chambon-sur-Lignon. They offer room and board in their home to make ends meet. Magda becomes involved in the Union chrétienne des jeunes filles in the community.
1937	At the insistence of the local parish council, André is appointed senior minister in Le Chambon-sur-Lignon.	Magda suggests starting a Protestant secondary school for both girls and boys in Le Chambon-sur-Lignon, on the same model as one she had seen in Italy.

	ANDRÉ TROCMÉ	MAGDA TROCMÉ AND THE TROCMÉ FAMILY
1938	The Cévenol school is established.	Magda teaches Italian at the Cévenol school; she continues there until 1948.
1939	September: When France enters the war, André declares he will not bear arms. He offers his resignation to the parish council because of his pacifism. The council rejects his resignation.	
1940	André travels to Marseille to meet American Quakers about helping prisoners in French internment camps; by the end of the meeting, he has decided to organize shelter for refugees in Le Chambon-sur-Lignon, which is located in the Vichy-ruled portion of France rather than the area under direct Nazi control.	As well as lodging their boarders, the Trocmés begin hiding Jewish and other refugees in the manse. From 1940 to 1944 Magda is deeply involved not only in the care of her family, teaching, and parish activities, but also in assisting the refugees who come to stay in her own home and in the surrounding area.
1941	Paul Trocmé, André's father, dies.	1941–42: The Trocmés' activities intensify. The shelter given to refugees becomes an ever larger part of their work.

	ANDRÉ TROCMÉ	MAGDA TROCMÉ AND THE TROCMÉ FAMILY
1943	February 13: André Trocmé, Édouard Theis, and Roger Darcissac are arrested and detained in a prison camp near Limoges. March 16: After several influential figures intervene with the Vichy regime, André is released. July: André and Édouard Theis are told their lives are in danger. André goes into hiding. He suffers from severe back pains. He writes a book on theology, *Oser croire*, which is finished in 1944 but would not be published until after his death.	January: Alice Reynier, nicknamed Jispa, arrives to stay with the Trocmés and help with their work. She becomes like a member of the family and remains so until her death in 1989. June 29: André and Magda's nephew, Daniel Trocmé, is arrested by the German police, along with eighteen students, ten of whom disappear or die during their deportation.
1944	André is arrested at the train station in Lyon-Perrache but escapes. June 14: He returns to Le Chambon-sur-Lignon. Autumn: Allied troops capture the south of France, ending the war in that region.	August 13: Their son Jean-Pierre dies following a tragic accident. He is buried in Le Chambon-sur-Lignon.

	ANDRÉ TROCMÉ	MAGDA TROCMÉ AND THE TROCMÉ FAMILY
1945	The war finally over, André takes part in a conference of the Fellowship of Reconciliation, an international organization for non-violence, held in San Francisco at the year's end. He raises funds for Cévenol school thanks to the efforts of an activist American couple, Carl and Florence Sangree, and meets Tom Johnson, a teacher and conscientious objector whom he invites to Le Chambon-sur-Lignon.	
1946	André's time is divided between his pastoral duties and his work as European secretary of the Mouvement International de la Réconciliation (MIR), the French-speaking section of the International Fellowship of Reconciliation (IFOR). He travels to Sweden and the USA as part of an extensive series of lecture tours which he continues until 1960.	December 1946 and early 1947: Magda goes to Italy on behalf of the Mouvement International de la Réconciliation, renewing contact with pacifists there.

	ANDRÉ TROCMÉ	MAGDA TROCMÉ AND THE TROCMÉ FAMILY
1947	May–June: He travels to Germany. In July, he takes part in a workshop at Le Chambon-sur-Lignon led by the philosopher Paul Ricœur, on "education for peace."	
1948	July: second workshop at Le Chambon-sur-Lignon, on the theme of violence and non-violence. August: a trip to Finland.	The Trocmé family moves out of the manse in Le Chambon-sur-Lignon, into a rented villa. Magda works with André for IFOR.
1949	Trips to Germany, Japan, and southeast Asia. July: third workshop at Le Chambon-sur-Lignon. André's work as European secretary of IFOR becomes a full-time position.	October: Magda goes to India as one of France's representatives at the "World Pacifist Meeting." She then travels to Pakistan before returning home in February 1950.
1950		André and Magda move to Versailles and open the Maison de la réconciliation, an international centre for peace. Magda, along with Jispa and other volunteers, becomes even more deeply involved with IFOR's work.

	ANDRÉ TROCMÉ	MAGDA TROCMÉ AND THE TROCMÉ FAMILY
1951	March: a trip to Spain. April: trip to Italy and then England. November-December: lecture tour in the USA.	
1952	Two trips to Germany. 1953	
1953	October-December: trip to the USA.	Spring: André and Magda travel to Tunisia, Algeria, and Morocco (all still under French control).
1954	April-May: trips to Israel, Lebanon, and North Africa.	Summer: Magda travels to the USA on a lecture tour for IFOR.
1955	Trips to Algeria, Vietnam and Cambodia, and the USA.	
1956	Attends a pacifist congress in Italy. Travels to Kassel, Germany to lead a workshop on non-violence.	April 10 to May 22: André and Magda go to Algeria, where they help to organize literacy classes, especially for women. October-December: Magda travels by ship from Naples to New York. She gives a series of talks in churches working with Martin Luther King for civil rights.

	ANDRÉ TROCMÉ	MAGDA TROCMÉ AND THE TROCMÉ FAMILY
1957	André joins with members of the Church of the Brethren (a German movement dedicated to pacifism and social justice) to create a group for conscientious objectors in Morocco; he returns to Morocco in June and September. Spring: Travels to Germany and Italy.	
1958	May 24: André gives a forthright interview about Algeria in *Le Monde.* July 31 to August 31: Trip to Japan. Late 1958: Trip to the USA.	April: André and Magda organize a protest in Marcoule, an enormous nuclear site in southern France. May: Trip to Algeria, where they witness horrific events in Algiers. July: Travel together to Germany, Poland, and the Soviet Union.
1959	Travels in England, Germany, Austria, Switzerland, Italy, and Spain. April 16-19: Attends a peace congress in Prague.	

	ANDRÉ TROCMÉ	MAGDA TROCMÉ AND THE TROCMÉ FAMILY
1959	Co-founds the Fédération française contre l'armament atomique. October: Trip to the USA.	
1960	January: Trip to the USA. André looks for a new parish in France, but without success. May: Appointed pastor of the Church of St Gervais in Geneva, Switzerland.	Magda moves with André to Geneva. Over the next decade she will teach in three Geneva schools.
1961		Their son Daniel dies. He is buried in Le Chambon-sur-Lignon.
1964	André starts a vocational program to train diesel mechanics in Algeria.	
1965	June 27–July 12: Trip to war-ravaged Vietnam and Cambodia.	
1966	April–May: Trip to Algeria.	
1970	André retires in Geneva.	

	ANDRÉ TROCMÉ	MAGDA TROCMÉ AND THE TROCMÉ FAMILY
1971	January: The Righteous Among the Nations medal is awarded to André. He asks to receive it at a ceremony in Le Chambon-sur-Lignon on May 31. However, he is hospitalized for back surgery and dies following several unsuccessful operations on June 5.	June 12: At André's burial in Le Chambon-sur-Lignon, Magda is given the medal on her husband's behalf.
1972		Magda and Jispa move to Paris. Every summer, until 1986, they spend a month in Le Chambon-sur-Lignon, where they continue to have many close friends.
1980	John Yoder, an American theologian and pacifist, asks that André and Magda Trocmé's archives be given to the Peace Collection of Swarthmore College, near Philadelphia, which has Quaker roots. The request is granted.	

	ANDRÉ TROCMÉ	MAGDA TROCMÉ AND THE TROCMÉ FAMILY
1981		Magda is awarded an honorary doctorate from Haverford University in Pennsylvania, for her own work during the war and on behalf of the residents of Le Chambon-sur-Lignon. Rosa Parks is honoured on the same occasion.
1984		September: Magda receives the Righteous Among the Nations medal from Yad Vashem at the Israeli Embassy in Paris.
1987		Magda and Jispa move into the home of Jacques and Leslyn Trocmé in Vernouillet, about 40 km northwest of Paris.
1989		April 29: Jispa dies. She is buried in Le Chambon-sur-Lignon.
1996		October 10: Magda Trocmé dies.
1997		Magda's ashes are buried in Le Chambon-sur-Lignon.

Magda's father, Oscar Grilli di Cortona, as a soldier in 1916.

Magda's mother, the beautiful and short-lived
Nelly Wissotzky Grilli di Cortona.

André as a baby with his mother, Paula Schwerdtmann Trocmé.

André's father, the domineering Paul Trocmé.

André's difficult childhood can be glimpsed in this family shot from 1911. Sitting, from left: André; Louise Trocmé Dumas (his widowed half-sister); Paul Trocmé; Étienne Dumas (André's cousin and friend). Standing: Yvonne Dumas (Étienne's sister), Pierre Trocmé (André's older brother).

André Trocmé, 1925.

Magda Trocmé, 1925.

The four Trocmé children, July 1934.

A parish outing on a Sunday afternoon in 1936. André is holding the hand of his daughter, Nelly.

Hôtel des Roches (Maison des Roches), Le Chambon-sur-Lignon, one of the places where Jewish adolescents were hidden during the Second World War.

A wintry photograph of the Protestant church at Le Chambon-sur-Lignon, where André served as minister.

The interior of the Protestant church at Le Chambon. Engraving from the 1930s by Evelyn Bridge, an Englishwoman who vacationed there.

MAGDA
AND ANDRÉ TROCMÉ

1

The Beginning

André Trocmé's childhood and adolescence unfolded in a stable, protected, middle-class setting, but also in a rather lonely atmosphere. His father owned a lace factory in Saint-Quentin, a small town located in Picardy, northern France and, in this well-to-do Protestant family, there was little room for fantasy. In this passage André, as an adult, remembers the atmosphere of his early years.[1]

I considered my childhood home normal: eighteen rooms plus the kitchen and the service rooms … So large for me as a little boy that I only got to find my way around it gradually. Duty was the key to everything in my house. A sense of duty that prevented us from expressing our feelings, talking about our dreams, or showing our enthusiasm. I remember feeling enthusiastic then, just as I do now. My mood or my interests would rise to a peak and then, it seemed to me, come crashing like waves on the overly smooth banks of a river that was too narrow.

However, personal and international events eventually shook up this orderly and tranquil routine. First, there was the death of André's mother in 1911, when he was ten years old, then the horrors of the First World War, the occupation of Saint-Quentin and the requisition of their family home by the German Army, then forced exodus to

Belgium. Finally, as a teenager, he discovered Christian faith and pacifism. All this marked and shaped his personality. And yet, André Trocmé would need to wait until he was an adult and he met Magda to negotiate the necessary distance from his upbringing. At that point he was able to begin his life as a non-conformist minister, a man committed to the Word, and an independent thinker. As we learn about his life, his ministry, his causes, and his struggles for peace and justice, we will see that they were deeply affected by his childhood, his background, and his education.

Late in his life, in 1968, looking back at everything that had happened to him, he wrote:

> Today, I still live as if I were hanging … from what? From my faith. Not a naive faith inhabited by angels, Christ-figures, miraculous shows of divine intervention, but a faith in which action and free will play a large role. I have learned to deliberately turn my gaze from what is absurd in order to focus on what is intended, what *must* be now and in the future. Why will peace come one day? Why will the truth be revealed? Why will justice win out? I do not know. I have found no proof for these things in the past, in the present, or in the foreseeable future of humanity. The major obstacle does not seem to be the mean-spiritedness of men, but their stupidity, their social climbing, their incommensurable naivety. In such conditions, why do I still have faith? For two reasons, probably. First, because I was raised in a simple and austere religious climate, without any bells and whistles or any need to question the harsh circumstances of earthly existence. My faith, in order to survive and sustain me, needed to have a global lens, to wager not only on the existence of God but also the possibility of goodness on earth… In order to maintain my faith, I had to be able to see that everything could be embraced by it: society, the Church, my family, my children, the members of my congregation. This meant that there was a practical side to my ministry, even though I have never considered myself a practical man. If something cannot be translated into deeds and actions, then it doesn't interest me.[2]

As for Magda, her background was also quite privileged, and was international: the people around her were Russian, Italian, and English. Her difficult childhood and adolescence made her an independent young woman, sometimes anxious and lonely but with a resilient and strong disposition. Magda's life was marked by the loss of her mother only three weeks after her birth from problems related to the delivery. Her mother's death, for which she was held responsible, resulted in a sense of guilt that only made her feelings of isolation worse when she was ignored by her father's new wife. She was also torn between several cultures and religions. These experiences sensitized her to suffering and injustice in the world, so that she was understanding and compassionate very early in life.

Her sense of human connection and very practical notion of solidarity were similar to André's, but André was more mystical and introspective. Here is André's description of his wife:

> Magda, alone in the world, would become my wife, and became closer to me than would have been possible for any woman who was nostalgic about her childhood home. Her life was my life; she married not only a man, but his career and his vocation. She did it with rare passion and intelligence, because the temptation to look back in regret did not stand in her way. And I, who had never liked the past, whose eyes were firmly turned to the future, I now had a helpmate whose acute sense of the present moment and the importance of human beings could fill the gaps in my character. And, in turn, I could bring Magda a sense of security and a calmness that she sorely needed. Happily married couples, I believe, are not idealistic. Happiness comes mainly from the ability to put each other's interests before one's own and to appreciate the way each one's temperament complements the other's. There is also the balance of equality: it seems to me that Magda and I had equal weight in the marriage. Sometimes she would take the lead, when things had to be *done* quickly and properly, when it was time to take the risk of starting something new, when we had to recognize the true and distinguish it from the false. At other times it was my turn, when we had to distinguish what was essential from the feverish and somewhat

futile activities that got in the way, to set the direction of our ship and crew, to stay on course and stay on schedule.[3]

I have included here a few passages in which Magda and André give retrospective accounts of seminal moments in their lives, beginning in childhood and adolescence and continuing into their early adult years. In the following excerpt from her autobiography, Magda explains how – much too soon – she became aware of the reality of death and the fragility of life, and also talks about the childhood years she spent far away from those she loved.[4]

The Death of Magda's Mother, Nelly Grilli di Cortona

Lalli [her cousin] and I played with the other children and sometimes, out of breath and dripping with sweat, we stopped running and talked. Here is something we realized together: "Baby" (that was what people called me) has a father, and Lalli has a mother. But that isn't enough. Other children have a father and a mother. And then we began to understand.

The mysterious silences, the sentences cut short that we often heard, began to make sense to us. Georges had been Aunt Olga's husband. Now he was married to another Olga, a Russian princess. When people talked about him they minced their words and had a rather disdainful tone, even though he was Lalli's own father. We didn't know what a divorce was, but we knew that this Georges had abandoned Lalli's mother. He had abandoned Lalli right after she was born [...] And Baby's mother, my mother, where was she? Well, she was this Nelly that no one dared mention in front of Grandmother! That explained Grandma's tears, which dripped down her face so often, and her sad expression when she looked at me. There were photos of this Nelly, a tall, pretty woman, blond and fair with blue eyes, slender, a little distracted and dreamy-eyed, as if she was dreaming of the life she never had, the husband she had for only ten months, and the child she could hold in her arms for only twenty-five days!

Yes, Nelly died at the age of twenty-three years and four months, despite the promising future that lay before her, despite the true love of her husband and the deep love of her mother and despite the fact (which I found much more tragic) she had a newborn baby! Why had she died? What did it mean to die? And why would death take away mothers who were so young and beautiful? But who was there to talk to about these things? How could I even try? What would I say? How could I ever understand?

And then it was old Maria who died, the caretaker's wife. People were tip-toeing around the entry-way, at the bottom of the staircase, in front of the big coloured-glass door. They took Maria away. I didn't see anything, and this mystery, this silence were almost more terrifying than the real explanations would have been. So this was death. I was afraid and couldn't sleep.

With Maria gone, Giovanni was alone. But it wasn't long before he married Genoveffa and had a son, Enea. Genoveffa was much younger than Giovanni, but she had a wandering eye, perhaps from an injury. That is why she married an old man like Giovanni. Enea was born anyway. And there you are, death and life, the loss of some people and the birth of others. Why?

One day, one of the housekeepers, I don't know which, told me: "É lei che ha ammazzato sua madre!" ("You're the one who killed your mother.") I knew very well that it wasn't true, that it wasn't me, but I was afraid. It was sad, it was vile, it was mean to say that, more stupid than mean, actually. Words like that stay with a child.

The Death of André's Mother, Paula Trocmé

The day he turned fifty-seven, André Trocmé wrote to his children: "The would-be philosopher that I have always been made it hard for me to be fully aware of the reality of the people and things around me."[5] He was totally immersed in his ministry and his numerous obligations, and his life was, as he said, a "whirlwind." Occasions to stop and reflect on his life were rare so, as with Magda, it was only in the last years of his life, and usually during holidays, that he worked on his autobiography.

The book, referred to here as *Mémoires*, is a valuable source of information about their life together, and helps us better understand some of the details about the Trocmés. The following text from the 1960s tells us, in a very personal manner, about the circumstances of André's mother's death in 1911 and his feelings about them. André, who witnessed this painful event, was only ten years old at the time.

A home as deep as a cradle, maids to wash and dress you, a garden like a green bed, surrounded by walls, and nothing beyond it. Toys, a car that came up and parked alongside the sidewalk. They packed you up and put you into the car, and took you down the same roads. At the end of the trip was another house, lighter, another garden, and an endless forest. And there was, of course, Mother.

Mother entered every morning by the side door. I realize now that is what she did, because she doesn't do it anymore. She sang, she was tall and strong, in a nightgown with long sleeves. She opened the curtains. Was I ever held in her arms? Of course. I don't know. She must have had heavy, soft breasts. Her face must have been clear and pleasant. Did I see her? Didn't every child in the world, at that time, have a mother like mine, who came in singing and opened the curtains? All this I only discovered later, by looking at photos and touching souvenirs. I didn't realize it before that day, because I had always lived the same way.

The weather was splendid on June 24, 1911, the day I was born. High wheat stalks blew in the breeze in the country. Wheat ready to harvest. I didn't know that. I have learned it by experiencing June 24 in other years.

The car was parked alongside the sidewalk. I can barely imagine what the antique car looked like. I was a child during those pre-war years, and to me it was beautiful. Nothing better existed at the time: it was as pleasing to the eye to the men of the day as whalebone corsets were to my mother.

There were three children in our family, two boys and a girl behind Daddy, and Mother in her veil. And if nothing had happened that day, I would never be able to remember the minuscule details that I want to share and that are engraved on my memory, because that was the day I was born.

So Daddy didn't take the regular route that day, the long boulevard between two rows of trees that continued straight ahead for thirty kilometres. He didn't take it, he said, because it was such a fine day, and we shouldn't miss the flowers in full bloom in the countryside, and we would go to pick honeysuckle near the woods. He didn't take the regular route because destiny had carefully set up the scene that would play out that day. The railroad crossing just outside town happened to be closed, which always upset Daddy, and that made it possible for a little jalopy to squeeze ahead of us on the narrow and dusty road we were driving on. Fate had decided to make Daddy angry that morning, and he was having one of those tantrums, superficial and stupid in nature, that vanished as soon as the driver's hands left the wheel and his feet touched the soft grassy ground, and which never bothered anyone. And when the gate went up, the jalopy took off and Papa, amidst our shrieks of joy, took off right after him. Oh, let me tell you, what a great race it was, and how magnificent and determined our Daddy was, behind the wheel of his "limousine," showing the jalopies of the world they would be left behind. The jalopy sent a thick cloud of dust up from its tires and we drove through it, unaware of the landscape, the spring, the road, danger.

And then it happened, inscribed in history long before it happened, since the beginning of time: Daddy would cause Mother to die.

I have died a hundred times, a thousand times since then, died in that accident. A hand that grabs another, raises it and lowers it again, crushes it. An atrocious howl of agony from five suffering beings. A jackhammer. Where did it come from? Immense, infinite, brutal, and so ironic, so indifferent. The thing that we call death, that is nobody, not even a skeleton with a scythe that we can discuss things with. This thing, this nothingness, ravaged us, crushed us, left us in a twisted heap of metal. And then there was nothing except for the crickets singing in the fields and the drops of gasoline dripping. Every time I hear about a train derailment, a plane crash, a shipwreck, a shell exploding, I think that it is the same thing, the same nothing, brutal and devastating.

A thousand times, I have died along with Mother.

Motions of people struggling, climbing, moaning. Desperate efforts to loosen the grip of death. The three children, and Daddy, clasping his shattered wrist, all standing near the twisted metal, shaking, laughing like idiots because we had lived through it.

And then one of us saw Mother. No, already it was no longer Mother. On the road, ten metres behind, covered in dust, a body lay motionless. The legs were slightly parted, and there was a thin trickle of blood from the right corner of her mouth. Eyes closed. Not closed like someone asleep, though: closed like the windows of a house left empty a long time ago. A facial expression of pride, indifference. The mark of the thing that is nothing. And the nervous laughter of those who had escaped death was transformed into silent tears, jaws clenched to hold in the screams, to keep from trembling even more.

People came. Where did they come from, in this deserted countryside? And from the odious jalopy (oh, how I hated the people from the jalopy), the jalopy stopped on the road, people came and fussed over us, full of pity and compassion.

Mother was laid on the bank, with the reddish foam around the mouth of this bobbing head. A doctor. A taxi from out of nowhere. Life had resumed, in spite of everything, and there was movement. It was in that instant that, in a sudden cry, I understood. It all hit me: I no longer had a mother, I had an aching body, an aching heart, an aching soul. I was a man.

At home, in the big bedroom next to ours, for hours and hours, Mother moaned. She did not come into the room, in her nightgown, to open the curtains. I was born. The horrible, raspy sound of her shallow breathing, interrupted by endless pauses, still echoes in my ears. A machine. An automaton. A thing. Not my Mother.

I saw her again a few moments before her death. Her real death had occurred on the road, but for the doctor, and on the death certificate, that was the day she officially died. I could no longer recognize her in the white linens wound around her head.

Mother, I know today that you left, you obeyed, because you had to, because I had to be born that day, as one day, when it is time, I will have to leave so that others will be given life through my death.[6]

Discovering Freedom

In the following account, André remembers his encounter with the realities of war and the emotions he experienced during a vacation in August 1914, when German troops arrived at his family's country residence in Saint-Gobain, about thirty-five kilometres south of Saint-Quentin. He then describes the shock of discovering the occupied city when he returned to Saint-Quentin. When he considers his mother's German family, his inner conflict deepens and he becomes very emotional. In retrospect, we can see that these troubling events were formative for the thirteen-year-old boy he was and contributed to the pacifist he would become.

A faint grumbling from the north, so faint we weren't even sure we had really heard it. Our hearts stopped beating, and the air stopped moving on that sweltering afternoon at the end of August 1914. The children stopped playing in the yard. For three weeks, France and Germany had been at war. I was thirteen and I was both exalted and crushed about what I was hearing: men going to war, soldiers fighting near Liège.

Was it possible that the Germans who had savagely attacked France were the same people I had known since childhood? The same uncles and aunts and cousins from Germany I knew so well, who had gone swimming with me the year before in a river near Braunschweig? No, the Germans who attacked us and who were the soldiers in the stories told by grown-ups in the parlour were other people, people with pointed helmets who fought for a Kaiser who was intolerable and a braggart.

I was enraged against the Germans. In my notebook, I drew war-like figures facing French uniforms (red pants and gold ribbons). I fought against them. I was the general, leading a hundred thousand Tommies with irresistible weapons. I surveyed the enemy forces from an airplane, watching as they turned tail and ran away. But these cannons, far away in the north?

Newspapers reported nothing. The man in the street said it was a military exercise. Papa, so wise, so different from the others, who had fought in the Franco-Prussian War, said that the situation was serious and people were hiding the truth from us.

The British had arrived. Someone had seen them. They had shouldered their rifles in the woods near Vandricourt. So the battle was drawing nearer. Something was going to happen. My exaltation transformed itself into determination: I felt compelled to do something, to take decisive action. Outside, I appeared to be the same calm, big boy I always was, relegated to the clan of children kept away from the adults who reigned in the parlour and whose discussions were not supposed to concern me. I was not allowed to read the newspaper. The message from the parlour was distilled for me, "a child who cannot yet understand." Pierre, my older brother, who was fifteen and a half at the time, was allowed into the "upper chambers." I had to be satisfied with the gossip of the maids. How insulting! While tea was served in the parlour, while Pierre cut out a map from the newspaper and put little flags on the Belgian border, while the cannons rumbled faintly in the north, I was preparing to undertake a major action.

I was torn between two impulses. Part of me wanted to fight against the Germans in their pointed helmets, show them what a young Frenchman was capable of [...] We had to impress them and show them we were not afraid of them. But the other André, the other child was still there. This was the André with happy memories of Germany, who knew, on some level, that the soldier wearing the foreign uniform might be cousin Wilhelm. It was said that Germans burned and shot and cut the hands off children. Everyone knew that. Yes, this is what I would do: when the Germans came in, I would go and meet them alone. I would have a white flag. I would talk to them, using the German words I had learned from my governesses. I would explain to them that they must not destroy this village or shoot its inhabitants. The Germans would understand. I would be a mediator, like the young woman from Jericho in the Bible. She hung a crimson cord from the window in her house.[7] I would put a white flag at the entryway into the village. A white flag or a French flag?

It was the red, white and blue flag that won out. Why? Because I found a little flag in the attic, one we used for Bastille Day. It was already there, and I would have had to sew a white one myself. It would have been complicated. So while the parlour discussions continued and became more vocal as the cannons became louder and we knew the Germans were really coming, I went to work. I did not say anything to the grown-ups about it; adults never understand anything about children's ideas. I climbed up the tallest apple tree in the orchard and tied the French flag on the highest branch. There, Germans! You see? We are French and we are not afraid of you.

The next day, when I got up, the flag was flying cheerfully in the sun, and Papa had left for the train station to get money and news. It was an anxious day. The parlour had lost its composure; people were fighting only sixty kilometres away. The cannon rumbled constantly, and the rhythm of its thunderous shots echoed through our overwhelmed and silenced hearts.

Four o'clock. Papa came back with a little two-seater car that he had to buy in Saint-Quentin. The last trains had left the city. The Germans were coming. Papa could not leave his little ones alone in the country, and in wartime no expense was too great. To get back to his family, he had no choice, and a few thousand francs did not matter. It was a blur of activity. We had to leave Saint-Gobain right away, the countryside where no one knew anything, where the crickets were singing as if nothing was happening. We got ready and left for the city, in two cars, in the space of half an hour. We had to take our valuables, some linens, close up the house … and all the while the cannon was thundering in our ears, drilling our nerves like a wasp buzzing endlessly, putting the parlour's nerves on edge.

It was at that moment that the grown-ups noticed the little French flag flying from the top of the apple tree …

"Who put that up there?"

"I did!" I announced. I stepped forward, proud as punch. I had made sure the Germans knew they could talk to someone here. I was expecting the praise of the parlour. Hadn't they been igniting my patriotic fervour for months?

But today the adults were ignited by the rumours they had heard, stories of hands being cut off and villages being burned down. They did not understand. "A flag!" "It's like an alarm!" "You'll attract the Germans, and make them mad!" "Have you lost your head, child?"

The engines were already revved up, ready to go. Too bad.

"Hurry! Climb up and get your flag down! You'll get us all shot!" […]

On the road, the two cars were trembling and the parlour people, already settled into their places, were waiting impatiently for the perpetual latecomer.

It took two and a half hours to travel the thirty kilometres that separated the village, in the south, from the city. An endless stream of pitiful refugees and impeccable British troops on dazzling vehicles, were moving south. Stupefied, they watched the crazy people marching to the sound of the cannon in the opposite direction. Saint-Quentin was as empty and stiff as Sunday clothes. The inhabitants had shut themselves into their houses, while the roads shook from the thunder of cannon fire and the stammer of rifle shots nearby. A few kilometres north, a battalion of French troops, scantily armed, was sacrificing itself to cover the retreat of the British Expeditionary Forces.

Then I understood what had happened. The French flag had failed and it was time for the white flag. The support of the parlour had abandoned me in my heroic gestures. Now they would approve of me in my call for peace. I would go to see the Germans. I could not let Saint-Quentin burn and its citizens be massacred. I would go …

It took a long time to get to sleep in my little winter bed. When I finally did, it was because of all of those little things grown-ups do to make children feel that life is continuing normally and they are safe while the ground is shaking. Meanwhile, the parlour people stayed awake and talked in the room upstairs.

The next afternoon, the bloody remains of the regional battalion were strewn throughout the city and the Germans had moved into Saint-Quentin. All morning, there had been an absurd sense of optimism. The Germans were dispersed, or surrounded. Defeated. The story was repeated all over town. At five o'clock in the afternoon, a regiment, marching in perfect order as if in a parade, marched down the boulevard on the other side of the public gardens. There was no doubt; they were British. We could hear the bagpipes of the Scottish troops. Running up and down paths in the park, I was ready to go and greet them. Alas, ironic destiny takes pleasure in reducing our grandiose plans to nothing […]

The crowd came to life, took foot and fled: "Go! Quickly! It's the Germans!"

Panic-stricken (but also eager to be the first to announce the sensational news to the parlour), I rushed home. The shutters were closed and the Persian blinds lowered: orders from the parlour. Everyone was sent rushing to the cellar. One crash after the other in the streets. Gunshots? Yes, and also the blows of German axes smashing down doors that were not opened right away. I only knew what the noises were later. All I could hear then were the heavy boots and the rough voices of soldiers in the courtyard, looking for snipers on the ground floor.

And that was it. I did not see anything, I did not know anything that was going on. My heart was beating fast, and I heard only one noise. It was only two or three days afterwards that I found out what had happened and I saw, in the streets of the city, big trucks from the country loaded with hay and with pale wounded bodies, all that was left of the Saint-Quentin regiment. And it was only later that I learned (from the parlour people) that my own father had been taken by some Germans on patrol and pushed from one street corner to the next in front of them as a shield in case any of the French decided to shoot. But when I learned that, the Germans had already taken over from the French. They were in charge; their black, white and red flag had replaced the red, white and blue in front of public buildings, and German guards were posted in front of government offices instead of French ones.

It would continue this way for four and a half years. My dreams and my plans had vanished: not only had the parlour forbidden me to act, but the reality did not look anything like what I had imagined. It never does. The man that we want to be – independent, courageous – is completely different from the little boy we always are, shaking and cautious.

But it was on the day of my personal defeat that I began to love freedom with great passion, and to long, with my whole child's heart, to set my true being free from any rules imposed by others and, what is more, free from myself.[8]

Magda's Religious Background

In order to better understand the existential path Magda Trocmé's life took, it is important to understand some of the relevant aspects of her religious upbringing and education.

As a child in Florence, Magda was baptized into the Protestant Church. However, for reasons that she will explain herself, she was baptized again in the Catholic Church. According to the people who ran the Catholic institution in which she was placed, "Protestant ministers baptize with water that is not pure, rosewater, even! Their baptism is not valid for us. So we have to baptize you again, just in case, by saying: 'If you are not baptized, I baptize you in the name of the Father, the Son and the Holy Spirit.'"[9]

Many years later, when Magda wrote about the rather unusual circumstances of her second baptism and her change of denomination, her description is rather comical.

The more I think about it, the more this second baptism seems a ridiculous imposition. I was born on November 2, 1901; my mother died on November 27. She had said she wanted to become Protestant, like my father, although my father was actually a Protestant very much on his own terms and she, too, was Orthodox on her own terms. Father Lewitzky, the Russian Orthodox priest, had heard nothing about this decision, so he came to bury her. His daughter, a good friend of my mother's, did not know either. So everyone was utterly surprised by the fact that, on November 29, Reverend Guymonat, the founder of the Waldenesian church in Florence, also came to bury my mother. The Italian Vaudois or Waldenesians are considered the first Protestants, before even Luther and Calvin; they were French who had come to Italy in the 16th century, after the Luberon massacre. I was there, and he baptized me as a Protestant. *This baptism, that took place while I cried, that resulted from a serious decision made by my father and my mother, this baptism was not valid?* I still cannot believe it! The baptism was registered by the Reformed Church of France, in Florence: the church wrongly called the Swiss Church, because so many French Protestants, persecuted in their homeland in the 18th century, had fled to Switzerland. I certainly started life with a bizarre religious beginning![10]

Protestant? Catholic? Orthodox? What was Magda's true religion? The future would decide.

So I said that I wanted to be a Catholic. Could a child between eight and eleven years of age make that kind of decision? Grandmother did not say anything; she did not dare to, given how complicated the family situation already was. Papa admitted later that he thought if I became Catholic it would make the family situation less complicated and, as we were living in a Catholic country, it would make it easier for me to marry later … Deeply troubled by the fear of Hell, I did not want to change my mind, despite the challenges I faced.

I had to take religious education classes that contradicted everything I had learned without realizing I was learning it. In my sad room on Via Leone X, trembling with fright each morning at the thought of what I would go through in the evening, I copied out long Catholic prayers that I recited with more fear and distress than joy.

How could I really concentrate on the bizarre words I recited? How could I not think about other things instead? […] I was always alone. It was only at school and at Grandma's house that I had any company.

It was not a simple thing to go from "heresy" to "truth." Who should be chosen to teach me? […] I was to receive instruction from a great prelate, a great theologian, who was also an expert on the *Divine Comedy*: Padre Magri. Despite his good intentions, how could such a man understand the horror, the terrors of a little girl who was seeking security rather than Theology with a capital T?

The beautiful Or' San Michele church is one of the splendours of Florence. But for me, it remains a chamber of horrors. There used to be an awful little vestry in the left corner of the church. It is not there anymore. It was poorly-lit, musty, with an acrid smell. This is the room where Padre Magri was. He would take a snuff of tobacco powder, and suck peppermints, and combined with the humidity in the room and the incense wafting in from the sanctuary, the odour suffocated me morally and physically; I was frightened.

Grandma asked to go with me to the lessons. Padre Magri refused.

This is where I made my first confession "in visu," without the benefit of a confessional. This is where I began to question my scruples. What did it mean to be good, to live a proper life? Where was the line between good and evil? And what a lot of sins existed to tempt us … Which ones had I actually committed?

We decided I would have my confirmation at the same time as my cousins in the private chapel of the Archbishop of Florence, rather than in a crowd of ordinary mortals! The ceremony took place: I carried a candle in my hand and a ribbon of white silk with golden sparkles was placed around my head, covering the spot on my forehead where the Archbishop put some holy oil […] And now I was a Catholic, safe from the dangers of Hell, but still a little ashamed I was not like the rest of them, a "convert" rather than born into the fortunate lot of the chosen. I was one of the unhappy ones condemned to be better than the others, and grateful for the "grace" I had been granted.

And yet, I was not really Catholic. Not yet. The obstacle course was not over. The priest who was supposed to prepare me for my first communion questioned the validity of my Protestant baptism. He was "more Catholic than the Pope"; despite being simply a priest, he was stricter than the Archbishop of Florence […] I was only about twelve years old, and I had to renounce my former religion, by myself, and in Latin. The word "renuntio" still rings in my ears. What in the world could a child like me renounce? […] So I was baptized. It was "mandatory." I was embarrassed, frightened, sad. The next day was my first communion. What anguish I suffered before the ceremony […] The priest came up to me, with tiny little quiet steps, wearing colourful and elaborately embroidered robes. I did not know why he was dressed that way. He held a Host between two fingers. He placed it on my tongue. The linen hanging from the railing was there to make sure that no crumbs fell on the floor, but if they fell on the linen, what would that mean? This time it was a real Host, consecrated, the real body of Jesus … but … I did not feel anything. Nothing at all. The Heavens did not open, my body was not struck and did not shake, my spirit remained the same as always, worried, expectant, disappointed.

So?

So … nothing.[11]

Besides these stories, which reveal something of her early years, we also have abundant evidence of Magda's faith, and know that she was inspired by a strong religious conviction for the rest of her life. As she once put it: "Yes, I was a Protestant, perhaps more of a Protestant than those who called themselves that. My religion was a true protest, and still is."[12]

A German Friendship

This story, about which André wrote during the 1960s,[13] took place in 1916, when part of northern France was still occupied by German troops, Saint-Quentin served as a rear base and hospital centre for the German army, and the Trocmés were forced to receive officers as guests in their home.

André's conversations with Kindler, a young Christian pacifist in the German army, are especially surprising considering he was only fifteen years old at the time. He managed to overcome conventional hatred of the enemy and realize that the young man who shared his ideas could be a friend. This discovery led him to introduce Kindler into the *Union chrétienne des jeunes gens* circle that he was attending, at the risk of dishonouring himself.[14] This was an important step in establishing a link between Christian faith and conscientious objection. Consequently, their meeting is essential to understanding the commitments André would make later.

I was the accidental intermediary in the UCJG's discovery of Christian pacifism.

The ever-changing stream of German officers and soldiers who lived on the second floor of our house was of no interest to us. Sometimes we would meet the men on the stairs, and their heavy boots would give off a strange odour of leather, sweat, damp fabric, and tobacco. The Battle of the Somme was well underway. After the first hopes of liberation, a sombre mood and deep-rooted hatred had taken over the population. The entire city had been converted into a hospital. The smell of carbolic acid and occasionally of gangrene hung in the air. At night, trains full of bodies returned from the front to the rear base, where they were incinerated.

The true horror of war was revealed to me one day when I met a miserable column of injured Germans making their way from the train station. Transportation, both horses and automobiles, had become so rare that anyone who could still walk had to get to the hospitals to which they had been assigned on their own. In the first row, I saw three men, all wounded and bandaged. The one in the middle had a ball of bandages instead of a head. He was obviously unable to see, and stumbled and dragged himself along with the help of his comrades. When he got closer, I realized, with horror, that his lower jaw was missing. In its place were bandages from which clots of dried blood hung. My heart was in my throat. I did not know what the war was before that moment. Young men inevitably have a sense of illusion so that they believe that war is a heroic duel, a boxing match, and that courage will send the opponent down onto the ground. It takes a spectacle like the one I have just described to make them confront face-to-face the truth of what they have done to their brothers, to make them realize that they are guilty of these brutal murders and there is no turning back. I could no longer hate this man without a face. I walked back home, disgusted and devastated.

A few days later I met a German in our staircase. He stopped, looked at me kindly, and touched my arm with his hand.

"Bist du hungrig?" ("Are you hungry?") he asked. He awkwardly held out a chunk of black bread, the famous Kommisbrot marked with a K for Kartoffelbrot (potato bread) and which we called KK (caca).

"No," I answered in German, "I'm not hungry, and even if I were I wouldn't take your bread because you are an enemy."

"Nein, nein," he said, "Ich bin nicht dein Feind." ("No, no, I'm not your enemy.")

"Yes you are," I persisted. "You are my enemy. You are wearing that uniform, and tomorrow you might kill my brother, who is fighting you and trying to get rid of you. Why did you come here, to our house, and bring us war, suffering and misery?"

"I am not who you think I am," he replied. "I am a Christian. Do you believe in God?"

My face lit up. This kind of language was what filled my whole life, and I understood.

"We found Christ in Breslau, and we turned our lives over to Him."

Then he gave me the details, told me the name of the denomination he belonged to (I forget the name now) and continued: "Men cannot raise their hands against anyone who has put his faith in God. One day, a man who hated our group and what we believed in came into the room to kill the leader. His pistol caught a ray of sunlight, and we knew it was a sign from Heaven. I will not kill your brother. I will not kill any Frenchman. God has revealed to us this truth: that no Christian shall kill. Never. We will never carry weapons!"

"But how do you manage that, if you're a soldier?" I asked.

"Well, I explained what I believed to my captain, and he gave me permission not to have a weapon. Ordinarily, telegraph operators like me have a pistol or a sword, but I don't have anything. I'm often in danger, and between messages I will sing a hymn and pray to God. If He has decided to keep me alive, He will do so. If not ..."

I was thoroughly impressed. The sincerity of this man was evident. For the very first time, I found myself looking what would later be called a conscientious objector in the eye. If he had been French, I might have become indignant: "What? You refuse to defend your country, which has been invaded and trampled on by the enemy?" But I was dealing with a German, a man who refused to take part in an obscene mission. His faith and courage were plain. I trusted him without any hesitation. I had met a true Christian, a Christian like all of us in the UCJG should be, like God, Who has revealed to us what we should be.

My friendship with Kindler – that was the courageous young man's name – gave me the solution to the contradictions adults had presented to me, which had poisoned my soul. In that brief meeting my nationalism and my respect for the military collapsed. I saw the war for what it was: a frightful chaos in which belligerent men, alternately criminals and victims, disobeyed God and took what they claimed was justice into their own hands, meting it out in His place with each shot of their cannons. Without considering the consequences, I invited Kindler to come to the UCJG the next Sunday. He accepted [...]

My UCJG comrades were visibly surprised when I introduced the German soldier. Some of them put up a wall of distrust. But when I explained that this man was a true Christian, that he did not kill because he wanted to obey the teachings of Jesus Christ, Kindler was accepted into the group. He said a few words, which I translated, and taught us a hymn that I can still remember. The "newcomers" to the UCJG giggled a bit when they heard *Alleluia Alleluia A-men! A-men! Alleluia Alleluia A-men! A-men!*

In any case, it was easy to remember and soon everyone was joining in cheerfully with Kindler. We knelt down to pray, according to our custom. The thunder of the battle in the distance never let up. Men were killing each other. Here, however, several Frenchmen and a German were opening their eyes to the tangible reality of God's kingdom. Kindler prayed in German. I think it was one of the first times that I prayed out loud, delivering my secret thoughts to God.

Kindler left for the front a few days later. He brought me up to his room. We prayed together. Then he gave me some papers and photos, a roll of duct tape, and a pair of cutting pliers.

"Keep this for me until I come back," he said. "You'll see us when my regiment gets back from the front. If I'm not there, it means I've been injured or killed or taken prisoner. If I'm injured or taken prisoner, you'll hear about it. If you don't hear from me, it's because God has taken me back to Him. In that case, please send these things to my wife, at the address I've written on the paper."

I never heard from Kindler again. After a month's time, I sent the papers back to his wife, and that was that.

Many years later, when I was studying theology, I heard

about Christian pacifism and I had the same experience of direct revelation that had happened when I listened to Kindler. Of course he refused to shoot! That was what the Gospels of Jesus Christ said to do, and anything men add of their own accord is a corruption of His teaching.

Towards Liberation

Given his austere Protestant upbringing and the fact that he had grown up without his mother, who had left him much too soon, it is understandable that André became a timid and introverted adolescent. Taking part in the Protestant youth movement and undertaking an increasing number of duties gave him an opportunity to gain self-confidence. In particular, his experiences in the Federation led to his active involvement in community work, a heightened sense of responsibility, and many close and lasting friendships.[15]

André describes a period which he considers a turning point in his life. He decided to begin his studies in theology and to become a minister, and moved to Paris with his family.

Every morning I walked to the Lycée Buffon […] This was the first time I had lived in a really big city: a rapid-transit train, lots of traffic, the Babel of soldiers of every colour and nationality, enjoying demobilization … all of this thrilled me.

I was seventeen years old, tall and heavy. A photo of me taken at this time shows me with heavy, angular features, dressed in a tight blue wool jacket cut from a Lycée uniform worn in Saint-Quentin before the war! […]

Two of my teachers were very good to me and taught me so much. One was my literature teacher, an odd-looking man whose name I have forgotten, with a little goatee, constantly suffering from a cold, so that he had a red knitted scarf tied around his neck and a drippy nose. But when he talked about Jean-Jacques Rousseau or the Romantics, the magic of his lecture enthralled us. I got good marks in his class and that encouraged me. Then there was Mr Sauvage, a redhead with tousled hair who taught English. He had fought in the war and had emerged from it a revolutionary, rebelling against violence. His passionate rhetoric echoed deeply in my conscience.

Papa lived by a set of principles which included going to church on Sunday morning in Plaisance, a little building in the 14th arrondissement, because he had a prejudice against "Parisian gentlemen." Papa, who had been seen as such a bourgeois in Saint-Quentin, disliked the important bankers from the right bank of Paris whom he had met at the church synods.[16] So we went to Plaisance.

The minister, Reverend Édouard Sautter, was an energetic, bearded man who spoke eloquently and overflowed with affection. He was one of the few ministers I have met who was adored by his congregation.

He picked me out of the group and "hooked me up" with the UCJG members at the Plaisance. That is how I came to meet up with the young people I loved to be with, for the first time in two years [...] We had fervent prayer meetings, heartfelt hymn-sings, long and frequent (perhaps excessive) talks about purity. I remember certain Sundays, coming home by myself late at night after a UCJG meeting, walking along Boulevard Pasteur where the festivities under the sky train were in full swing: shooting galleries, an anatomical museum, merry-go-rounds, swings, freak shows, nougat candy, roulette ... Boys my age had their arms around the waists of young girls who shrieked with fear and delight. Girls approached me; I hurried away, stiff-necked, my head high, avoiding them with a mixture of fear and disdain, confusing vice with innocent fun. Papa told us: "I know I can trust you." Oh, how right he was! He had marked us for life. Life was black and white: pure and righteous at church, at the UCJG, on walks in the Meudon woods; and corrupted at the movies, the circus, and brothels. In any case, Babylon[17] held no attraction for me.

On Sundays when there were no UCJG meetings I would go with my family to Aunt Pauline's and Aunt Alice's [...] Children owed everything to their elders, while the older generation owed nothing more to the young than a cup of tea and some cookies.

But going there was a family ritual. In my aunts' parlour, the family criticized (not meanly, of course, no, never!) all the boys and girls who did not descend directly from our lineage [...] Woe to those who were only second or third cousins; they were all "characters" or good-for-nothings. As for those who were not related to us, why, they were never mentioned. They did not even exist for us. Well, we did talk about ministers, who got what was coming to them: the "excellent" Henri Monnier, Wilfred Monod who was "in the moon" and the "excitable" Henri Dartigue, and so on. What connection there could be between morning worship and these conversations, I had no idea. One day I exploded and stormed out the door because Aunt Pauline had expressed her stupefaction about "those bare-headed women, those working women who dared buy chicken now!" My visits with my aunts became fewer and further between once I was labelled a zealot and a socialist.

At the end of the 1918–1919 school year, I wrote my first baccalaureate exams. The end of high school was quickly approaching.

At the Lycée Buffon, I had two friends, who took me to a meeting of Christian students at the Lycée: the "Left Bank" group, a junior branch of the Federation. Diény was (imagine!) the president of the entire Paris chapter of the junior branch. He was a thin, nervous boy with eyes that darted all over the place behind heavy glasses. He was filled with a deep and inexhaustible religious enthusiasm, and his mind (he was, in fact, brilliant), buzzed with prophetic visions and grandiose plans.

One day, the "Left Bank" met and I was put in charge of the "laïus" or introduction. The Federation loved using "argot" or Parisian slang. I talked about the "use of vacations" and, true to form, I tried to put things as simply and clearly as I could. Papa reminded me constantly to do this, and I am grateful to him for it. Diény, like a whirling dervish, was in constant motion on his chair, his cheeks feverishly red. I stammered from time to time, afraid of being rebuffed. When I finished, Diény opened the discussion. When it was time to leave, he took me aside and told me, "Hey, what you said was so interesting! We need you for our magazine!"

"Our magazine": I still have a few yellowed copies of *Notre Revue*, a minuscule magazine containing sixteen pages edited and printed for the Christian Lycée students. The *Revue* represented, in my mind, the Holiest of the Holy, and only the Anointed had the right to write for it.

But this was not the last time I would be surprised. Diény extended a warm invitation to go with him to the Domino Camp.[18] The idea had Papa's blessing, because he had sent Pierre to Domino in 1914. The vacation would not be too expensive and would be good for me. The war had loosened Papa's principles a little; he would now allow us to sleep in a tent. Besides, the camp counsellors at Domino kept an eye on everything.

Domino was on the island of Oléron, huddled in the midst of kilometre-wide dunes and little white farms in the interior, an acre or so of torrid sand. A long, low warehouse was used as a kitchen and cafeteria. A dozen comical tents called "Marabout" were installed in a small pine-wooded area. At Domino, we pranced about half-naked (I was reminded of the refugee boy in Saint-Quentin, who always wore a tie but still had straw-soled sandals; the first time I bought a pair of shoes that did not lace up to my ankle I felt light and frivolous.)

We spent happy parts of the day sunbathing in our "swim shorts," releasing gleeful catcalls into the summer air. We came into contact with the Anointed. One of them, on the very day the camp directors decided to charge a fine of 1 franc (to be donated to mission work) to anyone who swore, collected us all together at lunch and had us shout a loud SHIT in a chorus of 90 delighted voices, collecting 90 francs for the Missions. The scandal and glee was such that, for the rest of our stay at the camp, we would say "Mission" every time we wanted to swear. It cost nothing and meant everything. Having this kind of casual and humourous exchange with the Anointed changed my feelings about authority figures.

There was André Nick, a handsome Greek god, and his

brother Pierre. There were little theological and literary gaggles. Albert Léo, a man with skin as dark as a Moor's, with a profile like an eagle's and eyes as sharp and deep, taught us lessons about the historical Jesus I will never forget.

There were scouting exercises in the dunes, where actual little mountains appeared alongside deep valleys that were perfect for climbing. And last but not least, there were swims in the ocean with its rolling waves that crashed the full length of the beach. Only the best swimmers ventured across the bar that separated the less experienced campers. At low tide, we collected oysters hidden among the rocks. At sunset, we started sing-alongs with familiar folk songs and ended them hours later with hymns, psalms, and prayers.

For the first time in my life, I learned to enjoy myself.

In September, after my summer at Domino, I went home to a new place. Papa had bought some furniture and rented an apartment on the third floor of 30 Rue Jacob, right in the heart of the Latin Quarter!

Despite the lack of creature comforts, the apartment on Rue Jacob has good memories for me. I had finally broken out of my shell, and went from one extreme to the other. In 1919, I was admitted into my first year of theology, an exception to the normal rules because I had not yet completed my second baccalaureate diploma. Along with my Hebrew and Greek courses in the Faculty of Theology,[19] I took collegiate philosophy courses (logic, moral philosophy, and psychology) at the École alsacienne, and studied natural history, cosmography, German, and English on my own at home. I was busy: I was the president of the Paris chapter of the Federation of Christian Lycée students (which meant visiting Rouen and Le Havre), and the representative for the local group in Clamart, a suburb of Paris. In July, I caught the mumps two days before my baccalaureate exams, and was bedridden due to complications. However, I passed the final exams that marked the end of my secondary education that October with 18/20[20] in philosophy. I had certainly made the most of my philosophy classes.

Letter from Morocco

In September 1921, André Trocmé interrupted his theology studies to complete his military service. He was first posted to Compiègne, a city on the Oise River in northern France, and assigned to the 54th Infantry, where he took his training, and then sent to the north of France and to Morocco until the summer of 1923 to work with the Army Geography Division. He undertook his military service after already being exposed to Christian pacifism but justified this decision by saying he wanted to test his religious vocation by participating in the experiences of other men.

The time André spent working under the flag of France was valuable, enriching him by distancing him from a somewhat stifling family and student environment. But he also encountered major challenges, for instance when he refused to use a rifle or when he explained to his superiors that he did not want to wear the corporal's ribbons they had awarded him. When an explanation was demanded, André replied that he was "a theology student who had made a commitment before God not to kill, and that he could not teach others to kill."

In 1923, the French branch of the Mouvement International de la Réconciliation (MIR) was formed out of a group of students at the Faculty of Protestant Theology in Paris. André had returned to his studies and joined the company of Henri Roser, Jacques Martin, Jacques Babut, Jean Bresch, Robert Chéradame, Charles Vallée: a large group that stood in determined opposition to the war. Certain of them were imprisoned at the beginning of the 1930s for being conscientious objectors and refusing military service.

In these paragraphs from a letter published in January of 1923 in the *Bulletin des isolés* (a newspaper published by students from the Faculty of Protestant Theology in Paris who were dispersed throughout various regiments during their military service) André denounces the atrocities perpetrated by the French while Morocco was a protectorate.

Facts that I have realized, little by little, about the behaviour of colonists and especially of the military, leave me transfixed with horror: Arabs hanged on the cross, brutalized, whipped to death, their wrists slashed, others beaten with boots in their private parts, stomachs, and face! And eyewitnesses have told us these stories, matter-of-factly, as though they are natural and sensible. What a monstrous debt of sin the French are accumulating. Alcohol, too, has been making strides over the last four or five years, invading a population already ravaged by syphilis. Here, too, missionaries are needed, apostles like Charles de Foucauld, and there is no one![21]

Abandoned by Christian missionaries, Morocco is suffering from what appears to be the sole influence of French industrialism and commercialism. The previously humble Moroccan is becoming greedy. Western civilization is progressing at a desperate pace, in a frenzy like a gold rush, to replace an Islam which has become modern and decadent. Nothing can come of this but a terrible collapse of society. On the other hand, we cannot deny the positive role Europeans could play if, along with their love of money, they brought health and the knowledge of Christ.[22]

2

A Couple's Commitment

1925 and 1926 were very significant years in the lives of Magda and André Trocmé. Both made trips to the United States where their paths crossed. By the spring of 1925, André had completed his studies at the Protestant theological school in Paris and was due to start work as a pastor, but instead he decided to continue his studies. He won the scholarship awarded every year by the Union Theological Seminary in New York to a French student and left for New York at the end of the summer of 1925.[1] Like his predecessors (including Édouard Theis), he was hired as a French tutor to the children of the billionaire philanthropist John D. Rockefeller Jr. The year André spent in the United States enabled him to make valuable contacts who would help him during the Second World War, when he provided a safe haven for refugees in his parish, in Le Chambon-sur-Lignon, France. Some of the contacts also made generous contributions to his settlement work and to the school he established there, the Cévenol school.[2]

As for Magda, she found out that she had been offered a scholarship to the New York School of Social Work while she was travelling with an American tourist in Switzerland.[3] It was late August 1925 when she landed in New York, evidently with some misgivings. "The hardest thing," she wrote, "was probably the fact that I wasn't leaving anyone who was truly close to me, anyone I couldn't live without. I felt dreadfully alone."[4] Magda took courses and made ends meet by giving private classes. She also spent long hours teaching the

Italian immigrants who were clustered in the inner-city neighbourhoods of New York.

Magda and André did not find each other until six months later when they met at International House, the student residence where Magda was living. Soon afterwards, they took part in a tour of Washington, DC and discovered they greatly enjoyed each other's company; they became engaged on 18 April 1926. Three months later, after the end of the university year, they abandoned their plans to either continue their studies in the United Studies or go to India to work alongside Gandhi, and instead returned to Europe because André's father insisted he marry Magda in Saint-Quentin and begin serving a parish.

The Trip to Washington, DC

Over the Easter weekend in 1926, the Cosmopolitan Club arranged a tour to Washington for foreign students. When he found out that Magda was on the list for the tour, André decided to go too. Here is his story of spending his first few days with the woman who would soon become his wife.[5]

From the very beginning, the invisible link that joins two beings who are meant to understand each other and be together connected the young Italian woman and me. Christen (a friend of André's) came outside wearing a thin suit; it was chilly, and Magda immediately told him: "Hurry and get a sweater!" I thought, "Now there's a girl who looks out for others. She's not interested in turning heads; she sees them as they are, and cares." I didn't know at that time that my Italian friend was always too hot or too cold when others were, and that she would spend the rest of her youth putting blankets on our children or taking them off.

We visited the Washington Cathedral (which wasn't finished yet), the military cemetery in Arlington, the country home of General George Washington in Mount Vernon [...] But most importantly, there were the evening meals in a little bistro not far from the Potomac Falls which were still very wild at the time [...]

Little by little, as we talked, we got onto the topic of God, of Jesus Christ, and I felt that my words resonated in the Italian's heart. Her eyes looked straight into mine, unwavering in their gaze, and I was able to look her in the eye. Her eyes were magnificent, intelligent, and expressed a range of emotions in quick succession. Then she began to talk, and it was as if we were alone together. The others fell silent while we continued our dialogue. She, I, in the lamplight, and around us the blur of everything outside of us.

"So, she's Protestant," I thought, and I felt my heart leap. "This is the one; she's the one who will understand me! And she has the same thirst for freedom and adventure as I do, the same hunger for truth. She's brave and hates conventional rules."

But Magda continued to talk. "I wouldn't call myself Protestant," she was saying, "because I've never been able to affirm my belief in something I wasn't sure about. I would rather not define what I believe. Too much has been laid on top of what is essential, burying it under our human ideas."

Back to Europe

Half a century after the events, Magda Trocmé described their departure from the United States and her first impressions of André's family.[6] The story began in May 1926, when she was beginning a rest cure in a sanatorium: her engagement present from Mrs John D. Rockefeller Jr.

Clifton Springs Sanatorium in northern New York state. A sad, flat property [...] A main building, like a hotel, with parlours, a dining room, a ballroom, etc. Another building that housed the nursing school, and then all kinds of buildings in every direction for the various categories of patients. An odour of sulphur throughout, from the waters of Clifton, a little stream that crossed the compound, which spread a slightly nauseating, but apparently curative, odour. A large garden with carriages and chairs, patients lying down or being wheeled around. Some of them were really ill, and others were just on a rest cure. The latter sat in wheelchairs arranged in rings outdoors, if weather permitted.

I spent hours lying there, waiting. Waiting for what? To be healthy, but especially for André to come. He would visit every other weekend, when it wasn't his turn to look after the Rockefeller children. It took him all Friday night and then he had to leave again Sunday night to be back to work on Monday morning. Two nights on the train, two days together, a night at a hotel. A huge expense of money and energy, but what lovely visits! What wonderful conversations we had, two beings who loved each other and were discovering each other! And how odd our engagement was, with the bride-to-be in hospital!

How could we announce such a strange engagement in Saint-Quentin, especially to the pater familias, Paul Trocmé? How could we tell him that his only son planned to go to India for a year before taking up his parish duties?

André had written to Gandhi and Tagore. He had already received an answer, but it was more complicated now, with an engagement. And he had to announce his engagement to a person who needed to be taken care of, and who, besides, was an unknown quantity from a completely different background. What would Paul Trocmé say? "I have already made enough money at the Rockefellers' to pay for my trip to India and back," André wrote. "True; now there are two of us. But we're going to work over there or on the ship [it was still possible to do that in those days] to pay for our return to France."

It was a return for him, but not for me. I had never been to France. I had seen the French mountain ranges in the distance when I was on the Swiss side of Lake Leman. From Montreux, actually, you could see the stiff peaks of mountains, but no villages to speak of, only a soft dusting of houses around the lake that were often hidden by the fog. But the mountaintops looked beautiful on sunny days.

In my case, when I announced my engagement to my father, he replied: "Be careful. He said he was a theology student, that he was going to be a pastor, but how do you know it's true?" He didn't know that Union Theological Seminary was right across from International House and that André, the Rockefeller children's teacher, was very well known already. He also didn't know that the students from France said that André was the most intelligent student in their group.

Italians weren't afraid of the French, but the French bourgeoisie at the time considered Italians to be dirty, inferior, backward people, toting a rifle or at least a hidden pistol. These imaginary Italians were people who were as likely to murder hapless travellers in roadside ditches as to sing to mandolin tunes. They were also bicycle thieves.

There were also French people who had been to Italy, of course, and who had seen beautiful artwork there. In fact, they all knew about Dante, Leonardo de Vinci, and an adequate collection of popes. But that wasn't enough to reassure the French. The Italian Renaissance was hardly reassuring, either. There had been two young belles from Florence who had come to France, two young wives, but they weren't reassuring either: Catherine and Marie de Medici! Who was this Florentine woman André was bringing home from New York? And why from New York?

Paul Trocmé decided to compromise: "All right," he agreed, "you can marry the young woman you love. But the foolishness ends there. Forget about India. America was enough. We need you desperately in the Reformed Church in France." And that was it! His wish was our command. Farewell Gandhi, farewell Tagore, farewell our eastern dreams …

For the time being, I was on bed-rest in Clifton Springs.

Magda recovered from her tuberculosis and the couple sailed back to Europe. But it was not easy for her to step into André's world.

It was evening; we had arrived in Saint-Gobain and entered the vast dining room. As it was rather late and meals were always served on time, everyone had already eaten. There had been no question of waiting for the fiancée from America to arrive. Two places were set at the big dining-room table, and all around an impressive quantity of Trocmés were assembled: big ones and little ones, young ones and old ones, all sitting on chairs lined up against the wall. Just picture it! It was frightening for me, but I tried to put on a brave face. People were staring at me and I didn't know what to say. I'm told now that when I arrived I said, "André, I don't know what to say!" And now that everyone knows I talk a lot, people are surprised and amused by the fact that those were my first words.

The weeks before our wedding were an odd time. First, we had many, many problems. There was a lot of paperwork involved in order to get married. In America, we could have got married under a tree in a second; in France, the preparations were dramatic and drawn out. We had to wait thirty days to get an authorization from the Italian consulate. We had to write to Italy and request all the documents and have them translated by certified translators. It was a comedy of errors. And I was a guest in my father-in-law's house … It was an embarrassing situation. He was charming, but for me, having no family, it was a touchy situation. I was there waiting to be married, and we couldn't plan the wedding because without the paperwork we couldn't set the date. Jeanne and Marie were there, the cook and the chambermaid; they were good little chaperones and wanted to "keep an eye on us." When we wanted to be alone we went out to the very end of the garden and sat on a bench that we called "the moonlight kissing bench." There we could sneak a few kisses and talk to each other. The rest of the day, we had no privacy; there was always someone around.

Early Days in the Ministry

Early in 1927, André was named assistant pastor of a church in Maubeuge, a small city in northern France near the Belgian border, and began working under Pastor Paul Perret: "Perretto, as Magda quickly nicknamed him, was Swiss, and came from the area of La Sagne. The inhabitants of La Sagne have a reputation for being frank and forthright, and Perret was a perfect example of this character. He worked hard and expected others to do the same. His theology and his social values were similar to mine."[7] In Maubeuge, one of the most industrial areas of France, André and Magda found themselves in a difficult situation. André could still remember it vividly years later:

> The rust-coloured smoke from the steel mills fell on the rooftops, the walls and the ground and formed a greasy crust; it even penetrated the walls of the houses, getting inside them. The population … still wallowed in a crass existence that would be difficult to imagine if I hadn't seen it so often. It wasn't because they were poor – it would be hard to attract men to a job that ruined their health in twenty years without luring them with high wages – but the population wasn't interested in anything outside their life of forced labour and liquor. They would go to the shoddy local tavern and drink until they collapsed. The Maubeuge mission was, first and foremost, to lift these drinkers up.[8]

Magda's comments in this passage show how precarious the conditions of French pastors were in the period between the two world wars.[9] Nonetheless, the vocation of the pastoral couple grew stronger and deeper, not least because of their humour and tolerance of less-than-ideal circumstances.

> The honeymoon had ended; we went back to Saint-Quentin and left for Maubeuge, that is to Sous-le-Bois, which was a working-class area on the outskirts of Maubeuge. André was to look after Sous-le-Bois, and Perret, the head pastor who was in charge of the mission, looked after Maubeuge and supervised everything André and the missionary evangelist, Mademoiselle Jouvet, did.
>
> Our address, "1 Hermitage Row, Sous-le-Bois," struck me as wondrous. I got a letter from Mrs Jalla, in the Vaudoises valley,

who wrote to me "I can imagine your beautiful presbytery in a remote hermitage in the woods."

Well! Sous-le-Bois was hardly a wooded paradise; it was a rundown part of town on the wrong side of the tracks. But it was also very interesting because of its population: especially interesting for people who have a religious or social mission.

There were huge steel mills with large factories there. It was hellish. The workers came and went up a long, long street lined by an endless row of houses and stores. Sometimes people came to work in the plant for a week or two weeks, then left again. The population was very transient. A lot of them came and left without paying their bills, and that caused serious financial hardship for everybody.

There was also a stable population centred on the church and the local community centre, which André also looked after. As a result, we were quite involved with the comings and goings of that unfortunate population. They were the by-products of human progress, desperate people, drinkers, really the dregs of society.

Our house in Sous-le-Bois was located in an old *estaminet*. In the North, this term means a tavern or bistro, and is usually a rather shoddy establishment. When you came in the front door, you were in a big room that had originally been the lounge; it had been divided into two rooms by a partition. It was damp and musty and old-fashioned. The floor of the office was rather unstable, but fortunately there was no cellar underneath, only a space between the floorboards and the sod floor.

One day André was writing his sermon. He turned around in his chair a bit abruptly and the floor boards gave way. There he was, lying across a rickety chair with two legs still inside the office and two others in the little space under the house! In this office there was also a bed, a kind of couch we had put in a corner so I could lie down and rest sometimes. We had some photos, some souvenirs of Assisi. André had already collected various books for his growing library.

In the dining room we had a table and a buffet in whitewood that we had bought with the money Aunt Pauline had given us as a wedding present. We figured it would be better to have something simple that wouldn't shock the workers when they visited, or make them think we were bourgeois. However, we were mistaken. As soon as the townspeople could afford it, they bought elaborate Louis XV- and Louis XVI-style furniture, and thought ours was cheap.

People (even a housekeeper we had for a while) would say things like: "I don't know where you're from. You speak several languages, but we can't tell if you're working class or upper class." Indeed, our situation was hard to nail down.

When we started inviting people from the Fraternity over, they usually wouldn't come. Or else they would come and say, "We've already eaten." They were afraid to eat with us. Our background wasn't exactly the same as theirs, and they were uncomfortable with us. I was a foreigner, and André stood tall; he seemed a little austere, you might say … They really didn't know us at all yet.

The kitchen looked over a "little yard," a horrible little square of land that you got to by going under an awning that led into a storage shed where we put our tools and bicycle. Between the shed and the kitchen there was a little stream that came out of the kitchen sink! So when I threw something into the sink or emptied it, it flowed through and out into the street. When André came home, he could tell if I had burned something, for instance if I had scalded the rice pudding again! There was no running water in the sink, but in the yard there was a pump. First you had to prime it, and then you had to pump and pump to get anything out of it. So André decided to use some of the money he had earned at the Rockefellers (the money he had been saving to tour the world) and he installed running water, drinking water, in the kitchen. It was the height of luxury! I didn't have to spend all that time pumping.

[…] Then André decided to use the rest of the money on something rather luxurious: a little garden. He brought in some workers, had them plant a little lawn that never did grow, and a little skeleton-like tree that tried to grow but couldn't manage to, even after two years; it survived and even sprouted a few leaves in the spring. André had a few flowers put in, and some of them even grew! It was a good try, all the same.

On the other side of our garden were the yards behind the workers' houses and, right next to our little garden and shed, a dance hall. There were dances there every Saturday and Sunday … and a racket loud enough to wake the dead! André was furious because he had to write his sermon and couldn't; it wasn't pleasant music at all, and it drained all our energy. And that wasn't all: the street was noisy with shouting and comings-and-goings all night long, and a French fries vendor in front of the dance hall gave off a dreadful smell and smoke […]

One day we had a strange visit from Mr Heuzé, a minister with the Reformed Church of France, which was at the time a member of the *Société chrétienne du Nord*. My father-in-law, Paul Trocmé, was the president of this group. Mr Heuzé had come to talk to André in a fancy frock coat more suitable for a ball than a visit. It was Monday, which was supposed to be the minister's free day. We never seemed to get the day off, though, because the Perret group met on Monday and there was always something to do.

So there he was, Mr Heuzé, arriving in his fancy coat. Why was he dressed this way? Why, this was part of the typical pastoral wardrobe! Ministers were so poorly paid (there were no benefits or family allowance in those days) that the wealthy Protestants gave their pastors their old clothes. And the old clothes that were the newest (or the least worn-out) were their fancy dress clothes, like tuxes and tails. The richest and most generous parishioners believed that these were the most suitable attire for ministers; shouldn't ministers dress differently than others, to stand apart? So that was what the pastoral wardrobe was like. Fortunately, André never wore this kind of clothing. But Heuzé did. He was a rather short and stout man, and looked a bit like he was from the country; his voice was loud and his eyes bright and sharp. He was a very nice man and he had a beautiful singing voice. Sadly, he died during the Second

World War, just as the concentration camp in which he had been imprisoned was liberated.

Heuzé had come on behalf of the members of the *Société chrétienne du Nord* to have a serious talk with André. He had come to tell him that he should be preaching about Jesus Christ and nothing else. André couldn't hide his astonishment. "I became a minister to preach about Jesus Christ. It's my vocation! Why did you come here to talk to me about it?" There had probably been rumours. What were people saying? Was it Perret? Was it other well-meaning people, people who were old-fashioned or misguided and believed that because André was a conscientious objector he must be a bad pastor? Did André's pacifism play a part? Was it because André had asked to work as a labourer?

[...] When André was brought to Maubeuge, he was told that there was an urgent need for him to be there. In fact, that wasn't the case at all. André had been put in a difficult position, and it was impossible for him to refuse Maubeuge. He had been told that going to Maubeuge was an absolute necessity. He'd had many other offers: Rockefeller had asked him to stay in America; the Faculty of Theology wanted him to stay another year and finish his doctorate; André had plans to travel around the world, to go to work with Tagore and Gandhi; he could have gone to Ivory Coast, where an African Christian revival movement had begun. All of the possibilities were exciting, but André was compelled to give all of them up and go to Maubeuge. It was only later that he realized that he had been tricked. Conord, his predecessor, who didn't get along with Perret, wanted desperately to leave but couldn't until he was replaced. And the replacement was this rather naive minister who had been in America, the youngest son of Reverend Paul Trocmé, a young man full of vocation but who had been somewhat sheltered, who lacked experience in the real world and didn't suspect the kind of ruses people could invent [...] When we figured out what had happened, we were crushed. But we were together and very much in love. We decided to look at this difficult time with Perret as a learning experience that would last two or three years, because such apprenticeships didn't last too long, and then we would leave. Too bad if we had been tricked.

Two Sermons

In the Protestant Reformed Church, Biblical commentary and interpretation and their application to contemporary life hold a central place in worship. The following excerpts are from André's early days as a preacher. His interest in speaking simply and in making a connection between Christian faith and the daily life of his congregation are easy to recognize. He gave the sermons from which these passages are taken in Maubeuge on Sunday, 13 February 1927, and Sunday, 17 July 1927, respectively.

And the second is like unto it[10]

Just a few days ago, I was asked this question: "What is religion?"

This is the same question Jesus was asked by a learned man, a lawyer, the equivalent of a university professor in those days: "Which is the great commandment in the law?" And Jesus replied, "Thou shalt love the Lord thy God with all thy heart, and with all thy soul, and with all thy mind. This is the first and great commandment. And the second is like unto it, Thou shalt love thy neighbour as thyself. On these two commandments hang all the law and the prophets."

The first and second commandments, on which all the law and the prophets depend: in other words, the most important principles of the Gospels. If Jesus had condensed His complete teachings into a book, they would be the summary.

[...] Today [...] my purpose is very simple. I want to show how a little phrase that is often ignored – "And the second is like unto it" – is an effort by Jesus to connect these two commandments.

The word "like" in Greek is much stronger than our translation; it means identical. Jesus tells us that the second commandment is identical to the first. In other words, Jesus has made a link so strong between the two commandments that the two phrases mean the same thing: loving God *is* loving one's neighbour.

Even if we do not go quite that far, we must understand that these two commandments cannot be separated from each other without their meaning being lost. We cannot love God without loving our neighbours, and loving our fellow men is impossible if it is not founded on our love for God [...]

In the Middle Ages, our monks would have said that it is possible to love God without loving our neighbours. Our modern-day monks, who close themselves off in a seminary to escape the vain turmoil of the world and worship God, would say the same. And the ninety-five percent of Christians who hold a grudge against one or two or ten of their fellow men would also agree.

But Jesus said: No, it is not possible. The Gospels and the entire New Testament affirm this. The Apostle John, who was among those closest to Jesus, asks: "If a man say, I love God, and hateth his brother, he is a liar: for he that loveth not his brother whom he hath seen, how can he love God whom he hath not seen?" John is saying that someone who does not love his brother is wrong, and cannot see clearly. He is unable to love God, the Father of Jesus Christ.

Because of what we are taught, we have a fundamental belief in our faith that God is One, the same for everyone. However, it also true that there are big differences in the ways we see and describe God. Different people may think of God as a Being that may be whole or not, ideal or not, a higher power or not. In a sense, there are different gods: there is the god of the Hottentots, who worship a talisman; Allah worshipped by Muslims; the God of Buddhists who adore emptiness. There is the God of theologians, who believe in a God who is the Creator, and then there is our God, the life-force, who comes to rescue us from our trespasses and our weaknesses. The "Father" addressed by a man who does not love his neighbour is not the same as the God of Jesus Christ [...] for Jesus has said: "You cannot, it is impossible to love God, to love the same God as I do, or to even know Him, if you don't also love your brothers."

The second commandment is the same as the first. And for all of us, who suffer from not being able to pray, from not being able to find or love God, who always doubt God, Jesus said this: "If you do not love your neighbour, you will be unable to pray to or to believe in God." He said, "Therefore if thou bring thy gift to the altar, and there rememberest that thy brother hath ought against thee; leave there thy gift before the altar, and go thy way; first be reconciled to thy brother, and then come and offer thy gift."

In the Gospel of Luke, in which this story is told a little bit differently, the lawyer, after reciting the two great commandments himself, asks Jesus, rather nervously: "And who is my neighbour?" When I read this verse the other day, the words were a little painful for me. Certainly, there is love in me toward the people around me, pity for those who deserve it, but how am I to overcome the vague indifference, the disdain in which I hold five-sixths of humanity? All of these men and women whose life, aspirations, ideas are so different from mine that I cannot find any reason to be interested in them?

And aren't we all in the same situation? Apart from family and friends, the great figures we admire, we find the ordinary people we see every day dull or uninteresting. But the truth has been revealed to us: "For if ye love them which love you, what reward have ye? do not even the publicans the same?" We cannot love our fellow men if we do not respect them, consider them equal to ourselves or even superior, desire for them the same things we do for ourselves. Respect is what makes it possible for us to see others as good, and not evil. It has nothing to do with the attachment we feel towards those who are close to us, with whom we enjoy happy relationships. It consists of seeing others as people as worthy of attention and consideration as we are.

To truly love a fellow man, whether he is close to us or distant, like an Arab or a Black, we must first respect him. How, then, do we free ourselves of the disdain with which we are all afflicted? There is only one cure, and that is the love of God. Not the God we see in pictures in Catholic churches or we hear in Protestant churches, but the inner God [...] who can only enter into an open heart.

This God is the one of whom Jesus speaks, the God who can only be heard by someone who has gone into a quiet room and listened.

Those of you who have heard this God inside yourselves themselves, have had this rare privilege, have emerged from this experience trembling in awe. God alone can cure us of our disdain for others.

This God can be found deep in the soul of any man. Every man, without distinction of race or class, has inside of himself the ability to hear God and see through God's inner gaze, which enables us to feel respect and love for those we disdained in the past. Everyone carries God's star.

Those who do not love God will always choose men according to categories, races, and classes. Only the inner love of God can teach us to love. Those who have found God in themselves can love their neighbours as themselves [...]

Therefore be full of love for others; give love to your brothers, freely, fill your lives with the life of all the lame and the poor and the miserable you meet. By doing so, you are simply doing part of what Jesus Himself has shown you.

Since Jesus came, we cannot love God without loving others, nor can we love others without loving God, for Jesus has reconciled His two commandments for us.

On the Gospel of Luke

We can rejoice in the fact that the Gospel of Luke has been saved for us, for without it we would never have known some of the most beautiful words of Jesus Christ. We sometimes wonder, when we read the first three Gospels (the Gospel of John is rather distinct) without paying too much attention, what each one really adds to the others. Think of it this way: if we didn't have Luke, we would have neither the parable of the Good Samaritan nor that of the Prodigal Son, two gems of the New Testament. In fact, nearly half of the stories in Luke are not found in the other Gospels. Without the Gospel according to Luke, in fact, a new facet of Jesus would have remained hidden from us.

In the Gospel according to Mark, we see the man Jesus, suffering and struggling in the crowd, collapsing in exhaustion, feeling helpless against the doubts and ignorance of those around him.

In the Gospel according to Matthew, we discover, in the Sermon on the Mount, the most beautiful portrait of Jesus that exists, painted in his own words.

In the Gospel according to Luke, we find something new: the feelings of Jesus.

After reading the Gospel according to Luke, oh, how tedious the other portraits of Jesus seem! The other Gospels show him in the countryside of Judea, rather listless and humourless ... In Luke, we learn that Jesus wasn't an incomprehensible, implausible being who hung between heaven and earth. Instead, we discover a Jesus who is vibrant, whose feelings change from tenderness to enthusiasm, from enthusiasm to indignation. Nowhere except in Luke does Jesus show so much love for men: not only Jews or the peasants of Galilee, but all men everywhere. Jesus is seen to be a universalist and an internationalist (the Roman centurion, the Samaritan, the tax collector). And Jesus is particularly interested in those who have been shunned and mocked; these are the people he talks about in his parables, and who, time after time, accomplish the most valuable and remarkable actions.

In the Gospel of Luke, Jesus appears more vividly than ever as a friend of the poor, the weak, the downtrodden, children. Nowhere is the story of the sinful woman, illustrated by the parable of the unpaid debt, as colourful and as touching as in Luke. Open Luke's Gospel and see the strange procession that follows behind Jesus, a procession of victims of disdain, infirmity, and ignorance. The centurion's servant, the widow of Nain, the prostitute, the good Samaritan, Martha and Mary, the woman searching for her piece of silver, the prodigal son, poor Lazarus, the widow of the unjust judge. Among the poor, women occupy a large place. Jesus seems to delight in their company and they admire the delicate, sensitive, understanding man he was.

Jesus is portrayed as a vagabond in Luke. Mark and Matthew show him in Galilee in his homeland. Luke shows him as a traveller, going to Samaria, across the Jordan River, or crossing the border, having nowhere to rest while he is pursued by Herod's outrage or hatred.

Luke is the Gospel of the poor, but has also been called the social gospel because, curiously enough, this Gospel of tenderness, pity and forgiveness is also that of anger, outrage and condemnation.

Jesus, who could spend hours in conversation with Mary, was also capable of shouting down the rich and powerful on the town square. If Jesus were a political leader, his threats would be of no consequence; they would only be noticed for their oratorical effect. But how they must have thundered from the mouth of Jesus, friend of the humble, the meek. What indignation he must have felt to cry out so violently!

"But woe unto you that are rich! Woe unto you whose bellies are full! Woe unto you that laugh now! Woe unto you, when all men shall speak well of you! […] Woe unto you Pharisees, scribes, lawyers …" Jesus shouted these condemnations in the face of the very people who were mocking him. He was outraged that they had kept knowledge out of the hands of their people, had been unfaithful and unjust to their flock. When you read these words yourself, late at night, have you ever felt you were hearing a condemnation of our own European civilization, rotted by riches and blood? That we are as deserving of criticism as the wealthy man Jesus rebuked?

But after the storm, the calm returns. Jesus turns his attention once again to those he loves and understands, the poor and the downtrodden. "Fear not, little flock; for it is your Father's good pleasure to give you the kingdom." Jesus cried for the people of Jerusalem, who would not listen.

This, then, is the portrait of Jesus as Luke drew it: his love, tenderness, wanderings, rebellion, anger, pity. How dull and mediocre our own lives seem in comparison! Our petty desires, our minds that are not open. Our hasty and harsh judgements, our hypocrisy. Our hearts, dry and shrivelled, keeping track of the costs of our friendships. Our complacency in the face of evil, wealth, force, pretence and power, in the face of those who rest while, all too often, others toil to make them rich. Our pleasure in the unjustly gained riches we often hide under our mattresses ... What a long way all of this is from Christ's example, from his love, his kindness, his passion, his suffering! Next to him, we are not even alive; we are already dead. And our placid acceptance of the life our people lead, the calamities and the shame in which we take part, none of this has anything to do with the fervent devotion shown by our Master, Jesus Christ.

This is what the portrait of Christ in the Gospel according to Luke has to teach us. The Gospel of love, of struggle, of the awakening of our conscience. When we read Luke's Gospel, we cannot help but cry out: "Oh Master of life, this is the true life, loving, generous, strong! Oh Master, how I long to follow your example, to be like you and to see your face.[11]

Concrete Action

Magda and André Trocmé were not the kind of intellectuals who follow ideological fashions and protest for the sake of attracting attention to themselves. Nor were they like those ministers who do not act on their words; who, as Jesus said "say, and do not." Quite the opposite: the Trocmés spoke out for social justice, were committed to the cause of those less fortunate, and worked enthusiastically for peace. In 1930 and in 1932, in Sin-le-Noble, a town in the Pas-de-

Calais area of northern France where he was called after his time in Maubeuge, André, who had just turned thirty, was passionately involved in social action. Clearly ahead of his time, he was already facing challenges. He was able to overcome the obstacles in his path thanks to the tireless support of Magda.

Still preoccupied with the need for the Church to be a witness in social and international affairs, I had channelled the energy of our enlightened men towards practical matters. While the economic crisis and unemployment spread misery through the homes of miners, I turned to Mayor Foucault and suggested setting up a community kitchen where everyone could eat. All that was needed was to collect potatoes from people who had them. Foucault put one condition on my proposal: I would have to get the extreme right (i.e. the parish priest) and the extreme left (the Communist party) to co-operate. "It's the kind of thing that a mayor has to do with full co-operation," he explained. "Otherwise, we're going to be attacked from one side or the other during the next election campaign."

The parish priest declined: "We have our sisters to help out; we are doing what is needed."

The leader of the local Communist group was friendly, but said he had to consult his members. Eight days later, he told me their decision: "Given the state of decay into which capitalism has led society, the Communist party sees no reason why it should try to bolster capitalism through charity work. The working class needs to understand the corrupt nature of the oppressive system that has victimized them. Only when they are aware of this will they be ready for the revolution which is our goal."

When I went back to the mayor, he shrugged his shoulders and said, "I knew that would happen. Everyone just pulls the covers over to his side of the bed." I had to put my plans aside, because the fifty Protestant families didn't have the resources to carry out such a large-scale project.

But a few days later, hearing bells ringing in the street, I went outside to see what it was: a hand-cart, identical to the one we used for the "Old-Timers' Christmas," with large signs proclaiming a collection of potatoes and other vegetables organized by the "Red Aid" to benefit exploited and starving working-class citizens.

I have never been able to get over the hypocrisy of the Sin-le-Noble Communist group. However, it did teach me one thing: an act of charity should never be performed as propaganda, but only as work done in the interest of those who benefit from it. Otherwise, it is a point scored for the wrong team.

The "Old-Timers' Christmas" was an idea we borrowed from projects we first learned about in the United States. Now they are common throughout Europe, as well. A "Santa Claus" collects food or gifts for old people with no resources.

For our tiny congregation, it was not an easy feat. There weren't many of us, and people didn't know much about us. We had to send around a notice about what we were doing, make a Santa Claus costume and, one Sunday afternoon at least seven or eight weeks before Christmas, go out and push a little hand-cart up and down the endless streets lined with dismal mining cottages, knocking at every door to gather up what the good people had ready for us. We didn't turn anything away. We got old household items, shoes, clothes, food. We set up a warehouse in the manse to sort and pack two or three hundred Christmas boxes. We started one Sunday in November, to keep everything on track.

Benjamin Bocquillon, a big black-haired boy who looked a little scruffy, had agreed to "play Santa Claus," but just before it was time to put on the heavy red cloak he panicked and ran away. One by one, our young people begged off, leaving Magda and me alone with my horror of disguises. Cancelling the activity would have been a disaster. So I wrapped the red cloak around me and put the white hemp beard on my face. Magda got the little cart ready and off we went, knocking on doors as the children gathered around us and heckled us. Nobody knew what we were doing; people asked us what business we were advertising. It was raining; we were soaked, dirty, cold and generally miserable. Meanwhile, the young people of the congregation were lurking not more than 200 metres away, elbowing each other and waiting for us to fail. I decided to approach the children in the street, playing my role half-half-heartedly and asking them, "Have you been good? Do you deserve candy in your stocking or coal?"

One group seemed a little intimidated. An unkempt boy must have had something on his conscience and was about to burst into tears when an older boy shouted at him: "Stop crying, stupid! Can't you see it's just the captain of the temple?"

In the end, all the children got candies and year after year, in good times and bad, the cart would be full of donations. We went back to the manse and unloaded the wares: chocolate, cookies, oranges, figs, old shoes, wool mittens, socks with holes in them. Once we even found a corset in there! The young people who came to help were soon jostling each other and fighting over the privilege of pushing the cart and playing Santa Claus. And they went back into the streets for more donations, the victorious Santa Claus leading a straggly group of collectors. It didn't take long for the "Old-Timers' Christmas" to become a proud tradition of the community.

On Christmas Eve, I told the story of the Good Samaritan to a large crowd in the town hall. When I reached the part about the Samaritan caring for the wounds of a passerby, a keen old man cried out: "That's wonderful!" I knew that this was more than the voice of a shy man who had been moved to speak up; my call to the townspeople had really been understood.

When I was leaving Sin-le-Noble I went to say my farewells to Mayor Foucault. It was the Old-Timers' Christmas that he mentioned when he thanked the Protestants for their generosity.

Our little Protestant parishes soon began bending over backwards to try to bring the Good News to people everywhere. Sometimes all it takes is a bit of imagination and a sense of what moves crowds to win them over. True, ads and radio commercials have become very successful in their appeals to people's generosity today. But that doesn't mean the Old-Timers' Christmas wouldn't still be successful. As simple an idea as it was, the volunteers' desire to contribute and the young people's infectious good humour had as much of an impact (or perhaps even more) as the practical result of our work.

I had kept up my international contacts with the "Reconciliation"[12] from time to time, enough to be able to send two of our men wounded in the war, to the Bade area in southwest Germany, near the French border. They came back marvelling at the welcome they had received from the German veterans.

But it was really the "Gerhard Halle" affair that turned the Protestant "North" upside down and jeopardized my future as a clergyman in the region. Halle, a German Quaker[13], wrote to us one day to announce that, as an officer in the Engineering Corps during the Great War of 1914–18, he had carried out orders to systematically destroy a number of villages in Cambrésis. Regretting his actions, he wanted to visit the site of his errors and ask for the forgiveness of the population living there. I was deeply moved by the prospect of a German finally feeling and expressing his remorse, and replied that I would make myself available to help him. Moreover, I arranged three engagements for him, one in Sin-le-Noble, a second one in Douai, and the last one in Arras, under the responsibility of Reverend Lestringant.

The meeting in Sin-le-Noble was a great success. A full house. Halle spoke in French and explained his inner conflicts. In 1914, when war was declared, Halle decided to leave the church he belonged to. "Fighting a war is incompatible with Jesus's teachings," he argued. "I want to have a clear conscience to enlist and fight." However, doubts overcame him one day in the trenches. "What am I fighting for?" Halle asked himself. "To defend my country. And what about them? To defend their country." He was struck with the absurdity of these two groups of men destroying each other for identical reasons. He wasn't yet brave enough to refuse to bear arms as an officer, and he ended the war as a member of the Engineering Corps. "I was just following orders, blowing up villages to make it harder for the enemy troops to advance; but my conscience was troubled by the fact I had obeyed such barbaric orders."

After returning to Germany from his tour of duty in 1918, Halle was called back to suppress the "Spartacist"[14] uprising in Berlin. Finally he had the courage to refuse to follow orders. "Violence is a crime," he said, "a collective madness that will never cease."

It was then that he began looking for a Church which was faithful to the teachings of the Gospels. He found the Quakers. After his conversion to Jesus Christ and his repentance, he wanted to ask the French, victims of his earlier actions, for forgiveness. My readers will be hard-pressed to relate to the degree of hatred that still reigned in the public opinion of France in 1932, fourteen years after the end of the war. The conflicts of 1914, the invasion of Belgium, the four and a half years that our boys had spent in the trenches cut out of the ground of occupied France, their desolate, ravaged homeland, had left deep scars that would not be easy to heal.

"If there were only one single German who would express his remorse for what happened to us!" This sentiment was on the lips of many throughout France. "But no, we don't hear anything of the kind," people would lament. "They consider themselves victims of the war, and are almost ready to start up again!"

Admittedly, by signing the Treaty of Versailles, Germany had accepted and declared its sole responsibility for starting the war. But the German people had not confessed. In fact, out of a sense of loyalty and patriotism, none of them had ever admitted, at least not to any foreigner, that Germany was guilty, in whole or in part, of wrongdoing.

But what about the other side of the coin? You can only imagine Wilfred Monod, a well-known French pastor, a liberal and a pacifist, refusing to shake hands with Sigmund Schultze, his colleague and former friend from Germany, who was no less well-known, liberal and pacifist than he, until the latter confessed the sins of his country![15]

In short, then, Gerhard Halle was, to my knowledge, the *first* German to return to the site of his ill-considered actions and ask his French victims for forgiveness. As such, he should have been welcomed, heard, understood, and even celebrated.

And indeed, in Sin-le-Noble, which was a working-class community, people listened to him and were moved by his words. They applauded him. The next day, however, in Douai, the evening was much more dramatic! [...] A man named Joly, a reserve officer who had been badly injured in the war and the president of the local Veterans' Union, decided to sabotage the event I was hosting.

"This meeting is a scandal!" Joly shouted from the back of the large room in the city hall, where he was sitting with a group of veterans. "You have no right to bring a German in here to talk, when our country is soaked in the blood of our martyred compatriots! Shut up! Go back to where you came from!"

The crowd began to join in with him. I tried in vain to calm them down. A minority wanted to hear what Gerhard Halle had to say. He did manage to say quite a bit, but the atmosphere was so negatively charged that everything he said ended up being taken the wrong way. His emotional confession inspired only shouts of hatred and derision from the majority of the audience. I had to conclude the meeting abruptly.[16]

The next day we were supposed to go to Arras, but early in the morning the newspapers announced that the authorities in Pas-de-Calais had prohibited the meeting. I discovered later on that they were acting on the request of my colleague, Lestringant, who was so horrified to learn about the meeting in Douai that he had found a loophole to prevent the same thing from happening in Arras. However, Gerhard Halle's visit had an unexpected benefit for Sin-le-Noble. It galvanized my circle of parishioners who, in a show of their faith, stood steadfastly behind their minister. This group of uneducated men could understand the meaning of the Gospels more clearly than the more privileged, educated people in the area. As for the reactions of the bourgeois Protestants in Douai, I will only say that my career as a clergyman had been seriously jeopardized by my actions, which were considered to be those of a "militant." I was now under the surveillance of the secret police.[17]

A Conscientious Objector

After he finished his military service, André Trocmé's belief in pacifism and non-violence became stronger. In the following passage, taken from an article published in 1930, he officially takes a position on the side of those who reject war, murder, and the use of violence.[18] We need to remember that, at the time, ministers were forbidden from being conscientious objectors.

We often believe that a conscientious objector is a rebel who reveals his attitude by taking part in a showy protest against compulsory military service. The noise and attention surrounding a few cases of conscientious objection helps validate this impression. But the impression is false.

The problem with war, for conscientious objectors, is killing.

When a man resists the obligation to kill, it is nothing more or less than a personal rejection, based on his conscience, of an evil that has confronted him.

The external apparatus of this conflict is secondary. An arrest, legal proceedings, scandal, imprisonment, notoriety: none of this really matters to him.

After all the Gospels, from beginning to end, are the story of Jesus' protest against evil. Christ's religion is a rejection of evil and wrongdoing, a rebellion, but a rebellion that leads to the victory of God.

[...] We must avoid the idea that conscientious objection is a goal in itself, a badge of glory. We can't let it be swallowed up by politics and become a partisan issue. Any political party would be more than happy to hide its backroom scandals under the noble cover of their commitment to defend these new victims of conscience.

The legal recognition of conscientious objectors is a political absurdity. How could our law-makers consider disobeying laws a legal act? What would be logical, politically, would be to call for the abolition of compulsory military service, or at least the introduction of a system of optional military service (which would make the war effort suffer considerably).

Conscientious objection does not have political aims. There are objectors in every party. I might even go as far as to say that conscientious objection has no goal at all. In any case, it has no earthly goal. He who obeys God obeys without attempting to understand.

Only religious reasons can explain conscientious objection. For those whom God has enlightened, it represents fairness, clarity and humility.

On the happy day when military service becomes optional, conscientious objectors will immediately be called to object to other iniquities.

The March for Peace

In 1927, at Magda's insistence, André took part in the Congress of the Reconciliation Movement, in Oberammergau, Germany. Five years later, he participated in the "March for Peace" in Europe. This commitment meant that he abandoned his vacation plans and could not spend time with Magda and their three young children.[19]

If I'm not mistaken, it was in 1932 that the "March for Peace" was held across Europe. The first of its kind, it had modest resources. In France, Philippe Vernier, Pierre Vernier, and Jean-Jacques Bovet walked from one town to the next, carrying placards and gathering people together in the town square. In England and Holland, similar teams spread the word. In Germany, particularly, simmering under the turmoil of Nazism, a vigorous call to action rang out. All of these teams converged upon Geneva, where they were welcomed by Arthur Henderson, the secretary general of the World Disarmament Conference.

But this initiative was a disappointing failure and incited a backlash of German support for armed conflict.

For a couple of weeks I took part in the march through Germany. We formed a solid team made up of Germans, English women (Muriel Lester, Lilian Stevenson), Americans (Nevin Sayre), and one Frenchman (myself). Every night, in packed rooms, we addressed assemblies convened by the Deutscher Friedensbund, an association with socialist leanings. In Frankfurt, we were incredibly successful, and the audience nearly carried us on their shoulders in triumph! In Offenbach, Pastor Goethe, the organizer of the meeting, invited us to his apartment, which had been pillaged by Hitler's Brownshirts. He had called the police when the SA were there, before they cut his phone lines.[20] The police didn't respond until it was over, because they were in cahoots with the Nazis. They wrote up the minister for being guilty of "disturbing the peace" because he had organized a meeting to call for peace! Naturally, the meeting was cancelled.

In Heidelberg, the meeting nearly turned into a brawl. Two groups of young people, one Nazi and the other Communist, confronted each other. Each of them accused us of siding with the adversaries. The two groups came to blows pretty well every day in the outskirts of Heidelberg. At the end of the evening, we nearly fell victim to the Brownshirts ourselves; they accused us of coming to "einseifen, damit später England und Frankreich uns besser rasieren können" ("to clean us up so that the English and the French can shave us better later on"). Taken aside by one of them, who was waving a revolver in my face, I offered to kill myself then and there, in front of the crowd. My offer seemed to calm him down. He quickly disappeared into the crowd, but it turned out that it was probably only the fact that I was a foreigner that had saved me from his rage. He was already known for assassinating four Jews. The German justice system hadn't prosecuted him, because it didn't dare react to the growing brutality of the Nazi movement.

In Reutlingen, in southern Germany, we had the chance to see Mr Braun, a German we had met in Douai. "Holding the meeting here tonight is impossible," he announced. "The Brownshirts have occupied the theatre where it was supposed to take place. They have sworn they will not let you speak. It would be best to forget the idea." After a prayer meeting, our team decided we wouldn't back down. We entered the theatre through the stage door. We would address the Brownshirts with all the civility and courtesy we could, because these boys were men like ourselves – despite the collective madness to which they had succumbed. Because I spoke German better than the others, I was asked to speak first.

Never will I forget what it was like to stand behind the curtain in that theatre. I could hear the audience buzzing with anger. I had been told, "there will be a little podium for you; don't waste any time, just get up there!" As soon as the curtain was raised, I strode quickly over to the platform. Before the four or five hundred Brownshirts had a chance to react, I shouted out Hitler's own words in a booming voice: "Deutschland erwache!" "Germany Awake!"

For a few seconds, there was a stupefied silence. I took advantage of it to launch head first into the issue of the day: the need to awaken in the face of the looming danger of the Second World War. I, a Frenchman, was in favour of equal treatment for those defeated in 1918. It was the French who had suffered most cruelly during the war, but the hour of forgiveness and reconciliation was at hand! "Down with arms! Today, the Christian who is responsible is opposed to war and the actions that prepare for war. He is a conscientious objector." A thunder of applause answered me! The match had been won.

The speakers after me had no trouble sustaining the mood, and their comments were warmly received. By the time we left, we were nearly hugging each other. The local head of the SA, a very young man, came up to me and said, "You said exactly what our Führer does: Justice for all, equal treatment, peace." "Yes," I replied, "but I didn't say it the same way, and why does he persecute the Jews if he believes that?" The young man retorted that it was because "the Jews are the Number 1 enemy of peace." I didn't manage to convince him otherwise.

I often think about that stupefying scene in Reutlingen. Hitler had managed to fascinate the youth and exploit their fresh enthusiasm for his unthinkably vicious purposes. The naivety of the Germans, their candour about the good as well as the bad, their tendency to mix all their values together, will always seem inexplicable to the French, who remain incredulous, clear-sighted and critical.

In 1940, I once again watched as German soldiers marched into France. As in 1914, they came to deliver France from its vices. Their naivety was equal as that of the SA in Reutlingen. But then, aren't some racist Americans just as sure they are defending Christian values in the face of sin and vice when they lynch Blacks?[21]

Refusing to Teach

Here, Magda explains the reasons that led to her refusal to teach Italian in a school in Sin-le-Noble. The following stories reveal Magda's social concerns, her integrity, and her commitment to improving women's lives.

I have to tell you my stories about the Italians living here.

I'll start with the Italian women. We have many Italians around Sin-le-Noble. In the village of Dechy, there were only Tuscans, a whole lot of Tuscans, on every corner. When they found out there was an Italian woman who was interested in Italians, when they realized that I could even go to the consulate and help them with their problems, a steady stream of Italians began flowing through our door. Even later on, several years after I left, they still remembered me. One day I came back to visit Sin-le-Noble, and when I was simply crossing the street, a man came up to me and asked for help! He didn't even realize that I had left, and no longer lived there.

When we were living in Sin-le-Noble, I invited the Italian women in town to a meeting. I already held meetings for women in the congregation. I also had the UCJG, the Young

Christian Women's Union, and I decided to add another weekly meeting for the Italian women. As I had done with the other women, I took one of Nelly's big baby dolls and used it to give lessons to the women about child care, diapering, bathing babies, and so on. The women were very interested in this. I also shared with them biographical sketches of interesting people, told stories, talked about my travels. It worked well – so well that people as far away as Saint-Quentin heard about it! My father-in-law was very proud to learn that his daughter-in-law was beginning to perform her duties as a minister's wife "by the book." But it wasn't quite that easy. I'm going to tell you the tragic ending to the story.

I found out that in the primary school in Sin-le-Noble, where there was an enormous number of Italians, they were looking for a teacher, an Italian woman who could give the children of immigrants Italian lessons and classes in Italian history and geography, once a week, every Thursday. Classes like these were offered in almost all the schools in northern France. There were also Polish classes. I even thought of organizing something of the sort at the Alliance française, to help Italian immigrants keep up their mother tongue. It was something I was very interested in. So I wrote to the consul, told him about my qualifications, sent my papers and transcripts to show what education I had. He replied that I was, of course, better qualified for secondary school teaching, but that this was actually an advantage for the children. They wrote to Italy for papers; the consul was extremely charming with me. I went to see him with André; he asked me who my father was: a colonel … an engineer in Florence. And as far as the consul was concerned, everything was just fine! I was hired for the following year, and all set to begin in September. A while later, I was sent a large carton containing all the books I needed, magnificent books with splendid illustrations. They even sent me papers explaining what should happen at the end of the year, how to give out the prizes and what prizes the consulate would send; everything seemed perfect.

As soon as I had a moment, I opened the books and … what did I see? Magnificent pictures. Even the font and the paper were beautiful. But – sprinkled generously throughout the book, like salt and pepper, was a seasoning that was 100% Fascist! It was impossible. I couldn't teach Fascism. The books spoke of Mussolini as Italy's saviour. There were stories of the Virgin Mary. Everything was mixed in: God, the Holy Virgin, Jesus, Mussolini, the Pope … It was an unacceptable mish-mash. Basically, it was Fascist brainwashing.

The consul had already visited our home once or twice. His chauffeur-driven limousine awaited him on the other side of the iron fence around the church, so it was clearly an official mission.

André and I decided to go and see the consul. But first I wrote him a letter telling him I was resigning before even starting my job. I explained that I was not in the least Fascist, that I disapproved of the government, and that I absolutely could not teach this material. I apologized for my mistaken assumption that the class would be strictly cultural in nature, when in fact it was political. At the same time, while my letter was making its way to the consulate, an article appeared in an Italian newspaper published underground in Belgium by Italian immigrants who had gone there for work or for political reasons. The article claimed that the Italian wife of a minister in Sin-le-Noble had ties with the Fascist government in Italy and the Fascist consul in Lille. People had seen his limousine parked in front of her house! Moreover, this woman invited Italian women to her house and the pastor visited Italian women in their homes while their husbands were at work! Imagine! Actually, André had never called on the Italian women in their homes. I received a notice from the consul, asking me to come to see him. Because of the way it was worded and the scandal that was developing, André announced: "I'm coming with you, then, because I have a feeling he's going to make trouble for you."

Indeed, the consul was furious. How could I, the daughter of a colonel, possibly be opposed to Fascism? I told him, "My father may be Fascist, but I'm not. People don't always share the opinions of their parents. Obviously, I was wrong not to have got more information before. I was wrong to think it would be a cultural activity, but I assure you: that is what I really and truly believed it would be." I defended myself as best I could. André, sitting beside me, said almost nothing. He was there to protect me from the consul's attacks.

And that is how my career teaching Italian in Sin-le-Noble came to an end, and how, once and for all, I got rid of Fascism, which had been persecuting me up until that day.

Being Italian was a lot of work. Not only was there the story I just told and my classes for Italian women, but there were also my personal woman-to-woman relationships.

There was an Italian woman who didn't have any children. She had married a Polish man. She was desperate. I took her to the doctor who couldn't understand it. I took her to a special clinic where they did extensive and thorough tests; they tried unsuccessfully to unblock her tubes. One fine day her husband arrived on my doorstep and told us he was out of work. He asked us what he had to do to become a minister! He thought we had a nice house and a car; he assumed we must be rich and he wanted to be, too. So he figured he should become a minister! We had to explain to him why that wasn't possible. You can imagine how complicated things could become, how hard it was to explain our work: what we did, why we did it, and how it was, in large part, unpaid volunteerism.[22]

3

A New Parish

After spending seven years in the north of France, Magda and André Trocmé wanted a change. So in April 1934, André applied for the position of minister in Montrouge-Malakoff-Clamart, in the suburbs of Paris. He was somewhat familiar with this church because he had helped build the parish hall approximately ten years before, while still a theology student. But his appointment, first in Montrouge-Malakoff-Clamart and then two months later in Thonon-les-Bains, was blocked by the authorities of the Evangelical Reformed Church, who disapproved of his pacifism.[1] "I will end up in the street," Trocmé said, "or on the steps of the church … all that will be left for me to do is play dead, which means becoming encrusted in the soil of Sin-le-Noble. I'm sure they wouldn't dare expel me!"[2]

It was then that he received a letter from his former classmate, Reverend Roger Casalis, who was leaving his position in Le Chambon-sur-Lignon and suggested that André replace him.[3] The adventure of Le Chambon was about to begin.

Nevertheless, nothing could have prepared Magda and André for what they found when they settled into this town in the Haute-Loire. As André wrote in his *Mémoires*:[4]

1934. The town of Le Chambon-sur-Lignon is ugly. Dreary granite facades alternate with dilapidated hotels covered with dirty yellow or grey stucco […] The whole thing looks unbearably sad […] I swore I would not be a pastor in the country. It has always

> been the city and its urban problems that drew me. But there was no other solution for me but to apply for this position. [...] My former classmate, René Herdt, president of the regional council had [...] appointed me on a temporary basis for a year, thus dispensing me from the necessity of agreeing to stop spreading propaganda on the cause of conscientious objection. Le Chambon was a take-it-or-leave-it situation. I took it.

Magda, André, and their four children arrived in Le Chambon-sur-Lignon in September 1934. They remained there for more than fifteen years, learned to love the area and its inhabitants, and accomplished a great deal there.

Their first important project was the establishment of the Cévenol school. When the Trocmés arrived, Le Chambon already had dormitories and summer camps for children, and a tradition of welcoming students already existed. However, founding the Cévenol school, an international college for peace education, would permanently change the life and spirit of the town. The idea of creating it came from Magda, who had good memories of the open learning approach of the Protestant school she had attended in Torre Pellice, in the Vaud Valley in Italy, as an adolescent.[5]

The college project was a collaborative effort. Here is how André pays tribute to the contribution of his colleague, Édouard Theis:

> As for the Cévenol school, I would have got nowhere had it not been for Édouard Theis. He has all the qualities I lack [....] a broad vision and high aspirations for the project, tireless determination to accomplish every goal he sets out, no interest in financial gain, complete absence of personal ambition to appear brilliant or be popular, conscientious dedication to the most mundane and fastidious duties incumbent on the director of an institution. On three points, Theis dared to imagine what I could not. First, he had a picture of the college in a beautiful setting at the foot of the Peybrousson hill [...] Second, he knew how to establish and maintain valuable contacts with the ecumenical training council in Geneva [...] Third, after the Second

World War, Theis envisioned the college as a great educational institution with residences, an idea that frightened me a little.[6]

Besides this major achievement, the daily life and the personal qualities of the Trocmés need to be considered. These qualities were put to excellent use in serving their parishioners in Le Chambon and people much further afield. André was never at a loss for ideas. He could just as easily awaken a child's imagination (he wrote Bible stories and Catechism lessons for children) as he could open the eyes of adults to the important issues of the day. He organized trips and outings, formed a men's circle, started a choir, and even established a little folk museum: Pierre de l'Esclop. He held numerous meetings in the area, giving people an opportunity to gather and discuss current issues. As for Magda, she was known for her wonderful hospitality; despite her family responsibilities she welcomed visitors, and there were always guests in the manse. In addition, she had a special interest in helping women in difficulty. And, not least, she was in charge of programs for the young girls of the parish and taught Italian at the Cévenol school.

Facing the Clamart Council and the Church Authorities

The passage that follows gives the essence of the declaration André made before the Montrouge-Malakoff-Clamart parish council on 9 April 1934. In it, André describes the circumstances of his conversion to Christianity and his pastoral vocation. Out of a concern to be prudent, as he recognizes that he could only be called as minister if he signed a written agreement to "not spread propaganda about conscientious objection," he did not advocate the practice here.[7]

I have little confidence in ideas or doctrines. Our narrow minds can easily be distracted from them. I believe instead that God gives direction to our lives. God places each of us in particular circumstances and it is in these very circumstances that he calls us to act, if only he finds us among the men who are ready to obey His Word [...]

I am part of the generation that was marked indelibly in our youth by the war. At the age when our personalities were being formed, when adolescents are dreaming of the future that lies before them, between fourteen and eighteen years old, I was living in occupied territory, in suffering and sometimes in hunger, and in a state of such moral depression that even the most unaware of my friends were forced to turn their gaze to the heavens. The daily reality was life behind the German front, with its indescribable misery: a combination of deserved suffering, premeditated sins, innocence, and violence. German soldiers and French civilians were often mixed up together in this chaos.

But, in the midst of this darkness, God suddenly shone a pure light. Among the young people of the UCJG of Saint-Quentin, at the darkest hour, the light of the Awakening burst through. For the most part, they were simple, working-class youth. But God makes use of modest means to reveal His glory. Above the streets of Saint-Quentin, delivered to forces of destruction, among the young people – many of whom died in captivity – God made a new dawn arise. We loved each other dearly, we prayed together for hours at a time. We experienced the miracle of our changed lives in our everyday existence. God showed us the boundless power of His love and the possibility of a world regenerated by His Spirit.

Armistice came and life was restored to its normal course. I believed, as we all did, in the possibility of God's Kingdom on earth. It was not a dream without a foundation, because Jesus Himself had instructed us to pray: "Thy Kingdom come." There was disillusion and failure. Like all of you, I was thrown up against the indifference and the resistance of men. Pastoral ministry is difficult, and sometimes exhausting. But God did not allow His celestial vision to be erased. He always calls us to accomplish acts of our faith. He requires us to believe, to believe more and still and always, and the only way we can respond to this call is to surrender our lives to Him.

However, you must not assume that God would allow idealism to get in the way of reality [...] My years of study were a long struggle [...] I was, at times, on the brink of giving up the idea of pastoral ministry. I felt unworthy of my vocation. It was in these conditions that I completed my military service, aware of the gap that separated my military activities from a total consecration of my life to Jesus Christ. However, I did not feel able to protest, because of my sins.

Since that time, I have been a minister. I became one through an act of faith and I experienced, in the depth of my misery, the radiance of God's complete forgiveness of those who believe in Christ […] My ministry is to preach the Gospel […] I have therefore abandoned many of the worries which often afflicted me in the past, about my family's security, about money, and I have broken many of my worldly habits. In every way, this happened without any effort on my part, it was a side effect, a consequence of my sole faith in Jesus Christ.

Similarly, one of the consequences of placing my life into God's hands was that I feel incapable of taking up arms in the future and of disobeying the precise instructions of Jesus, who told us to defend ourselves, not with the weapons of men, with the weapons of the world, but with the force of His love, which shall be our only refuge, our only defence, our only safety, our only strength in battle.

In these conditions, you understand, there cannot be any question of me spreading propaganda about conscientious objection. That would be an error comparable to the one made by certain propagandists of the Croix-Bleue, for whom the Gospel can be summarized by a single sentence that does not even appear in it: Thou shalt not drink alcohol![8] The only essential propaganda we are asked to spread is the witness of Jesus Christ […] There is no question, therefore, in my ministry, to impose on others or even propose to them my own, personal ideas. On the other hand, there can be no question of me hiding the fact that God has shown me the power of His love in the world and in myself.

Despite these promises of good will and the approval of the Clamart parish council, his appointment was refused, without any explanation, by the authorities of the Evangelical Reformed Church. Anxious to understand their decision, André went to the Church headquarters in Paris, as he describes here:

I resolved to force the issue with the council, and went to the French Protestant Centre on Rue Clichy. I installed myself in the waiting room. At about nine o'clock, the councillors arrived. Most of them recognized me: wasn't I the son of the well-respected lay leader, Mr Paul Trocmé, perhaps a son who had "gone bad," but still, his son? Some of the councillors were even classmates with me at the faculty, who had pursued their careers to this level. When Pierre Durand-Gasselin [the chair of the regional council of Paris] arrived, he made an angry gesture. "I did not call a meeting with you," he told me. "I know," I replied, looking him in the eye, "but I will stay here until I have been heard." A quarter of an hour passed. The door opened. Fifteen men received me. They didn't ask me to sit down.

Durand-Gasselin interrogated me in the incisive tone of an officer: "Mr Trocmé, we have only one question to ask you, and we want you to answer only yes or no, without another word. In the case that war is declared, will you fight to defend France under the flag of your country? Yes or no?"

Me: "I refuse to answer yes or no to such a question without explaining myself. I have a typewritten page that I read to the presbytery council in Montrouge. I ask you to let me read it. Then I will answer."

Durand-Gasselin: "Only one page? Show it to me. What do you think, gentlemen?"

The heads of his fellow councillors nodded. Mr Gounelle offered a weak smile of encouragement.

Durand-Gasselin: "Very well. Read it."

I read my document, coolly and calmly, but inside I was trembling.

Durand-Gasselin (when I had finished): "Fine. Now, Mr Trocmé, I will repeat my question: in the case that there is a war, will you go to defend your country: yes or no?"

Me: "You have heard my declaration. No!"

Durand-Gasselin (fiercely): "Fine. Your position in Clamart will not be approved. You may be dismissed."

Me (red with indignation): "Gentlemen, it seems to me that when you are making such a decision, we could have prayed together!"

Fifteen jaws dropped. Fifteen pairs of eyes wandered, avoiding contact. But Durand-Gasselin, grasping how ridiculous the situation was, quickly took control. "Mr Paul Gounelle, would you please lead the prayer?"

Gounelle said the prayer. He was old, and his voice shook. He asked God to bless His Church and to lead the young pastor who had gone astray back to the road of righteousness. The young pastor was, of course, me.

On that note, I left the room. The men had not said hello or good-bye to me. I found myself in the street, in front of the door of the Reformed Church of France, not knowing at the time that another world war and the shame of collaborating with the conquering enemy would be needed to cast a shadow of doubt on the hearts of the good patriots of 1914, for whom France would always be right. How, then, could a Christian have any doubts about the cause of France, and refuse to bear arms? Was the cause of France not the cause of God?

--

The First Few Years in Le Chambon-sur-Lignon

In the following excerpt from her autobiography, Magda describes the conformity of the people she met when the family moved to Le Chambon-sur-Lignon.[9] Because of her open-mindedness and her refusal to adopt the attitudes around her, Magda continued to live freely and according to Christian principles, without worrying about the narrow moral judgments of others.

And meanwhile [...] what were we to do? André spent 100% of his time as a minister, running in every direction, his mind full of ideas and simmering plans for the future. But his ideas would come to fruition later. What was I doing at the time? Well, I was appreciated for the fact that I was very talkative, but there was still some criticism. Most of our detractors were outsiders who visited in the summer.

I never wore a hat (I have always hated hats) except in winter. I went to church without a hat, wearing only my braids on my head. So the fine Protestant ladies from Nîmes, Alès, Orange, said: "What? How can the minister's wife go to church without a hat?" This was repeated several times. I didn't know what foot to stand on, but I continued to go to church without a hat. A little while afterwards, fashions changed and no one wore hats any more, and no one gossiped about Mrs Trocmé's hats!

I also swam in the Lignon River, and apparently the wives of ministers who came before me never went swimming in the Lignon. I have no idea why. Were they cold? Did they not know how to swim? In any case, I went. And when I got out of the water I put on my cover-up, a thick terry-cloth tunic, very long and respectable. It covered me even more than the dresses I usually wore. But the parishioners would say, "My, my! Mrs Trocmé goes swimming in the Lignon, gets out of the water and walks back home in a shirt! What in the world?" and so on. They also said that, because I had a washing machine, our clothing and linens must not get clean. "She doesn't even rinse things in the Lignon! That's not how you do the wash, with machines! Imagine!"

In the summer, I went to "the Vogue," a miserable little fair that took place once a year on the town square in Le Chambon-sur-Lignon. There was a little merry-go-round, a little circus act, three or four little swings. I told my UCJG girls – the young women in our Christian group – to come with me to the carnival. We would make a little trip to the fair. Now, above the pharmacy next to square, a very strict Protestant woman from Morocco was posted at her window. Every summer she came and watched what was going on in Le Chambon. When she saw me at the Vogue, she was scandalized. "This is no place for a pastor's wife! And on top of it, she brought her UCJG girls with her! It's scandalous!" She spoke to André about it, but it did not upset us too much. In the north, on the contrary, the workers' families used to tell us: "It's a good thing you take our girls to the "Ducasse"! It's so much better than leaving the girls alone with the local boys!" So I continued doing my job of minister's wife in Le Chambon, and wasn't afraid of the outsiders' criticisms.

I made two very good friends in Le Chambon: Miss Matile, a charming and intelligent woman who was like a sister to me, and Mrs Marion, a minister's widow with two grown-up daughters who ran a boarding house. She was of enormous help to me in every way, sort of a mother to me.

The Creation of the Cévenol School

A few months before his death, in 1971, André Trocmé was invited to Le Chambon-sur-Lignon to give a speech at the official opening of a gymnasium in the Cévenol school. Too ill to travel, he dictated the following speech to Magda. In it, he recounts the history of the college from its initial conception until it opened. The existence of this college epitomizes the interests and concerns of the Trocmés, who valued open, mixed, pacifist, and international education, who wanted to engage in collaborative efforts and action, and who were willing and able to work with other people of principle, in particular Reverend Édouard Theis.

In the summer of 1937, in the room which is now used as the principal's office in the Cévenol school, a handful of people were gathered to discuss, once again, the possibilities for developing the Protestant town of Le Chambon-sur-Lignon, whose vocation as a focal point for youth was becoming more and more evident.

Doctor Henri Cambessédès insisted that a health spa be established; Reverend Charles Guillon, the Mayor of Le Chambon-sur-Lignon, was interested in an international camp for the Union chrétienne de jeunes gens, similar to the YMCA and YWCA camps he had seen in the United States; Charles Schmidt, the local inspector-general of libraries, was enthused about the idea of a sort of Huguenot Academy offering Protestant cultural activities. We were the guests of Charles Schmidt, who usually rented out the first floor of his farm in the nearby Luquet area during his holidays.

I was also there. A member of the Mouvement International de la Réconciliation (MIR), I had long dreamed of starting a secondary school that would be free of the narrow-minded nationalist teaching of history, where students from every country of the world would come to learn about peace in the spirit of the Gospels.

During the winter, the presbytery council of Le Chambon-sur-Lignon asked the Synod of the Reformed Church of France to hire a minister. Half of the minister's time would be devoted to serving the increasing number of young people who were coming into the area; the other half would be spent teaching Greek, Latin, and French. We would ask volunteers from the area to teach other modern languages. For the other subjects, students would attend classes in town.

In October 1938, the marvellous adventure began. A few rooms behind the sanctuary were transformed into a school. But what pastor would be fool enough to risk his future on such a fragile foundation? A young professor had already refused to take the risk, declaring the project "senseless and not viable."

It was Édouard Theis, the minister in Vézénobres, a former missionary to Cameroon and Madagascar, a former professor in the USA, married to a young American, who accepted the position. Strong pacifists, members of the MIR, we made an enthusiastic pair, bolstered by the same conviction. The Theis family already had seven daughters, and an eighth was born in Le Chambon-sur-Lignon. The first school year passed in a state of total financial insecurity. However, as the threat of war became closer and clearer, people from the cities where the danger loomed most visibly flowed into the Le Chambon area, and with them political refugees from central Europe and Spain.

This entire population, many of us inspired by very lofty ideals, came together to form a common identity we could soon consider "the Le Chambon spirit."

The new Cévenol college was an open and free education, rooted in faith in Jesus Christ. It provided what seemed, to us at least, the only appropriate education for its time. The horizon of the future seemed to be clouding over in the growing fear of a Nazi victory, with its funeral procession of lies and persecution. Among the teachers at the college were refugees, teachers from France who had been denied positions in public schools by the Vichy government for racial reasons, brilliant minds, enthusiastic spirits. They were a mixture of Christians who were strong pacifists, Jews, and idealists. Strangely enough, the diverse staff blended together and found in the words of Sunday morning worship their inspiration and guidance. For four years, they took the young people in hand, gave lectures, led study groups and Bible study and offered an exceptional program of activities to people in the area.

It is not necessary to go into detail about the war […] Through the historical adventures and misadventures of history, how did the "Cévenol spirit" take shape?

Unity of political viewpoints? Certainly not. Until the very end there were a handful of men who were faithful to Pétain; some who had been Gaullists at the beginning worked in the Resistance. Eighty percent were unsure of their political stance, but all had acknowledged that a human being, Jewish or Christian, friend or enemy, persecuted or decorated, had the right to refuge, protection, and sustenance in the Church of Jesus Christ, and therefore in the Cévenol school and under the roof of all those who found the guidance for their daily life in the Bible. Never was a "non-violent tactic," as such, planned in opposition to the "Devil's tactics." Every morning brought with it new risks and improvised solutions that were often inspired by God. When, in 1944, the Liberation lifted the crushing weight off our shoulders, only then did we measure the extraordinary distance we had progressed.

After the war a succession of human miracles led to our meeting with Carl and Florence Sangree[10] and dozens of Christian pacifists from the USA and elsewhere. Some arrived with food, others with clothing, still others with financial donations, and some brought only the strength of their robust muscles and their willingness to work, believe me, very hard! The gifts of their physical and spiritual energy and their financial generosity allowed us, in fifteen years, to offer bursaries for tuition and for room and board, to buy land, and to build a boys' dormitory, the principal's house, the classroom building, the girls' dormitory and now this gymnasium. All of this looks to us like a beautiful photograph that has replaced the negative of the tribulations we experienced during the war.

There is, throughout the entire world, a people of God which feels isolated and alone as it battles the skepticism of some and the opposition of others. But when this people unites without fear to do God's work, then extraordinary things can be done, things like the metamorphosis that began that day at the Luquet farm.

Magda at the Cévenol School

The experiences Magda Trocmé had as an Italian teacher were interesting for in several reasons. In the text that follows, she tells the story of her first days at the Cévenol school and explains why she suggested the idea of this college to André.[11]

As you know, I taught Italian, but Italian was a subject in little demand in France, except in the Mediterranean region. So I had very few students and I taught in unusual places.[12]

At the beginning, classes were sprinkled all over the town, wherever there was a vacant room to rent. I taught a small class in Mrs Marion's bathroom. There, I had groups of four to six students, and it was fun to teach in a bathroom. I had one or two classes at the Hôtel Sagne, which was closed in the winter. It was ridiculously cold. There was no central heating, only a few stoves. The one in the room I was in was so bad that when I lit it, the room became so smoky I had to open the windows! The windows also had glass that were gradually replaced by wood panels that let draughts in, but no light! But the lessons were interesting for all of us. I was told I was a good teacher, and I believe it, since the results the students obtained in Italian on their baccalaureate exam were very good.

Several students came and told me: "We passed because of our mark in Italian!" An examiner even asked who the teacher was because all the marks were so good. I was very proud. They were tiny classes, and much more pleasant and easier to work with. However, little by little the size of the classes grew and I had many private lessons to give, as well. The students had discovered that by taking Italian and private lessons they could do the whole program in two years.

I had some very interesting students. They were future theologians who were preparing their baccalaureate in order to get into the faculty of theology. From Batignolles, they had been sent to Le Chambon-sur-Lignon.[13] Since they had studied only one foreign language there, they had to make up the second one between their second-to-last and their last year. It was marvellous, because they were such intelligent, highly motivated students. And it was good practice for me, because later [...] I would teach students who had to learn their second foreign language just as quickly. Like my students in Le Chambon, they were motivated and proved to be strong students. One of them even learned Italian well enough [...] to obtain the highest marks in the language at teacher's college.

How did I come to suggest the idea of the Cévenol school to André? Many children came to Le Chambon-sur-Lignon for health reasons and had to leave again because there was no secondary school. As well, many students from the area, who took continuing education classes in the town, were not eligible or else were not prepared for admission exams to get into teachers' college, the post office, the railway, the revenue department ... There was a real need for good secondary education in Le Chambon-sur-Lignon. In the Vaud Valley, a Protestant region in Italy, I had experienced a fantastic school program, recognized by the state, Protestant, and which prepared students for the "licenza liceale," or the Italian matriculation exam. I thought that a similar school could be created in Le Chambon-sur-Lignon. André and I had a great time dreaming and planning! He was eager to keep people in the region, especially the young people who wanted to study and prepare for a career in the future.

There is an interesting book entitled *Alle porte de Italia* (Gateway to Italy), by Edmondo De Amicis. He talks about different borders in it, and when he arrives at the "Porte d'Italie" that opens into France, he also describes the French language spoken in these Protestant valleys of Italy. He nicknamed the town of Torre Pellice "the Italian Geneva." And that is where the very first idea of the Cévenol school came from.

"Do Not Stay for Two Weeks, But for a Year."

The following, written by André, is the preface to a brochure with historical and tourist information, entitled *Le Visage et l'Âme du Chambon-sur-Lignon* (The Face and Soul of Le Chambon-sur-Lignon). It was published in Le Chambon in 1943, the year after the German occupation of southern France began. The brochure describes the plateau as an active intellectual, educational, and social community. It is astonishing to see that several pages are dedicated to educational institutions and the children's homes that had recently opened, that there are many references to Jews and refugees, and that there is obvious pride in the town's vocation, as though the act of welcoming and hiding refugees was not only a legitimate occupation but also a factor that could be used in promoting the town and giving it a higher profile, with impunity.[14] Besides its geographical considerations and poetic tone, the preface reveals that André's attitude to Le Chambon-sur-Lignon and its surrounding area has changed. He has become attached to it.

Certain regions are destined, by their geographical position, to evolve in isolation. This is the fate of the upper basin of the little river that flows out of the Loire and is called the Lignon Vellave.

However, the area has nothing of the appearance of a wild gorge. It would be easier to compare it to a lush basket of forests and rushing water suspended at an altitude of a thousand metres. There, for four centuries, seven thousand Protestants have been marrying each other, settling in houses in the valleys and perpetuating a race of austere, melancholic, patient and pious people: the "Huguenots" of Velay.

Whatever route you take to get to Le Chambon-sur-Lignon, a threshold must always be crossed. If you come from Tence, you go through the passage of Beaujeu; from Yssingeaux, the furrows of the Auze; from Puy, the barrier of Meygal; from Monastier, the high desert plains of Mézenc; from Saint-Agrève, the Batterie pass; from Devesset, the wooded hills of Plafay. It is only after you have crossed over the obstacle that your gaze can encompass all the wonders of the landscape, the harmonious natural park [...] into which we invite you.

Do not expect a breathtaking revelation. This land is far from grandiose: the Lizieux is hardly a mountain, the Lignon is barely a river. Like its inhabitants, it will reveal itself gradually, as you become familiar with its many qualities. At first, you may find it sad, as are all lands where dark evergreen forests are the predominant vegetation. But melancholic countrysides have a secret that the sunny south and the Alpine valleys do not have. Here, you can see forever. Your eyes can travel over the vast, open territory, searching for a straight grey line on the horizon, resting on the spectacle in the foreground of a grassy rock in the middle of the short meadow grass, the sparkling water bubbling over smooth pebbles in a stream, the red glow of a pine trunk against a patch of blue sky, the austere, grey farm in a green valley ... And the landscape is constantly reinventing itself so that, after a half-hour walk, an entire story has taken shape.

[...] the mystery of pine forests, of rye fields and of country souls. Come to Le Chambon-sur-Lignon. Do not stay for two weeks, but for a year, and then you will begin to understand it.

4

Plunged into the War

In the 1930s, as the threat of war accelerated, André Trocmé became very active in peace and reconciliation activities throughout Europe. Lucid observers of the international situation, André and Magda worried about the ability of nations to maintain peaceful relations as hostilities increased. In consequence, they participated in several pacifist demonstrations in France and other countries.

In 1937, in one of his lectures[1], André declared:

> We have seen the rise of Italian, German and Japanese fascism, with their internal codes of honour and sacrifice, their social dogma and their philosophy of history. If anyone has any doubts about the subjective nature of the responses of these new social groups, all he needs to do is read, with an objective and open mind, the declarations of right-wing and left-wing intellectuals, and, especially, leaf through Alfred Rosenberg's famous book, *The Myth of the 20th Century*, which at least has the merit of being frank. For his adversaries, who criticize his philosophical bias in favour of the German race, to whose advantage he has rewritten history, Rosenberg replies cynically that he does not believe in the existence of objective truth and, according to his faith as a believer, is stating his subjective truth, the biological truth of the social group to which he belongs, the German race. We will find, in a philosophy of history outlined

by Marxists, a demonstration of the same spirit, except that the biological group, instead of being the German nation, is the international proletariat. Thus, we end up with astonishing parallels between political hatreds as well as individual hatreds.

After France entered the war in September 1939, and in the months that followed, André experienced a dramatic inner conflict. Despite the grave danger that Nazism presented for Europe, he knew that he could not take up arms. Contrary to his statements before the parish council of Montrouge-Malakoff-Clamart, non-violence was no longer a "corollary" to his Christian faith. Confronted with the reality of war, he had realized that commitment to non-violence was, in fact, the guiding principle of his faith. From this point on and throughout the entire war, with Magda's support and assistance, he would never falter in his Christian pacifism.

The following excerpts present the crisis of conscience André experienced.

"Therefore, Love the Stranger."

A brief article written in March 1939 for *L'Écho de la montagne*, a local publication of the Reformed Church, is indicative of his thoughts. The date is important: even if France had not yet entered the war, André is calling on his Protestant readers to respond and to engage in active solidarity. The tone is explicitly one of resistance to oppression.

"Therefore love the stranger, for you were strangers in the land of Egypt."

This exhortation to the Israelites, in Deuteronomy 10:19, strikes us as being timely and fitting today. It has special relevance to us as Christian Reformed people descended, at least spiritually, from the Huguenots who were persecuted in the seventeenth and eighteenth centuries.

Once more, atrocious persecution is taking place. Hundreds of thousands of Christians, Jews, dissidents and democratically-minded people are trying to escape the oppression and violence of totalitarians. But escape is possible for only a small portion of those persecuted, for many have no means to leave and free nations have barely opened their doors to them. Most of the people we welcome here as refugees are refused the right to work, condemned to unemployment, and all too often denied state benefits. Some, who were tired of begging and starving, are, at this moment, in prison for having committed the horrific crime of working. Others are desperate and have given way to vice or the mad despair of suicide.

In the midst of all this cruelty and indifference, the time has come for Christians to act in response to the words of their Master and Saviour: "For I hungered, and ye gave me meat: I was thirsty, and ye gave me drink: I was a stranger, and ye took me in."

"A Statement about My Attitude to War."

When war was officially declared, André reviewed and analyzed the essential elements of his life. This document, written in Le Chambon-sur-Lignon on 5 September 1939, was put into safekeeping at the home of Mrs Marion, a friend of the Trocmés, in case the manse was searched by the police. Forgotten even by André, this statement was only found and returned to his family in August 1974, three years after his death.

My father, Paul Trocmé, was born in 1845 and is still alive. He had nine children from his first marriage; after his wife's death he married my mother, who was of German origin. I am the youngest in my family. My two sisters have died. My brothers work as industrial entrepreneurs, engineers, doctors, ministers in France.

I was raised in the austere religious environment of a Huguenot family. My father placed the idea of duty above all else in the world. When I was still a young child, I learned to hate evil: not the evil you see others do, but the evil that you do yourself.

As a young child, as well, I learned the moral horrors of war. My father, in 1870, had religious scruples against killing his fellow men.[2]

The situation in my family became particularly difficult when tensions between France and Germany increased. My grandfather was a minister from Hanover. My grandmother was a descendant of Huguenot refugees. They had always resisted the "Prussianization" of Germany. I still have many relatives in Germany, my mother's six sisters, all wives of ministers, members of the German Confessional Church, a church whose clergymen prefer to go to prison or to die rather than to bow down before Hitler.[3] My visits to Germany, as a child, gave me an enduring love for the Germans, for their warmth, their family life, and their honesty.

In 1911, my mother was killed in a car accident. I was ten years old. In my child's mind, I idealized my mother. Everything that surrounds her memory is sacred to me.

For me, with my child's soul, the war of 1914–1918 was a scandal and a horror. The Germans had invaded Saint-Quentin. Their requisitions depleted my father's factories and ruined us. French and British airplanes, targeting military sites, dropped bombs that often hit their own countrymen. Starting in 1917, Saint-Quentin was under fire and ultimately destroyed. My half-brothers, particularly Robert, a captain in the infantry, for whom I have great affection, fought on the front in Somme in 1916, and were injured in battle.[4] Meanwhile, my German cousins were crossing through Saint-Quentin to the front. All of them were sincere, upright, eager to do their duty and convinced they were defending a just cause.

It was in 1916, amid great turmoil, that I found my religious vocation. It gave my spirit the clarity to rise above the moral chaos in which I had been struggling. During this period, I came to understand that Jesus Christ was the master of all mankind, and that His disciples (who called themselves Christians) could not continue killing each other, that this was unthinkable in the eyes of God. When I agreed to dedicate my life to serving this master, I became incapable of killing.

After the Armistice, since Saint-Quentin was uninhabitable, my family moved to Paris. I studied at the Protestant school of theology there. My university studies and, most of all, extensive and careful reading of the Bible, confirmed my convictions.

In 1921, I left for military service. Still young and inexperienced, I decided to do my best and I think my superiors appreciated my efforts. While I was in the regiment, I realized what a military leader could be like. I especially admired a particular commander and then a lieutenant under whose orders I worked in turn. In Morocco, where I spent six months, I was so attracted by the dedication of the intelligence officers that I had doubts about my religious beliefs. I even considered abandoning my pastoral vocation for a military career.

This is how I came face-to-face with the basic question of my future. From now on, it was all or nothing. Either I had to give everything to the community to which I belonged, to my homeland: not just my body but my mind, my heart and my soul. To obey it in every aspect, to take on an officer's conscience, and do everything I was ordered to do whether in times of peace or in times of war. But this would mean renouncing my belief in Jesus Christ, Prince of Peace, Son of God, the non-violent one who let himself be crucified for not having followed the orders of the men of his time. Or else I had to give everything to Jesus Christ, body, mind, heart and soul, and obey His commandments, to the letter, without further thought, even "Thou shalt not kill" and forgiveness.

I chose the second path. That I did is nothing to brag about. It was my vocation, and it was all-powerful.

From that time on, I have been a minister. I have served my country as best I could, as an educator of working-class youth and then impoverished rural youth. People will have to ask the parents of those I educated if I taught them to disobey the law. Today, I am still prepared to serve my country, with all my strength, as long as this does not require me to do what God forbids: to take part in war.

I have tried, like so many others, to envision serving in another form, as a stretcher-bearer, a chaplain, an orderly. Every time, I was stopped by the appeal of my conscience. The army is an all-encompassing unit. If war is, at a certain time in history, just and necessary, if God permits it, I will be neither stretcher-bearer, chaplain, nor orderly; I will be a soldier, a corporal in the infantry, in order to serve a just cause as best I can.

But if war is, as I believe, never part of God's plan, never permitted by God, then I am obligated to never take part in it, in any way, on or behind the front lines. My responsibility remains clear.

My marriage with Miss Grilli, the daughter of an Italian army colonel, made my situation even more complicated. At the time, France and Italy had shaken hands and were friends. I came to love Florence, my wife's home, and the spontaneity of the Italian people. Tomorrow, if Italy declares war on France, I would have to fight my father-in-law, my brothers-in-law. They are the ones I would be more likely to kill, rather than the head of state.

I believe that certain men have a particular destiny. Their life is traced out ahead of time, regardless of their intentions (we do not choose our mothers). They need to live it out to the end, and try to surrender to Divine Will joyfully.

I am not a man full of pride rebelling against the world. I am a servant who obeys the orders he has received since he was a child. I am not a zealot or a fanatic; I have never had a vision; I have a solid head on my shoulders. I am not exceptional in any way: I have a wife, four children, and material needs. I have my faults, my miserable character flaws, just as everyone else does. I do not believe I am better than other men. Like everyone else, I have to take some responsibility for wars. I will not make any excuses for Hitler; in fact, he is the incarnation of the Evil I detest. I am not accusing Daladier, or Chamberlain, of wrongdoing. I have no idea what I would have done in their place.

I have not discouraged any of the soldiers as they left for their posts, although my authority as a minister would have allowed me to do so. It has been a long time since I have taken part in any public action in favour of peace, because I know that *only* my example can count in such serious matters.

I have belonged to the Mouvement International de la Réconciliation for fifteen years now. We have numerous members in England, where the right to conscientious objection has been accepted by the Chamberlain government [...]

I have no partisan or political affiliations. I am free in every way, except in my submission to God.

I have no desire to return to the past, to my safe life. I only ask to be allowed to serve those in danger, the most pitiful victims of the war: women and children in the cities being bombed. I ask that my service be exclusively of a civilian nature. I am happy to give my life as others give theirs, without faltering in my faithful service to my Master, Jesus Christ.

So help me God!

Letter to the Reverend Marc Bœgner, President of the Reformed Church of France.

In this letter, written in Le Chambon-sur-Lignon on 7 September 1939, André Trocmé informed the president of his Church that he would refuse to comply if he were mobilized. Following it is the response he received from Reverend Marc Bœgner, dated 4 October 1939.

Reverend Marc Bœgner,
President of the Reformed Church of France.

Dear Sir:

I would like to inform you that, according to military laws, I am to be mobilized with the second reserve forces (recruitment class: 1921; mobilization class: 1913; four minor children; Recruitment Office of Puy; file number: L.M. 129).

I hold blue papers in my Mobilization Instructions (without posting) and am, therefore, not currently affected by the Order of General Mobilization. I will, at a later date, receive an individual notice to appear.

I also wish to inform you that, regardless of my call for military service, I am certain that God has called me elsewhere.

On the other hand, I am also certain that I have not been asked to flee danger. On the contrary: I sincerely wish to serve, *in a civilian capacity*, the women, children, and elderly in a city or village subjected to bombing, as a stretcher-bearer or a nurse in a non-military role.

I have notified the presbytery council of Le Chambon-sur-Lignon about my resolve and have offered my resignation. The council, which has been aware of my position since it discussed the matter with me five years ago, met on Tuesday, September 5. Ministers were not in attendance. Judging that I had not, over the last few years, failed to meet the commitments I made when I arrived, and noting that they were not in agreement with my ideas, they decided to go on considering me as the minister of Le Chambon-sur-Lignon.

I wanted to make you aware of this situation before my military orders are delivered. My only desire is to serve my brothers in this time of their suffering and to dedicate my life to them, without contravening the orders of God.[5]

[Reply from Reverend Marc Bœgner:]

My dear colleague,

Your letter touched me deeply. You will understand that I have no interest in entering into a debate with you about a point which, like a great number of your colleagues, I consider an error of interpretation of Holy Scripture and of Christian doctrine. As I have done with your friends, with whom I have met here, I will limit myself to assuring you that I will do everything in my power so that those who share your conviction are able to show they are not acting out of cowardice.

Your decision to submit your resignation was a good one.[6] It was the only action that was consistent with both the decision of the Synod of the Evangelical Reformed Churches and with the moral agreement you entered into with the Permanent Commission when you were named to the church in Le Chambon-sur-Lignon. In our opinion, you can only renew the agreement in the case of an appeal, knowing that in any case your household will not suffer any negative consequences from your decision.

Please accept, dear colleague, my sincere wishes.[7]

Registered Letter to the American Red Cross.

Sent from Le Chambon-sur-Lignon by André Trocmé, 22 May 1940.[8]

Dear Sir:

I wish to enquire about the possibility that the American Red Cross might need my services as a nurse or a driver, in particular in order to assist the civilian population in combat zones and in danger locations. I would, of course, work on a volunteer basis. I am a Protestant minister, of French nationality, and for the moment I have not been mobilized, since I am the father of four children. [A brief resumé and the names and addresses of references, Mr John D. Rockefeller Jr, New York, and Reverend Marc Bœgner, in Paris, follow.]

I expect to be able to benefit from a special leave from my congregation for the duration of the war.

"This is My Testament."

André Trocmé wrote his will in Le Chambon-sur-Lignon on Tuesday, 28 May 1940, after France was defeated. The sombre tone betrays his fear that he will not survive the war, and that his death will result in dire consequences for Magda and their children. Like the statement he wrote in September 1939, this will provides an overview of the important elements of his life and shows his state of mind at the time. This document was also placed in Mrs Marion's safekeeping, and was returned to the Trocmé family in August 1974.

This is my will and testament.

I know that my act of conscientious objection will not be understood. It cannot but be misunderstood by my fellow citizens, who have endured such suffering and humiliation.

I know that I will become the object of the most terrible accusations: of colluding with the enemy, of spying, of being part of a fifth column, of who knows what else.

I know that I am setting the wheels in motion for the terrible hours my poor wife will suffer, and for my children to be subjected to trials that should not be faced by children of their age.

However, there is nothing else I can do. I cannot kill, and I certainly cannot take part in this act of murder that is called war.

Why? Because I have received an order from God. This order does not take anything away from my passionate love for my country. I suffer its pain, its martyrdom.

I am from the north of France. My country has been invaded and laid to waste for the second time in twenty-five years. My father has fled, my family is ruined, because of German attacks.

I am ready to give my life for my brothers, and obviously for my closest neighbours, those who share my country. But I cannot kill or take part in an act of murder. I am well aware that there is a contradiction in these two duties. The contradiction is not between me and those around me; it is within me. Every report announcing more bad news makes me want to take up my gun, defend my country, and kill. But immediately afterwards, another voice tells me: "Thou shalt not kill."

I offered my services to the American Red Cross, I begged to be put in dangerous situations, and to tell the truth I would be very willing to die right now. But I am not willing to kill or to collaborate in an act of murder.

Some will wonder: "How can you be so certain, when

millions of other Christians are doing their duty as citizens without a second thought?"

The elements of certainty that I will share with you have at no time been the decisive factors in my decision. It is God, and only God, who directs me. If I were not a person of faith, I would not be a conscientious objector. No, I consider these elements of my life story only as a way in which God has led me to the place He wanted me to be.

[...] I could have left the country, become an expatriate. After all, *I always knew ahead of time*, with a clear and deep-rooted instinct, that my life would end in a violent manner, that I would die for the cause of Jesus Christ and His Gospel. So I resisted the calls from other places and returned to my country ... I am prepared to suffer anything.

But my children and my wife! With these words, I call upon some good Christians to help. Who? I do not know. We are living in a time when friends can become enemies and enemies can become friends. I am appealing to those who will read these lines and who perhaps will not even know me, to look after my wife, who will need help and support, and to keep her from being pressured in any way. My wife alone is worthy and capable of seeing to the care and education of my children. She is free and responsible for her decisions. It is to her that I bequeath all of my worldly goods and all of my parental authority over my children. Nonetheless, she will need help, true friendship, and that is what I am asking of others [...]

I thank God for the honour of being called to His service. Everything has been grace and happiness in my life, even my death.[9]

5

Refusing Violence and Rescuing Persecuted Jews

In 1940, while Europe was plunging into a new armed conflict that trapped millions of people, André Trocmé found himself confronted with a painful dilemma. Although he could not be called up, his sense of responsibility towards his family and his country were absolute. On the other hand, his commitment to non-violence on religious grounds would not tolerate any compromise. For such a man, the ultimate guidepost is obedience to Jesus Christ; making decisions on this basis was the best way for André to reconcile his duties as a citizen, a father, and a pastor. And despite the arduous situation the war had put them in, despite the dark and violent night they had to endure, André and his friends were guided by the light of the pacifist convictions they had forged in the wake of the First World War.

On 23 June, the day after France fell, André Trocmé and Édouard Theis exhorted their parishioners in Le Chambon-sur-Lignon to "resist the violence that will be brought to bear on their consciences through the weapons of the Spirit." In effect, their proposal became the watchword, the foundation upon which a vast project of civil disobedience would be based. Three months after the first Jewish Statute, a portion of the population of Le Chambon-sur-Lignon and the plateau had already been made aware of the problem of refugees, and for four years the pastors and their faithful parishioners resisted the orders of the Vichy government and the Occupation forces in order to save human lives.[1] The people of Le Chambon-sur-Lignon defied the Minister of Youth, Georges Lamirand, when he made an official visit in August 1942, giving him a glacial reception and publicly denouncing the "anti-Semitic persecutions." Trocmé and Theis also jeopardized their own safety when, imprisoned for four weeks in the Saint-Paul D'Eyjeaux internment camp with Roger Darcissac, they refused to sign an oath of allegiance to Marshal Pétain and to the "new social order," citing their rights as clergymen to remain neutral.[2]

In his rejection of both violent action and also passive resignation, André Trocmé denounced "the spirit of compromise that is often simply a screen to hide our personal egotism and our cowardly neglect of our social responsibility." A few years later, remembering this period, he wrote: "We learned that refusing to fight the war was only half of our duty; saying no to evil is not enough. Resisting the war means doing something more [...] it means saving the physical and moral lives of human beings."[3]

These quotations illustrate the principles that these Resistance members never abandoned: personal commitment, as well as commitment to engage all those who sought to follow Christ on the path of peace. Consistently and unfailingly opposing arbitrary power structures with active spiritual resistance, they were called to act courageously in order to provide real help to victims of persecution.

"The Weapons of the Spirit"

Delivered to their congregation in the church in Le Chambon-sur-Lignon on Sunday, 23 June 1940, the declaration André Trocmé and Édouard Theis made illustrates their characteristic Christian sensibility.

Brothers and sisters,

Yesterday, on the radio, the president of the Protestant Federation made a speech to which we must give our full support. Reverend Bœgner called on the Protestant Church of France to ask forgiveness for the errors that have led our people to the situation in which we find ourselves today.[4]

As it was in the time of Israel's great distress, the time has come to humble ourselves before God.

Let us humble ourselves as we think of our responsibility for this catastrophe. Let us bow our heads as we remember the trespasses we have committed and which we have allowed others to commit, for standing idly by, for our lack of courage that made it impossible to stand up against the impending storm, for the times we lacked love and compassion for the suffering of others, for our lack of faith in God and the way we idolized wealth and power, for all the feelings we have had that are unworthy of Christ's example and that we have tolerated or allowed in our hearts; in a word, for this sin, part of which we each carry and which is the only true cause of the unspeakable horrors which we are facing.

Let us humble ourselves before God, each one of us personally, in our individual roles as heads or members of families, as citizens and as Christians, as pastors, members of the session or the parish council, as Sunday School teachers, as members of church groups, as the faithful of the Church. It is to God that we raise our plea for forgiveness for the sin we are personally guilty of committing and for the sin of our people, of humanity today, and of the Church of today to which we are loyal. It is in God only that we can place our hope to be uplifted. However, we must be mindful of the ways we might humble ourselves that would be a disobedience to God.

First, we must make sure we do not confuse humility with discouragement, that we do not believe and cause others around us to believe that all is lost. It is not true that all is lost. The truth of the Gospels is not lost, and it shall be proclaimed freely from this pulpit, in meetings and during visits. The Word of God is not lost, and it is here that we shall find all the promises and all the ways by which our people, our country, and our Church shall be raised up. Faith is not lost: true humility does not weaken faith, rather it leads us to a deeper faith in God, a stronger will to serve Him.

Second, we must make sure that we do not humble ourselves by thinking not of ourselves and of our own errors but rather of others, and in a spirit of vengeful bitterness. These last few days, during our visits, we have heard numerous complaints of soldiers against their officers and of officers against their soldiers, of bosses against their workers and of workers against their bosses, of the rich against the poor and of the poor against the rich, of pacifists against patriots and of patriots against pacifists, of believers against unbelievers and of unbelievers against believers, each one accusing the other and each one attempting to deny his own responsibility by blaming his fellow citizens or the people of other countries and forgetting that God alone can judge and measure the guilt of each person. We do not believe that this kind of abasement is fruitful, nor that it can prepare the way for our country and our Church to be rebuilt.

Third, as our hearts become humble, let us not become humble in our faith and our convictions. Let us continue to live by the Gospel. We have not made good use of the free will granted to us, but let us not abandon freedom. In kneeling down before God, let us not become cowardly, and let us not allow ourselves to become slaves to new ideologies. Let us not be blinded by illusions. In the last few days the totalitarian doctrine of violence has acquired undeniable prestige in the eyes of the world because it has, from the point of view of mortal human beings, succeeded marvellously.

Humbling ourselves does not mean accepting this kind of doctrine. We are convinced that the power of this doctrine is comparable to the authority of the beast described in the thirteenth chapter of Revelation. This doctrine is nothing but anti-Christian propaganda. For us, it is a question of conscience to affirm this belief, today as much as in the past. It is almost certain that children of our Church have given their lives to fight against this doctrine, and humbling ourselves for our sins does not mean resigning ourselves to it now. It is by giving our lives to Jesus Christ, by serving according to His Gospel and His universal Church, that we shall live in true humility and faithfulness.

As we call you to this Christian humility, we also call you, in the name of Jesus Christ our Lord, to learn and remember something more.

Let us abandon all these divisions among Christians, and all the arguments among the citizens of France. Let us stop labelling each other, calling each other names, addressing each other with disdain by separating right-wing and left-wing, peasants, workers, intellectuals, proletariat and privileged, and laying the blame on each other. Let us learn to trust each other again, to receive and welcome each other, to remember, each time we meet, as did the first Christians, that we are all brothers and sisters in Jesus Christ.

And then, after abandoning our mistrust and our hatred along with the political passions attached to them, let us gather together around Jesus Christ, the head of the universal Church, and let us adopt as the source of our thoughts, our obedience, and our actions, His Gospel, nothing other than Christ's Gospel.

Lastly, let us understand that our return to obedience means leaving things behind, leaving behind the world as we know it, and the way we have been living in the world, that we have accepted as our life.

Heathen pressures will be wrought upon us, we have said this, upon us and our families, to try to lead us to submit passively to totalitarian ideology. If they do not manage to subjugate our souls right away, they will at least subjugate our bodies. It is the duty of all Christians to resist the violence that will be brought to bear on their consciences through the weapons of the Spirit. We call upon all our brothers in Christ to ensure that no one agrees to collaborate in this violence, and in the days to come, in the violence that will be directed towards the people of England.[5]

Loving, forgiving, doing good toward our adversaries, this is what duty means. But we must do it without resignation, without servility, without cowardice. We will resist whenever our adversaries will demand of us obedience contrary to the orders of the Gospel. We will do so without fear, but also without pride and without hate. But this moral resistance cannot be accomplished unless we let go of our own enslavement that we have carried within us for too long, that has taken over our inner courage. A period of suffering, of famine, perhaps, lies before us. We have all been serving Mammon to some degree, enjoying the selfish pleasures of our little families, comfort and idleness, drunkenness. Now we will be deprived of many things. We must let go of our pride and our selfishness, our love for money and our belief in earthly possessions. Let us learn to rely on our Father in Heaven, to depend on Him for our daily bread and to share it with our brothers whom we must love as we love ourselves.

May God free us of our worries as from our false security, may He give us His peace which no one can take from His children; may He comfort us in our grief and through all our trials; may He find us worthy to be the humble and faithful members of Christ's Church, the body of Jesus Christ, as we await His kingdom of justice and love, where His will shall be done on earth, as it is in Heaven.[6]

An Evening in the Manse

It is interesting to hear Magda Trocmé tell us that the first Jewish refugee who arrived at the manse did not receive a warm welcome. Her story shows the difficulties that have to be overcome to let strangers in, when the first impulse is to reject them out of fear. In Le Chambon-sur-Lignon it was no different than anywhere else.

The initial reaction of the main characters in our story to the prospect of helping the Jews needs to be judged in the context of what they did later. For instance, Charles Guillon, the former pastor and mayor of Le Chambon-sur-Lignon, played a decisive role in establishing an escape route to Switzerland that made it possible for the lives of numerous Jews to be saved.[7] The Jews worked diligently to save Jewish children, through organizations such as the OSE.[8] And it is widely recognized that the Trocmés, like other pastors and residents of the plateau, displayed great courage, much beyond what anyone had a right to expect or what anyone could have imagined.

When war was declared, André was waiting to be deployed. Meanwhile, we had to look after the refugees: the Spaniards who had come to Le Chambon-sur-Lignon, the German Jews who had begun to arrive, and then the French Jews, and then Jews from several other countries.

For years we had been waiting for André to get his conscription; as a conscientious objector he would have refused to fight. We were always worrying about it. In the end, he was never asked. Why? Because he had four children. Since there had been so many children orphaned during the First World War, it had been decided that fathers of large families would be called up later, two years later for each child they had. So with our four, André had aged eight years and was never called up. We still worried for a long time, though. Fortunately, I had finished my exams in Paris, and was qualified to teach. I knew I could get a job and earn enough money to raise our children if the worst happened.

So the period of the Jewish rescue had begun. André talks about it a lot, but I'm going to tell you what happened, especially inside the manse. The first Jewish woman who arrived was from Germany. She rang the doorbell. I didn't know what to do, and it was nighttime. She told me she didn't know where to go, she had left Germany and had made her way through France, zig-zagging east and west, because she wanted to get out of the occupied zone. She had been told that there was a pastor in Le Chambon-sur-Lignon who would probably take her in. I asked her in; outside, there was a lot of snow and it was cold. She had little summer sandals on, and they were soaked through, as you can imagine. There was a little fire going in the kitchen, with the kindling I could find, and I invited her to rest for a while, to eat something and dry out her shoes. I also made up the bed for her. I put her shoes right in front of the wood stove and I went back to what I was doing: I had so much work to do! Preoccupied and exhausted, she forgot about her shoes. All of a sudden she realized her shoes had burned! A hunt for shoes began; I knocked on several people's doors, asking if they had shoes about her size they could give us, because we couldn't buy new ones. We were only allowed one pair of shoes a year. I ran around the whole town and finally a young war widow, Mrs Monnier, gave us a pair that more or less fit our guest.

But what were we going to do with this refugee? I could certainly feed people when they arrived for a day or two; with the limited rations, any more than that would be impossible. Being rather naive, I decided to go to the mayor, Mr Guillon, who had been a pastor. He came to Le Chambon-sur-Lignon from time to time. I told him the whole story. I really believed he would help me. He got angry, told me it was ridiculous, there were already French Jews and I was bringing in German Jews, that the whole town would be in danger. He ordered me to send the lady away. Imagine: send her away. Away, where? I was devastated.

So I went off in search of an important figure, someone connected with the synagogue in Paris. She was living in Le Chambon-sur-Lignon because the large cities were too dangerous. I explained that there was a Jewish lady in my house, that I didn't know what to do with her, and that I had come to her for help. Just like Mr Guillon, not only did this woman refuse her help but she grabbed my arm and told me I was putting all the other Jews in France in danger by bringing in Jewish foreigners. I was so upset … André and I gave the German woman some information about how to get to Switzerland, through some connections we had with Catholic priests near Annecy. We had to tell her to leave.

And that's how we were pushed into clandestine activity, André and I. We started to get false ID cards with photos made by Mr Darcissac, giving people false names, telling lies. But they were justified lies, told to save the lives of the persecuted.

Then a woman named Berthe Grünhut arrived. She asked if she could stay with us, cook or do anything we wanted, anything to remain in hiding until the war was over. It wasn't easy. A cook? But cooking was far from complicated; there was almost nothing to eat! She was often anxious, wondering where her husband and children were; she didn't know […]

A charming man came. We stayed in touch for years afterwards. Doctor Mautner came from Vienna and had a terrible accent. He was a courageous man. Throughout the entire war, he cooked and cleaned so that his wife could work as a seamstress in Le Chambon-sur-Lignon. They were both in hiding.

We lent them our sewing machine, which was kept in constant use throughout the war. Mr Mautner couldn't be a doctor, but his wife was a seamstress. Every week he came to use the washing machine and the children would laugh, because he said "Matam, ze vashing machine, if you please."

Yes, they came in all shapes and sizes! One day, when I was alone in the house, a French woman arrived. She was in danger because she had helped the English in occupied territory … What could I do? I kept her in our home for a few days.

[…] Now I'll have to tell you about Simone Mairesse, who came to help me in Maubeuge just before our daughter Nelly was born. Simone came to Le Chambon-sur-Lignon with her mother and her sister Gabrielle. She was distressed because her husband had to go to fight in the war, and she knew he was in grave danger. One day, we received a letter; someone had enclosed a newspaper clipping in which they talked about a charming officer, Maurice Mairesse, who had been shot in northern France. A bullet had cut through an artery in his leg. He had died for his country […] We were in despair.

Instead of losing all hope and becoming paralyzed and idle, however, Simone got busy. She started working against the Germans to help the Jews. She did so much for us! She came every week with her sister to help us with the mending. The rest of the time she travelled up and down the mountain to hide Jewish refugees and worked with an organization in Marseille that helped Jewish children. We asked her to find places for the refugees to stay.

One day, a lady from Paris and her family arrived, and we asked Simone to "find them a place." She found a home for them between Fay and Le Chambon-sur-Lignon, high in the mountains near a mill, so it was well hidden. It was a miserable day, rainy with that thin but penetrating rain. I went to the train station to meet the lady, who was coming with her son. Her husband was to join them a little later. What a surprise I got, when I gave her detailed directions to get to the farm and saw her angry reaction: "Mrs Trocmé, you don't actually expect me to walk there in this weather, do you?"

"Yes, yes, it is raining. And what about my friend Simone, who runs around in the mountains all night long to find places for people to stay, and the rest of us who are trying to help people like you ... Do you think we only work when the weather is nice?" It's a good thing not all the Jews were like that.

Life did not become any less complicated. The children were hungry, we were all hungry, and the ID cards that our friends were making in secret took time. I remember a man arriving with his son, I can't even remember his name now, a German fellow we hid somewhere around Lizieux. He slept in André's office, on the couch, with his strapping son. There was always lots of company. Once we had a Mr Colin, whose name was actually Cohn. Mr Colin ran and hid every time anyone suspicious showed up at the door. When the Vichy police came to do their search, Mr Colin hid out in the attic, which wasn't very safe at all. When they arrested André, Mrs Grünhut was hiding in the cellar, and from time to time she would poke out her head and ask: "What's going on up there?" We certainly had some intense emotions at the manse!

We also had two young girls staying with us, Micheline and Martine, two Jewish girls who were studying at the Cévenol school. They didn't give us any trouble. They weren't in any immediate danger, but it was still worrisome, especially for Micheline who had no other relatives besides an aunt who was hiding somewhere else. We were completely responsible for her well-being. If anything happened to her, we would have to look after her. Her aunt said she would pay her expenses "later." Martine's father had managed to escape by feigning insanity. We liked Micheline and Martine a great deal; in no time, they were like sisters to Nelly.

The hiding places we found for the Jews we were looking after had to be changed frequently. We often used children to warn us of danger. Sometimes the telephone rang and a voice would say, "Hello; be careful tomorrow. Be careful tomorrow." We didn't know who was calling, but we figured out it was probably the police, who had caught wind of some impending event. Everything happened in secret and the secrets were well kept. For instance, once when Theis was staying in a castle between Le Chambon-sur-Lignon and Tence, below the highway, my son Jacquot took a message to him. I don't know who gave it to Jacquot, because he didn't say anything at the time. We only found out about it after the war.

Another time, I had to go to Saint-Étienne. Mireille Philip asked me to go to Mr Malécot's house (Malécot was involved in politics and went to Paris often) and bring back a large parcel he would give me.[9] I had no idea what was in the box. I was simply told it was full of oatmeal. Much, much later I learned that there were stamps to use for false ID cards in it. The stamps came from North Africa. Why from North Africa? Making ID cards was a complicated affair. As the Germans moved across southern France, occupying one town after the other, the false cards from southern cities weren't safe anymore. Why? Because now the Vichy police and the Gestapo could check whether they were valid in the municipal records. As a result, the same Jew who was originally said to be "born in Lyon" would then be born in Valence, and then in Marseille. His final birthplace would be Algiers, because that way he was better protected.

Obtaining enough food was a constant problem. The vouchers and ration cards did not always arrive quickly; we didn't have much food and the children were hungry. I became as thin as a rail; I hardly ate and I had too much to do. Even buying groceries took time that was hard to find. I would leave on my bicycle between noon and two o'clock, before or after school, and go to the farms to find food. Once, on a farm in 1943, I heard the BBC announce that two pastors from Le Chambon-sur-Lignon, Theis and Trocmé, had been arrested!

We could get extra tickets by trading. Sometimes I exchanged cigarette tickets for bread tickets. André wasn't thrilled about it, but he allowed it. With cigarette tickets, we could get wood and sometimes a few potatoes. The parishioners often brought us carrots, but they didn't have much to eat either. And then there was the black market. If we had traded our wine tickets it would have been much more lucrative for us, but that was strictly forbidden. We belonged to the Croix-Bleue.[10] André would have never given wine tickets to people in a town where alcoholism was so prevalent. We tore up the wine tickets, and I remember that one day, when we were expecting a big load of wood, the man told me "I'm not going to bring you any more wood because you won't give me your wine tickets!"[11]

Le Chambon-sur-Lignon: A City of Refuge

André Trocmé records the problems involved in granting refugees sanctuary and describes his meeting with representatives from American Protestant churches in Marseille. They suggested that Le Chambon-sur-Lignon be used as a "city of refuge."[12] In fact, the Plateau Vivarais-Lignon had already become a refuge for many people who were persecuted: Spanish republicans, German Jews, those who opposed the Nazis. In 1939, Le Chambon-sur-Lignon had nine hotels, thirty-eight rooming houses, and nine orphanages.[13] The town already had the means to house more children, adolescents, and adults in new buildings. Trocmé's manse was one of the exemplary links in the chain of resistance solidarity.

Very quickly, Jews began to arrive in great numbers. First there were French Jews, fine people, often well-off, who had lost their jobs, their factories, their own businesses. Many of them were able to buy high-priced farm produce to complement their meagre official rations. This was also true of non-Jewish refugees.

It wasn't long before the "competition" between "rich refugees" and the impoverished population of the town led to a palpable tension that wasn't limited to Le Chambon-sur-Lignon. Jews who were guilty of selling and buying on the "black market" were violently denounced by the Vichy press. Public opinion, rarely intelligent, made Jews the scapegoats people needed to blame for their own suffering.

However, Le Chambon-sur-Lignon continued to exist "in peace" on its mountain, while sinister rumours reached us from southern France. Tens of thousands of foreigners, stuck in camps called Gurs, Argelès, les Milles, were enduring dirty, disgusting and even horrific conditions. Although we were supposedly living in the free zone, the Gestapo had its inspectors everywhere. Already, at the end of 1940, they were organizing the deportation of political enemies and Jews to Germany. Families were separated without mercy. The Protestant CIMADE group [...] under the direction of Madeleine Barot had managed to slip a few courageous social workers into these camps.[14] In addition, the French Red Cross and American Quakers worked tirelessly to provide the refugees with food and clothing, while we, in Le Chambon-sur-Lignon, had everything we needed and lived in peace.

I called a meeting of the parish council. I pointed out the fact that we enjoyed great privileges. It was easy to serve our parish, because we could count on Édouard Theis, who was working as a part-time pastor at the time, Henri Braemer, a teacher at the Cévenol school, and Mr Poivre, a retired minister. I asked the council to send me as an "ambassador" to an internment camp; I would live there for a while and give out food and whatever goods our parishioners could collect.

Theis agreed, and the council allowed me to go. First, however, they asked me to make enquiries in the camps. So I left for Marseille, where I made arrangements to meet with a delegation from the American Friends Service Committee. There I met Burns Chalmers [...] who advised me not to go and live in the camps: "We represent several different organizations, and it's not always easy for us. But you tell me you live in a mountain town where it is relatively safe. Our problem is this: with the help of doctors and the French authorities in charge of the camps, we try to issue medical certificates to the greatest possible number of adults in the camps, declaring them incapable of working.[15] If we don't manage to save the father's life, we focus on the mother. If the parents are both deported anyway, we look after the children. Then we ask for the "reformed" prisoners to be housed outside camps. But it is very hard to find a place in

France where anyone will take the risk of providing sanctuary to these people – adults, adolescents, or children – who can compromise the safety of the whole community. Would you like to be the community which welcomes them?"

My unexpected duty was laid out clearly before me.

"But these children: they have to be housed, fed, educated," I said. "Who will take on that job?"

"Get space and assistants," Burns said. The Quakers and the Fellowship of Reconciliation will give you the money you need."[16]

Burns gave his word, and it wasn't broken when the United States entered the war in 1941. The Americans had long since left France, but the Quakers, the Fellowship of Reconciliation [...] and the Congregationalists continued to send us money, faithfully and secretly, through the channels of the Ecumenical Council which was being formed in Geneva and with the help of Charles Guillon.[17] The money was sufficient to operate our children's and teenagers' homes and to pay for the young refugees' education at the Cévenol school. Some courageous messengers carried money across the Swiss border. Many were arrested, and one of them was shot by the Germans. When I got back to Le Chambon-sur-Lignon, I won an easy victory with the parish council, who were happy to keep their pastor in town.[18]

A Synod

In May 1941, André Trocmé took part in the National Synod of the Reformed Church of France, in the southern town of Alès. On this occasion, André once more urged the Reformed Church of France to make an explicit commitment towards the Jewish people. His approach was quite distinct from that of Marc Bœgner who was, at the time, president of the Protestant Federation of France and the National Council of the Reformed Church of France. Bœgner made many public statements that were courageous, if cautious.[19]

Two strong personalities, Trocmé and Bœgner inevitably disagreed about some delicate matters. Nonetheless, Bœgner's personal comments about Trocmé clearly show his respect and admiration.

The German Confessional Church had long ago taken a stand against racism; the Dutch Reformed Church had just made an even stronger declaration. As the vice began to grip more tightly, it was becoming urgent for the Reformed Church in France to make a public statement.

Along with a handful of other delegates, I wrote a statement. The bylaws required five signatures to present a motion to the synod. The text of our motion stated that the Church strongly protested racial persecution, and opposed laws that went against the teachings of the Scriptures, in order to protect the victims of racism.

Oh, I was such a naive youngster (even at forty-one)! I should have sent off my motion in the middle of a session, like the blast of a cannon! But I thought it would be more courteous to let Reverend Bœgner read it first, so I showed it to him during a break between sessions. He read it, raised his eyebrows, and said: "It's very important! Very interesting! I'll look after it myself!" And then he walked off with my motion. I stood there with my mouth open, glued to the spot.

As soon as the session began again, Bœgner took the floor. "Some of our colleagues are very worried about the situation of Jewish refugees. It's a very serious matter that deserves our full attention. I am requesting an *in camera* session, with delegates' voting privileges checked at the door. We must not allow the members of the press who are here to interpret our decisions in their own way when they write their articles."

All right, let's go for the *in camera* session, I told myself, not yet thinking it might be a trap. The evening session took place behind closed doors. There was a tense, dramatic atmosphere. Bœgner talked, he outlined all his personal efforts to help the Jews, and a "letter to the Chief Rabbi of France" that he had written was shared. Generous and vague, the letter had given Bœgner the reputation of being a great resistance fighter. His personal discussions with Pétain "who has been won over completely by the idea of tolerance" and "who is doing everything he can to prevent the deportations." His efforts with the National Council of France, of which he was a member. Basically, everything that needed to be done had been done.

"But we want the entire Church to respond," I objected. "The Church is inconsistent; some parishes, pastors, regions aren't speaking up. Protestants everywhere need to be called to take action to protect the Jewish people."

"That's madness!" replied Mr Bœgner. "All that you'll accomplish that way will be to attract the wrath of Hitler's Germany to the Reformed Church of France, this little flock under my watch. We have to put the 'physical survival of French Protestantism' before all else. That's my business. Put your confidence in me." Then he called for an immediate vote.

The confidence vote passed almost unanimously, with only two or three votes, including mine, against it. My motion was not even read.

After this event, the suspicions and tension between Mr Bœgner and me became an open disagreement. I was furious that he had ploughed over my objections and I was ashamed by the decision of the Reformed Church of France to remain silent. The silence continued until the German Occupation was nearly over [...] It was in the local parishes where pastors were prepared to take a decisive stand that we could hear the courageous voice of the Church ring out loud and strong.[20]

In 1946, when Reverend Bœgner read a long report about the "Protestant Resistance during the war" to the annual general meeting of French Protestants, he spoke in detail about his efforts with Marshal Pétain, congratulated the CIMADE (rightfully so), and listed the many parishes which had exhibited courage in their actions. Le Chambon-sur-Lignon was missing from the list although, according to the Jewish organizations, the town had rescued and sheltered between 2,500 and 3,000 Jews. It seemed that Le Chambon-sur-Lignon, with its progressive ideas and its strong commitment to non-violence did not set a good example for other parishes.[21]

Church Bells

André Trocmé explains here how the members of the Chambon parish supported their pastors and joined them in active and, at times, non-violent resistance.

Our parish council (who had been warned, when I was appointed, that I would never carry arms if I were to be called to serve) had allowed me to declare such opinions openly, although they had never explicitly approved of them. They had also promised to support their pastor through thick and thin and had indeed remained entirely loyal towards Theis and myself. However, when resistance to the Vichy regime became necessary, and was followed, soon afterwards, by refusal to obey the racial laws, our parishioners became frightened. The first people in the region who agreed to receive Jews into their homes were Darbyists, who didn't belong to our denominational group, and whose doctrines required them to avoid any political action.[22] Our parish leaders followed, at first reluctantly, but gradually persuaded of the righteousness of their actions.

On August 1, 1941, the parish openly said "No" for the first time. The week before that, the mayor's office had delivered a directive from the government to us: "August 1, the anniversary of the founding of the Legion, is a national holiday. The clergy shall ensure that the bells of their churches ring loudly for a quarter of an hour starting at noon." It was an example of the ransom for favours that the State, from Pétain down, had heaped upon the Church. I showed the document to Amélie, our custodian, a tiny woman who sometimes came to work at our place. "Obviously," I told her, "you will do nothing of the sort, even if someone comes and tries to force you." Amélie understood completely. She was rather "Darbyist" around the edges.

On August 2, I ran into Amélie in town. The bells at the

Catholic church had rung out loud and clear. Those of our church had remained silent.

"So, Amélie, did everything go alright, yesterday? No incidents?"

"Everything went fine, Mr Tro-que-mé. Nothing happened."

"No visitors?"

"Actually, yes, there were," Amélie replied. "There were two ladies who came from up in the mountains. You know, where the villas are all colourfully painted."

"And?"

"They came to see me. They said, 'Aren't you ringing the bells today, Amélie? It's a national holiday!' 'The pass-a-tor didn't give me any instructions,' I answered. 'Oh, we would have been surprised if your pastor had asked you to ring them! Amélie, hurry, it's noon! It's an order of the Marshal!' they said."

As she told me the story, Amélie looked at me with a funny little smile on the corner of her lips.

"And what did you tell them?" I asked.

"I told them: the bells don't belong to the Marshal, they belong to God. We ring them for God, and not for any other reason."

"Bravo, Amélie. And what happened?"

"Well, they ordered me to open the door so they could ring the bells themselves, but I didn't want to. So I defended my church! I told them that I wouldn't open the door, and they didn't have the right to come in without the pastor's authorization. I stood in front of the door, like this ..." Amélie stationed herself in front of the door as she had done when the ladies were there. She bravely defended her church, stretching out her little arms as far as she could to protect the entrance.

"And how did the whole business end?"

She let out an ironic little laugh. "Oh, you know, yesterday at noon it was raining cats and dogs. I was sheltered by the doorway, but they were in the courtyard. It didn't take long before they were absolutely drenched and they left."

Amélie was right: nothing had happened, in the sense that

the bells had not been rung. As far as she was concerned, her bold resistance wasn't even worth the trouble of mentioning. If I hadn't pushed her, I would have never heard this story, which would have made the Huguenots of the past proud. Like her, they could not repudiate their faith because they didn't know how to repudiate it.[23]

An Icy Reception

In August 1942, the Minister of Youth of the Vichy government, Georges Lamirand, visited Le Chambon-sur-Lignon. In the following passage, André recounts how his visit turned into a ridiculous event. This story shows the spirit of Le Chambon-sur-Lignon and the plateau at the time. The people of the town and the region showed determination, refusing to accept injustice. At the same time they seemed rather carefree; this attitude was no doubt linked both to their sense of invulnerability and their conviction that their actions, because they were just, would be successful.

It was in 1942 that the police network began to tighten its grip on the area around Le Chambon-sur-Lignon.

In the spring, Marshal Pétain came on an official visit to the Haute-Loire, and it was quite a commotion! All of the car owners in town were given gas vouchers, and both townspeople and "tourists" from neighbouring areas came to Puy-en-Velay, the provincial capital, for the occasion, to wave flags and cheer him on. I can still remember the enthusiasm of one of my friends who kept insisting that I join him at the festivities. He was both astonished and scandalized by my refusal.

At the beginning of the summer, the prefect[24] of the Haute-Loire, Robert Bach, who was raised Protestant, wrote to me to apologize for the fact he couldn't convince the Vichy authorities to let the Marshal visit Le Chambon-sur-Lignon, where he could have seen with his own eyes the admirable work the young Protestants of France were doing. Imagine! This admirable work included the Cévenol school, which still didn't have a building of its own, the homes for refugee children, the YMCA camp, and especially the Protestant scout groups, called Éclaireurs et Éclaireuses. Scout groups had been set up in many rural communities, towns, and colleges by the wonderful Naho, aka Pierre Brès, a physical education instructor at the school. Mr Bach's letter also informed us that, to make up for missing the visit from the Marshal, we would soon have an official visit from Mr Lamirand, the Minister of Youth. He added, "I'm sure you will give this visit all the attention it deserves."

Theis and I were devastated. For two years we had been struggling to steer our youth clear of state domination. One of the first things the Vichy government had done was try to gather the young people into a blue-shirted herd of Compagnons de France. But with its fascist salute to the flag, its bugles, its parades, its social events, its work camps, its worship of the country and the Marshal, this group resembled the *Hitlerjugend* too closely to catch on in France. The Catholic and Protestant Éclaireurs were also demanding their independence. The State capitulated, but continued to give generous funding to various youth groups in order to keep them under control.

Meanwhile, in Le Chambon-sur-Lignon, we were teaching pacifism and opposing every type of totalitarianism. We had decided to refuse Lamirand's visit, although the "Powers that Be" were giving us to understand that the matter was out of our hands. The "Powers that Be" were named Jean Beigbeder (what a man he was), the Grand Chief of the Éclaireurs, also called "Owl's Eye," who came from Paris to tell us that he had matters well in hand. There would be a banquet in Joubert, an official procession to a sports field where all the youth groups would be assembled, and then a reception for the authorities in the church, where we would join together in worship.

"It will be fantastic! And on top of it, Lamirand is really great; you'll see," exclaimed Beigbeder.

We felt like we were up against a wall. Nonetheless, things went our way rather than Lamirand's, as you will see. The "banquet" turned into a very simple meal, consisting of the meagre rations the officials allowed us. I took part in it, and was seated next to the minister. "It's better this way," the "great" Lamirand told me, laughing. "It's more in keeping with the attitude of the Marshal, and more patriotic."

He had arrived dressed in a superb uniform, vaguely Germanic in style. He wasn't really laughing since, despite the rationing, he was used to lots of official hoopla.

The official procession was a rather sad affair. I was sitting in Lamirand's car. The town was nearly empty, there were no flags in the windows, no one lined up on the sidewalks: everyone had followed the instructions of the pastors. Lamirand was stunned.

Surrounded by the prefect, the deputy prefect and the deputy mayor, he got out at the field. The pastors didn't follow him; they wanted to avoid involvement in the event. No parade or receiving line had been planned. He was greeted by hundreds of curious children who crowded around him, trying to shake his hand: "G'day, Sir!"

"Good day, good day!" responded Lamirand, startled and charmed by such "spontaneity."

Pierre Brès gave a short talk, quoting Romans 13 about the respect we owe to the higher authorities.[25] It was cold. Lamirand, in the midst of all the commotion, offered a few words in return. It seemed that he had planned a long speech but was forced by circumstances to keep his thoughts to himself. Then he went back to the church where the pastors were waiting for him: because Theis and I refused to preach while the authorities were present, it was Michel Jeannet, a Swiss pastor (isn't it interesting that a citizen of Switzerland should be chosen to represent the French government?) and the president of the "Consistory," an ecclesiastic council composed of several different parishes, who spoke. He did a wonderful job, kept his sermon short, and summarized the position of the Church: obedience to the State, on the condition that the State did not obligate one to violate the laws of God. I was sitting next to Lamirand. I passed him a hymnbook and pointed to the verses. Awkwardly, he tried to sing, the poor man. And as if that wasn't enough, at the end of the worship service a dozen senior students of the Cévenol school, including several who were to become theologians in the future, approached him and handed him a written document. They asked Lamirand politely to read it. Here is the text of the paper, from memory:

"Minister Lamirand, we have found out about the horrific scenes that took place three weeks ago in Paris, where the French police followed the orders of the Occupation forces and arrested all the Jewish families in Paris, removing them from their homes and placing them in the winter fairgrounds.[26] Fathers were brutally torn away from their families and deported to Germany, children were torn from their mothers, who suffered the same fate as their fathers. We have learned from experience that the decrees of the Occupation forces are being imposed on unoccupied France. They are presented as spontaneous decisions of the head of the French state. We are afraid that measures will soon be taken to deport Jews living in the south. We wish to inform you that there are, among us, a certain number of Jews. We do not differentiate between Jews and non-Jews; doing so would be contrary to the teachings of the Bible. If our classmates, whose only fault is to have been born into a different religion, receive a deportation order or even a census order, we will encourage them to disobey the orders and will, to the best of our ability, hide them from the authorities."

Mr Lamirand turned pale and replied: "These matters are none of my business; you should speak to the prefect." And, with that, he strode quickly to his car.

Bach, the prefect, was furious. He had a good idea of who had written the letter. He turned to me and declared: "Reverend Trocmé, this was supposed to be a day of national harmony. Instead, you have made it one of divisiveness!"

I answered: "There can be no hope of national harmony as long as our brothers are being threatened with deportation."

Bach: "It is true that I have received these orders and will carry them out. The Jewish foreigners who are in Haute-Loire are not your brothers. They do not belong to your Church or your homeland! In any case, this is not a matter of deportation."

Me: "What is it a matter of, then?"

Bach: "My information comes from the Marshal himself, and the Marshal does not lie! The Führer is an intelligent man. Just as the English created a district in Palestine for the Zionists, the Führer has ordered the Jews to be gathered together in Poland. There, they will have land and houses. They will lead the life that is best suited to them, and will stop contaminating the West. In a few days, our administration will take a census of the Jews living in Le Chambon-sur-Lignon."

Me: "We do not know any Jews, we only know human beings."

Bach, with a threatening expression: "Mr Trocmé, you had best be careful. Seven of your fellow citizens have been writing to me regularly to keep me informed of your subversive activities. Until today, I have not taken action as a result of their letters but I am aware of what is going on. If you are not careful, it is you who will be interned in a camp. I will have no other choice. Forewarned is forearmed." [...]

And with that, he went back to his car. So, there it was! In 1942, no one knew what the Jewish deportation would result in. We only learned about Auschwitz, Dachau, and Majdanek after the Liberation. Nazi Germany had created such terror among the German people themselves that no one who knew anything dared speak. They didn't even dare believe it, they didn't *want* to believe it for fear of being sent there themselves. Where was "there"? The death camps, the gas chambers, the crematoria. So we knew nothing about this. What we *did* know was that handing over one of our fellow men, who had entrusted himself to us, was wrong. No one in Le Chambon-sur-Lignon in 1942 could agree to that.

How many Jews were in Le Chambon-sur-Lignon in the summer of 1942? Not that many, perhaps a hundred or a hundred and fifty at the most. We knew them all. Several farms had taken people in; others were living in the seven refugee homes or in other places in the town. We had two living in our own home.[27]

Jispa's Arrival

The following story, told by Magda Trocmé after the fact, gives good insight into her character. When an unknown woman arrives in Le Chambon-sur-Lignon to help her out for a few weeks, she becomes a faithful friend of the family and comes to share their lives and their commitment to change.

I'm going to tell you about something marvellous that happened to us during the war. It was getting close to Christmas in 1942. The war had been going on for quite a while already. We were waiting for Alice Reynier to arrive; she was planning to come for three months to help me, sent by Miss Butte, the director of the Pomeyrol spiritual retreat.[28] Once, when Miss Butte had come to Le Chambon-sur-Lignon for a visit, she had found me so thin and pale that she had asked André, "What is wrong with your wife?" André had explained that I was tired, that I really wouldn't be able to take much more of this, that there was never enough food and that I could really use some help. "Never mind," Antoinette replied, "in the winter, after Christmas, I can't keep my volunteers in Pomeyrol because there isn't any food or heat. I'm sending them to different places to help. I have a charming young lady there named Alice Reynier, a schoolteacher. Last year I sent her to Lyon, to help a pastor there, but this year perhaps she can come to stay with you. I'll ask her if she wants to come."

When I first heard about her proposal, I was scared out of my wits. What in the world was I going to do with a lady from the retreat centre, who would spend the whole day praying, think I wasn't a real Christian, and criticize everything? Then I thought more about it and realized it would be stupid to turn down someone who was willing to help. When I needed help, I shouldn't worry about being criticized and not getting along with someone who was simply different from me. So I said yes.

Miss Reynier arrived on January 8. It was a miserable day, snowy and icy. André was away at a meeting of colleagues and young people who helped him take care of the refugees. He had told me, "Listen, don't go to the train station tonight. After my meeting I will go and get the lady myself." My friend, Mrs Marion, came to the manse to help me get ready for her; she had even baked some cookies for the occasion. A few minutes later, the doorbell rang. Miss Reynier had come along on her own, without André. His meeting had gone on so long that he had forgotten all about the train station! She came in and said, with an affectionate smile, "Hello, friend." I was surprised by the greeting; she must be a rather unusual character, I thought. And this is how we met this person who became our friend and our mother, André's and mine.

I had always been looking for another "mother." Mrs Marion had been a bit of a mother-figure, and so had my teachers. As for my father's wife, Marguerite, I had always thought she might have a maternal quality, but no, that wasn't the case! That night, though, I had found a mother. What was even stranger was that André didn't have a mother either. His own had died when he was ten, and "Jispa" came to be like a mother to him, as well. It was amazing: we shared the same mother, so there was no mother-in-law, no tensions, no misunderstandings! In just a few days, Miss Reynier had become friends with everyone in the parish and the grandmother of all the children. Later, when the children got married, she became a great-grandmother to their children. People all over the place knew her, in Europe, in America, in several other countries, because she was indispensable wherever we lived, in Le Chambon-sur-Lignon, in Versailles, in Geneva. All our friends were hers.

Miss Reynier wanted to win difficult children over. The first time she went out with two of the boys, she lost one of them! She also tried to win over Jacquot, but couldn't figure out how. She made up names for them, invented cute little games, but nothing worked. Finally, she made up a nickname for herself: Jispa, meaning Joy in Service, Peace and Affection. It became the name everyone called her. As she told us, "when I feel tired, upset, at those times you get grouchy with me, this name reminds me of why I am here."

Jispa was only supposed to stay with us for three months,

but it went on to four, then five, and then I became ill. Miss Butte decided: "If Magda is ill, you should stay and help. Just send her to Pomeyrol, and we'll take care of her. You'll stay there and take care of the children while she rests." So that is what we did. I spent almost a month in Pomeyrol. Then Miss Butte insisted that Jispa return to the retreat centre, and it was very sad for all of us. She went away and took our son Daniel with her. He went to school there for a while. But André then had to go into hiding, and Jispa realized it wasn't possible to go on that way. Life was becoming more and more complicated in Le Chambon-sur-Lignon; the police were watching us now. Jispa told Miss Butte that she had to go back to the Trocmés; if that meant abandoning the retreat centre, it was just too bad …

That is how she came back to us for good. It happened in 1943 and she has never left since. Today, in October 1976, Jispa is 83 years old. She is still as sprightly as a rabbit, as keen as an eagle, and seems to get younger every day.

Jispa was there when André was arrested and during that endless year he was in hiding. She was extraordinarily helpful. There seemed to be nothing we couldn't do together; we were called upon not only to help the Jews but to respond to more and different situations than I'd ever have imagined.

Letter to Simone

This letter was most likely written by André Trocmé at the beginning of 1943, shortly before his arrest on 13 February. It is a clandestine letter addressed to "Simone" and actually intended for his half-brother, Robert Trocmé. This letter was delivered in secret because in it André speaks openly about his family life, his parish work with Magda at his side, and the assistance they offered to refugees. Moreover, the letter is of particular interest to us because it is a "raw" and real account of the events in which he was involved at the time.

My dear Simone,

We very much appreciated your letter of January 13. I really don't have much use for those little cards on which you can only write a short message, a few trite words: we're fine, Nelly has a couple more years of school, and so on.[29] Today I can write you at some length, and I am thrilled. If I have time, I will be able to write a report giving the latest news from the Trocmés of Le Chambon-sur-Lignon.

First, our worries. Health: the children are doing very, very well, but the parents are not in such great shape. Magda, still overworked [...] is quite thin, not eating well, getting old quickly, to the point that we had some concerns about the future. We went to see a doctor in Lyon and he reassured us. There is nothing dangerous about this aging process, but she needs to avoid exhaustion and nervous tension and get more rest.

And now I myself seem to have cracked. I've over-extended myself [...] and my mind went blank when I was giving the sermon on the Sunday before Christmas. I had to stay away from all my meetings for a whole week because of this mental exhaustion. Ten days with Magda in Dieulefit, after Christmas, put everything back into perspective. But hardly had I got home than I was struck with my old lumbago, which came back after three years and gave me fifteen miserable days with such pain in my stomach and legs that I could barely walk. All this served as a warning to me, because I am obviously overworked. The passing of my friend Cornier, the pastor in Caudry who left behind nine children, hit too close to home. Somehow, we have to find a way out of this whirlwind, but it seems impossible. So we have to deal with the burden and the commotion of a house where people are coming and going all the time.

Next worry: money. Since the first of January (before that, I earned less) I am getting two thousand francs a month, while the cost of living in Le Chambon-sur-Lignon, according to people who have moved here, is almost double that of Paris. Certainly, we're luckier than most. We have potatoes, a little butter, skimmed milk and a little meat, and even ration tickets besides! But the tickets aren't being honoured and we have to buy everything on the black market. With those prices, we've spent twenty-four thousand francs (yes, really!) to buy our potatoes! Nowhere else in France are things so costly. And we spent almost as much on wood for the stove: it costs *half as much* in the villages around us, but we have no transportation. Our farmers have so many buyers (with the refugees, children at the Cévenol school, and so on) that they have lost their minds. Our budget is completely out of whack. We are eating large mouthfuls of our savings. And if that was all it was … Magda is killing herself with all the work she is doing. She gives twenty-four hours a week of Italian lessons. She has three boarders […] not counting the refugees. All of this is a lot of worry for one family. We understand that others have their share as well, but we would really like to get out of this mess and get rid of the impression that we are throwing everything – our savings, our health, our future, our home life – into a big black hole, simply to survive.

That's it for the practical side. Now for the moral aspect: you may know that we have been able to help approximately sixty Jews this summer. We have hidden them, fed them, clothed them, saved them from being deported and often made it possible for them to find safe harbour elsewhere. You can imagine what struggles we've had with the authorities, what real danger that has put us in. We've been threatened with arrest, been subjected to long interrogations.

But since people all over the south of France have heard about our work, from Nice to Toulouse, from Pau to Mâcon, from Lyon to Périgueux, by way of Saint-Étienne, dozens, even hundreds of Jews have headed to Le Chambon-sur-Lignon. My regular work as a minister has come to a complete halt. I already had to turn my dining room into a waiting room every summer, with ten or fifteen people arriving every day to see me; now it's like that all year 'round.

I have told you about the atmosphere, the situation; you know it all, three thousand and three hundred parishioners, of whom two thousand live on farms in the countryside, seven hundred in town, five or six hundred people from outside of the region: a hundred and fifty refugees from Central Europe, adults, students, children in six different homes; three hundred students at the Cévenol school. About thirty teachers, fifteen people in charge of the dormitory, the band, the speakers, the choir, and four troops of Éclaireurs. A preparatory program for theology, a training program, and soon a farm education program. Everybody on the go, and going through the manse at one time or another. We can't even remember everyone's name any more. The Cévenol school is a victim of its own success! Students have come from far and wide; there would be four hundred if we could find room for them all. And they are no longer refugees but rather students that have been left with us by their parents, who want them to have an education.

Compared to most churches, we are spoiled in terms of what we have. There are approximately twenty pastors in training who act as group leaders, committee chairs, counsellors. When we have a youth pastors' meeting, we have thirty-five people attending. At Bible study teachers' meetings, we have twenty. Nearly two hundred men attend the various local men's circles; each of the fifteen leaders comes every two weeks to give talks on "the Christian individual, family, and community." Since November, I've had to find a secretary (a man who was involved in the church in Clamart) to help me sort my mail and look after my bookkeeping and other office work.[30] The magnificent generosity of our friends made this luxury possible: if you can call it a luxury. It's only because I've caught up with my correspondence that I could take the time to write you such a long letter.

But in this whirlwind of the activity, what happens to family life? [...] We are so rarely alone with our children, and we all suffer from it. Magda and I defend our Monday holidays as stubbornly as possible, and we still manage to read quite a few good novels out loud.[31] However, the children are in school on Mondays, and in the evenings we are so tired! The month of holidays compensates for this workload. The month goes by quickly, and because we have to take it when we can, we only have the children with us for two weeks of it. But the children are learning so much from everything around them. They learn what life is all about at a very young age. They watch the parade of interesting new people file by in front of them. Sometimes it will be a musician, sometimes a famous historian, sometimes an inventor, sometimes an artist …

And there you have it: the story of our life, as well as I can tell it.[32]

The Arrest of the Pastors of Le Chambon-sur-Lignon and Roger Darcissac

In this excerpt, Magda Trocmé describes the circumstances surrounding the arrest of André, Reverend Édouard Theis, and Roger Darcissac on 13 February, 1943. She then shares some of the details concerning their imprisonment, until their release on 15 March 1943.

In August 1942 my husband had already been warned by the prefect that the Vichy government had sent people to monitor what was happening in Le Chambon-sur-Lignon, that my husband had to release the names of the Jews who were living there, that there would be no dire consequences as a result, that the Marshal understood the situation very well, and that they would no doubt be sending some people to the centre of Germany where a new "state" was being established for them.

My husband was half-German, on his mother's side, and we had a lot of relatives in Germany. We had seen what was happening under Hitler and we couldn't be "brainwashed" that easily! Besides, I am Italian and I had seen what happened under Fascist rule, even if Mussolini was nothing like Hitler.

So we were already well aware that we were in grave danger. But no one else was afraid, and we weren't either. The work was so urgent, so pressing, and people were arriving so quickly. We had to find room for them, make arrangements for them. We weren't the only ones doing it; there were lots of people involved in a big operation like this. Initially, we thought we had rescued about 2,000 Jews, but last June some of the former Jewish refugees came to Le Chambon-sur-Lignon to present a plaque recognizing our work, and they said that approximately

5,000 ID card applications had been given out to the Jews and other refugees.[33] Everyone did his best to forge these documents, especially Oscar Rosowsky, called "Plunne," who worked day and night.

So my husband had been warned. The prefect had said, "You know, these Jews do not belong to your religion, nor to your race, nor to the community of Le Chambon-sur-Lignon. It is your duty to give their names. In fact, you will save them a lot of trouble if you do." My husband replied, "It's not a question of race or religion, they are human beings. I don't know all their names. They are people who have asked for sanctuary here, and they deserve to be treated with respect and compassion."

I had personally heard what internment camps were like, and I wanted to pack a little suitcase with André's clothes, so that if he were arrested there would be something ready for him. The suitcase was all ready in August. But it turned cold again, and I often took clothes out of the suitcase to give to André, who didn't have many. In the end, the suitcase was empty!

On February 13, 1943, there was a knock at the door and I found myself under the noses of two fairly high-ranking police officers who wanted to speak to my husband. Given that everyone was always looking for my husband, I wasn't surprised. I told them that he wasn't there but if they needed information, I knew about his work and could answer. "Oh, no, it's a very personal matter," they said.

My husband was at his youth council meeting. At these meetings, he could talk to the young people and the congregational leaders. It was where he shared all his ideas about rescuing the innocent and building a city of refuge. My husband got home very late. I was in the kitchen, knitting, and had even forgotten that the policemen were waiting in the office! When he came inside, he found himself face-to-face with them. A few minutes later, he came out and said: "That's it; I'm under arrest." I shouted: "Oh! The suitcase is empty!" "What suitcase, Madam?" asked one of the policemen. "We were expecting this arrest, you know. I had packed a suitcase for my husband so he would be ready, but it was so cold I used up everything I had."

"We're not in a hurry," they said. "You can do what you need to do."

After the suitcase was packed, it was time for supper. That night we were having vetch, and even after cooking for three hours it was so hard it bounced off the plate like marbles.[34] I told the police officers, "It's supper time; you can eat with us." They were extremely surprised; it was unusual for a police officer to be invited for supper when he had come to arrest someone. I didn't do it out of generosity. It was time for our meal, that's all. They were embarrassed; one of them had tears in his eyes. They realized that what they were doing wasn't exactly something they had dreamed of. I asked them if I could let some of the congregational leaders know what was happening, because it would be difficult for them if my husband left without warning. "Oh, no!" they said. "No one can know that Monsieur Trocmé is being arrested." In fact, I found out later that there were five cars circling our house and they had cut off our telephone. And that night, Suzanne Gilbert, my husband's god-daughter, had something to tell us.

She had arrived and found the police officers at our house. Immediately, she ran through the town to alert people, and they started to file towards the manse, carrying gifts. They came in, wished André luck, gave their offering and then left. It was really quite moving. At one point, someone arrived with a roll of toilet paper, an article that was rare and valuable at the time. It was only much later, when my husband opened the package in the camp, that he discovered it contained Bible verses, devotionals of encouragement, patience, trust in God. They were written hurriedly, every which-way, so that the pastor could have messages from his parish even in his camp or prison.

I should tell you that one of the last presents he was given was a candle, and it was very precious. But we didn't have any matches to light it, and the police officer, the one who had tears in his eyes, took a box of matchsticks out of his pocket, put them on the table, and said: "Here, I'll give you the matches. And I'll write a report to explain how things happened."

Meanwhile, unbeknownst to us, a young lady had collected a crowd of people and students from the Cévenol school who began to line the street outside our home, the Rue de la Grande-Fontaine. When my husband came out, he walked between the two lines of supporters, who began to sing Luther's hymn: "A Mighty Fortress is Our God."

It was incredibly moving. I asked the policemen if I could accompany my husband, and they allowed me to go with him as far as the end of the town. Once there, I was able to talk to him for a few minutes while they arrested Rev. Theis, the half-time pastor and school administrator, and the principal, Mr Darcissac. When they had all been picked up I had to go back to the manse and my husband left.

The first night, they kept him in the police station in Tence. The second night, he was in the prison in Le Puy, where he had to sleep without sheets or blankets in a locked room. Then he was taken to the Saint-Paul d'Eyjeaux camp near Limoges. To get there they had to go through Lyon and change trains. André wasn't handcuffed, but he had officers walking on either side of him. He said it was really strange to see how a man who was usually well-respected could be viewed with such suspicion by passersby; it was as though he was automatically condemned by public opinion simply because he was with the police. The same thing is true of people arrested for robbery and murder who, even if they are innocent, are presumed to be guilty. This gave André food for thought.

Édouard Theis, Roger Darcissac, and André were met with a lot of enthusiasm when they reached Saint-Paul d'Eyjeaux, because 75 per cent of the prisoners held there were Communists. This was the time when the Communists were all being rounded up: the true, dyed-in-the-wool Communists, the earliest and most earnest, and they were glad to have two pastors among them. There was already a priest there, and the men had begun to enjoy important discussions. Non-violence was of no interest to them; for important action to be accomplished, they said, a true revolution was necessary. After that there would be peace and joy. Until the revolution had taken place, they thought, my husband and his friend were mistaken about the course of action. Some of them were a bit suspicious because they thought the two ministers were "black sheep," traitors. Then they saw what they were really like, and that was when the men began to have experiences of real friendship and sharing. I went to visit when I could. My husband called the visit "love in the tram" because we had to see each other in a long, narrow room. We could bring all the provisions we wanted for the prisoners. The guards in the observation tower asked for food, too, but we did not give it to them.

Suddenly, five weeks after they arrived, the order came for their release. Why? We didn't know.[35] Their personal effects were returned; they gave back their mattresses and covers. At the last second, the director of the camp gave them a paper certifying that they were leaving on such and such a day and time. At the bottom of the page was written: "I pledge allegiance to the government of Marshal Pétain."

Darcissac signed it. The two pastors said, "We don't know why we are here, but it is probably because we didn't do what allegiance to Marshal Pétain required of us. So we cannot sign this paper."

"But it doesn't matter," the director said; "it's just a formality, just paperwork that isn't important and that everyone signs."

"Well, we can't sign it."

They did not sign it and were immediately returned to the camp. It was quite a drama. The prefect who had kindly told me my husband was going to leave the camp told me that there was nothing more he could do: my husband was to be imprisoned once more for refusing to sign the paper.

A few days later, a telegram signed by Pierre Laval, the prime minister under Pétain, arrived: "The two pastors must leave immediately." They didn't even allow them to say goodbye to their friends in the camp. They took them away quickly on the little train, so there wouldn't be any contact with the others. And that is how they finally came back to Le Chambon-sur-Lignon. A few days later, the Saint-Paul d'Eyjeaux camp closed. All of the prisoners were deported to Germany.[36]

Refusal to Sign

In order to be released, André Trocmé, Édouard Theis, and Roger Darcissac had to sign the following document:

I, the undersigned … released from the supervised residence camp of Saint-Paul d'Eyjeaux, Haute-Vienne, certify that I have been informed by the camp commander that I must make a pledge of honour to support the new social order, to respect "the work and the person of the *Maréchal de France*, the head of State," and not to take part in any anti-nationalist activities, and that any violation of this latter prohibition may be grounds for prosecution, without prejudice to any further administrative action that may be taken against me.

Darcissac, who was a civil servant and had a responsibility to obey the government, could hardly do anything else but sign the agreement. Trocmé and Theis, for their part, made a conscientious objection and refused to sign the declaration. Finally, a compromise was found and they were released the following day, on 15 March 1943, after each of them signed the following agreement: "As a clergyman, I cannot make a pledge of honour to support any social order that exists. I commit to respecting the person of the *Maréchal de France*."[37]

6

The End of the War

After two raids on foreign-born Jews in Le Chambon-sur-Lignon on 26 August 1942 and 24 February 1943, a new police operation took place on 23 June 1943. This time, the Gestapo arrested Daniel Trocmé,[1] André's nephew, as well as eighteen young students who were living in the Maison des Roches.[2] The people of Le Chambon-sur-Lignon were still in shock about these arrests when, in July, a member of the French underground who said he was a double agent came to warn André that the Germans wanted to kill him.

It is possible that the visit was a strategy by armed Resistance fighters to get rid of the non-violent ministers, who prevented them from recruiting young people from the area. However, André had good reason to take the threat seriously. At first he refused to leave but Maurice Rohr, vice-president of the Reformed Church, convinced him to go into hiding, telling him: "What good would it do to add another name to the list of martyrs? It's already long enough … And do you think the parish would remain non-violent if you were killed?"

In the end, André obtained false papers, shaved his moustache, put on a Basque beret and large glasses, and left Le Chambon-sur-Lignon. Mr Lespet, a Protestant hardware salesman from the town of Lamastre, in Ardèche (a region in south-central France about thirty kilmetres from the Trocmés' home), hid him first in the manse of Lamastre, then on a farm farther south in Chamos, then at a large, secluded place in the countryside between Lamastre and Vernoux. Finally André lived in a castle in Perdyer, about one hundred and fifty kilometres southeast of Le Chambon-sur-Lignon. This lavish residence was shared by the Deloche family (with whom André boarded) and Jacques Martin, a conscientious objector. During this period André was unable to participate in any clandestine action, as he was suffering from back problems that paralyzed him for days at a time. He kept busy by writing a theological text entitled *Oser croire* (*Dare to Believe*), but ultimately decided not to publish it.

When he returned to Le Chambon-sur-Lignon on 14 June 1944, he found that the town "had changed a great deal in ten months. The underground is no longer hidden. Young people parade in the streets, dressed in odd pieces of uniforms, with machine guns in their hands ... There were more refugees than ever."[3]

Although the war was coming to an end, this was still a very difficult period, especially for the Trocmés, who lost their son Jean-Pierre on 13 August 1944.[4] His son's death left André inconsolable; he described himself using the metaphor of evergreens which had lost their top branches and could never stand tall and strong again.

The following passages describe the chaos in Le Chambon-sur-Lignon and the surrounding area, and the atrocities which occurred there before and after the Allies arrived. They also relate André's efforts to resume his work after he got home, and to guide his congregation towards actions which were consistent with the Gospels and avoided the temptations of revenge and violence.

André's Creed

During the winter of 1943–44, while he was in hiding in the castle in Perdyer, André sought to clarify his spiritual convictions. Despite the tragedy of the war, the following credo reflects his optimistic attitude and his capacity to connect the individual to the community.

I believe in the reality, the value and the freedom of the human person.

I believe in the reality and the value of great ideals.
I believe there is only one goodness, the one displayed by Christ.
I believe that spiritual life is not destroyed by death.
I believe in the ultimate triumph of good over evil.

Christianity is almost too good. That is why we see numerous people raised as Christians abandon their faith and turn to pantheist, Eastern, or scientific thought. They prefer clear reasoning and obscure beliefs, would rather doubt goodness rather than reason. However, one dilemma cannot be solved by reason: why would eleven Galilean farmers' sons, discouraged and tired, go out into the world and preach the resurrection of their Master if Christ had remained buried in the shadowy cave where they had left him the Friday before? That, we believe, is one of the greatest puzzles in human history. Science has, in our opinion, been unable to solve it. The historical truth is crystal clear only to those who do not need visible proof. As Jesus told Thomas: Blessed are those who have not seen and yet have believed.[5]

The Gestapo at the Maison des Roches

The dramatic circumstances surrounding the arrest of André's nephew, Daniel, and the students at the Maison des Roches are described below by Magda. Two other witnesses have given different versions of the story.[6]

My story would not be complete without a crucial event that ended tragically. It was 1943; it was almost summer. We had left for Pomeyrol, Papa, the children and myself, leaving Jean-Pierre behind to finish his classes.

I had to go back to Le Chambon-sur-Lignon. I'm not sure why; perhaps I had to help my students get ready for their matriculation exams. Early one morning, Suzanne Heim came to the manse, obviously frazzled, shouting: "Come quick, Mrs Trocmé! Daniel Trocmé's been arrested!" "Where?" "They came to the children's house in Des Roches! Daniel could have gone into the woods right behind the house. But he said he couldn't do that, because he was responsible for the Maison des Roches."

While the Gestapo was arresting the older students in the residence, they asked who was in charge and went after Daniel.

I got on my bike, and Suzanne and I rushed up to the Maison des Roches. I went into the residence and Suzanne went back to the children's house. Why did they let me in? I don't know … The doors were open. The doctor had tried to go in because the child of one of the staff members was sick, but they did not let him. Reverend Poivre had tried to get in, too, but could not get in. But I could. In my rush, I had not taken my apron off. Maybe the Germans thought I was part of the kitchen staff? I went through the kitchen and into the dining hall. What I saw there was horrifying: on one side of the room, three or four Gestapo officers sitting at a table with some of the staff of the Maison des Roches, including the bookkeeper. The Gestapo were armed with machine guns. On the other side of the room, all of the students were lined up against the wall. The last one in line was Daniel Trocmé, the brother of Dr Charles Trocmé of Saint-Étienne. Did they realize that Daniel was someone important?

I tried to get close to him, but the Gestapo shouted so loudly that I stopped in my tracks, turned around and went back into the kitchen. No one moved; they must have thought I was a cook or a chambermaid. I sat down. After a few minutes, the students began filing by, one by one, into a little storage room on the far side of the kitchen. There, the Gestapo fellows had a register full of names. They questioned the students: their names, other details … When they came out, some of them had black eyes and seemed terrified. Some of them talked quickly and quietly: "I have a bit of money in my room, hurry and get it," or "Here's my mother's address" or "This is my fiancée's address, I have a gold watch, please take it to her." The poor boys did not realize that the Gestapo had already gone through the place and taken everything.

At around ten o'clock, the Gestapo was hungry. During the war, food disappeared quickly: eggs, butter, everything. But that morning they had brought two eggs for each of them and each of the staff members. I had two eggs and a slice of bread! The students, however, only got a ration of bread and we had to go and get them water.

We ended up using little pots to serve the water and, because there were so many students, we had to make several trips to fill them. I took advantage of one of the trips to take a pot of water over to Daniel, and talk to him for a quick minute. He said, "Remember how a student from this residence, a Spaniard, saved a German soldier from drowning in the Lignon River? Here's what you should do. Go to the Lignon Hotel, and tell them that the Gestapo is arresting everybody here, and remind them about that rescue. Who knows? Maybe because of him, we'll be safe. It's worth reminding them. Try it." I had no trouble leaving, getting on my bicycle, and setting out for the hotel.

What a beautiful day it was! The scotch broom was in flower; the sun was gentle and warm. It was extraordinary to see all this beauty, calm, and peace, and to know there were such horrors going on at the Maison des Roches nearby. I arrived in front of the hotel in Lignon, where Germans on leave came to relax in Le Chambon-sur-Lignon. I had to talk to the officers who had settled into town since this comfortable rest stop had been set up. Luckily, I knew how to speak German and I wasn't afraid. I went up to the guard, who simply said: "Verboten." I answered that I was in a hurry and needed to see one of the authorities who had been here for a long time. "Impossible," he said. "What do you want to tell him? I'll give him the message."

"No, it's a personal matter."

The messenger went upstairs and, a moment later, came to get me. On the second floor, sitting at a table near the window, were two or three officers. I went in and they asked me what I wanted.

"I want to know which of you has been in Le Chambon-sur-Lignon for a long time."

"It's none of your business."

"Well, then, I can't talk to you. I have something important to tell you but, in order to do so, I have to know how long you have been in Le Chambon-sur-Lignon."

Now they were intrigued. "Well, I have been here for X weeks," one of them said. "Longer than I should have been."

I asked, "Do you remember a German soldier who nearly drowned in the Lignon River?"

"Yes, yes, I remember that very well."

"One of the students from the Maison des Roches saved him."

"Yes, that's right. I remember."

"Well, this morning the Gestapo arrived …"

"We have nothing to do with the Gestapo."

"I just want you to talk to them. It's a question of honour. I am a lady, you are an officer, so we are both people with a sense of honour. I am simply asking you to tell the truth, to tell them that this rescue took place while you were here."

The officer looked a bit sheepish. "How did you get here?"

"I rode my bike."

"Go back there and I'll come later."

I refused. They had to come with me, on foot, while I walked my bike.

It must have looked very strange, to see Mrs Trocmé with a German on either side of her! When we got as far as the Pension des Marronniers, a girls' residence, I saw two young women from my UCJG group riding their bicycles. They looked shocked when they saw me with two Germans, and astonished when I told them I needed to borrow their bicycles for the two men. Fortunately, they liked me and trusted me, and handed them over willingly. So off we rode, me on my bike riding between two Germans on girls' bicycles! I had to say something to fill the silence. I mentioned how sad it was to hear about the German soldier and several French students who were killed in Clermont-Ferrand. "I think it's really too bad. It's not good for the population; it creates such a bad atmosphere." The older, and apparently harsher, officer replied: "You know, this is a war, and when a German soldier is killed you have to expect that someone is going to kill some Frenchmen in revenge." Silence. Finally I said, "There are some officers of the Gestapo in the hotel nearby, nice men who have come up from Clermont-Ferrand. Meanwhile you are officers in active duty in the army. In a few days, you will probably be on the front, or on your way back from it. You will be in danger … I don't know, what do you think?" The younger one looked at me with an odd expression, as if he wondered whether I was stupid to speak so frankly or I was right. But the older one had a face of stone; without moving an eyelash he replied: "All the members of the Gestapo were on the Russian front." More silence.

We got to the Maison des Roches. It had been easy to get in the first time, but harder the second. I was no longer "the kitchen help." I was someone who spoke German, who made decisions, who had gone to talk to the Germans and brought them back with me. I had even made them promise to tell the truth, as a matter of honour.

Then I said to one of the Gestapo: "I can't leave. I have to talk to my cousin, Mr Trocmé. He has been in charge of this residence and he has to tell me what to do."

"You can come back at noon. We'll be sure to let you talk to Mr Trocmé then."

I had said that I was Daniel's cousin, which was not as problematic as if I had said I was his aunt, and therefore André's wife.

So off I went again, through the flowering scotch broom, back to the manse where Jean-Pierre was waiting. He was furious with me. He did not want me to throw myself into the lion's den. He wanted to come with me. An hour or two went by, and, when I went to pick up my bicycle, Jean-Pierre was already out in the yard getting his. By the time we got to the Maison des Roches, everything had changed. The students were lined up on the stairs under the little balcony that no longer exists. Daniel was first in line. I could get to him right away and talk to him. While I was on the balcony, two or three members of the

Gestapo were whipping a young Jewish Dutch boy with a strap, shouting "Jewish pig! Jewish pig!" The atmosphere was horrifying.

At that point, Daniel said: "Don't worry. I'll go with the students. I'll try to explain things to them, to protect them as long as I can. Anyway, write to my parents, tell them what happened. But you know, I like travelling. I'm not afraid and this is my duty. Don't worry about me."

Jean-Pierre was devastated. He was pale and "green around the gills." He was trying hard not to cry. Then, one by one, all the students were put into trucks and driven away. I went into the dining hall. And there was Pepito, the Spaniard who had saved the German soldier. The Gestapo officers had been honest and had spared him. But my hope, and Daniel's, had been to save several, or even all of them. On the table, there were a few coins, scraps of paper with the address of a mother or a fiancé. It was pathetic.

There was also a woman named Mrs Meyer who had lost her husband in the Resistance. She said to me, "You know, Mrs Trocmé, it's dangerous! The papers that say my husband has been called for duty are upstairs in my bedroom. If the Gestapo find them, it's over! He won't be hard to find; he's hiding close by in the woods. He left when the Gestapo arrived. What should I do?" I went upstairs, found the papers, and gave them to Mrs Meyer.

We were on our way home from the Maison des Roches when, riding next to me, Jean-Pierre announced: "When I grow up, I'm going to get back at them."

"Now, Jean-Pierre, you know that we shouldn't try to get back at people. War might resolve a few conflicts, but it causes many more. That's how we end up going from one war to another. You know Papa and his ideas about non-violence and love for others. We have to understand and forgive. That's the only way we'll get anywhere. You can't think about violence."

"Oh, Mama, it's so awful!" After that he did not say anything else. We were home.[7]

A Trap in Lyon

At the beginning of 1944, as he was going out to the Perrache train station in Lyon to meet his son Jacques, who was to come and stay with him at the castle in Perdyer, André Trocmé was caught in a trap set by the German police. While he was waiting to be questioned, he managed to escape from the attention of the police. This episode, which could have had a tragic ending, shows how fragile human life really is.

On my way to pick up Jacques in Lyon, I almost fell into the hands of the Gestapo and lost this life which, for the first time, I was really enjoying.

I was supposed to meet Jacquot at the Paillots' house in Villeurbanne, about 20 km away from the station. On the way there, everything went fine. We spent the night at our friends', and got up early on Sunday morning to return to Perdyer. If I remember correctly, the train to Valence was supposed to leave at around eight thirty. We did not get there early enough, however, and I only had a few minutes to pick up Jacquot's luggage which Magda had sent along the night before.

When we got to the station, I told Jacquot to sit at the top of the big stairway into the train station. "Wait for me here," I told him. "I'll be right back." Then off I ran to the baggage check which was in the left wing of the station, down a long hallway.

I suddenly heard shouting behind me. At first I did not pay much attention because I had no idea the shouts were directed toward me. I continued to run until I found myself a few steps away from a German soldier, his face swollen and red, as though he was about to explode. He pointed his gun at my chest. Behind me stood another soldier, as menacing as the first. Terrified and mystified by this brutal show of force against me, I surrendered myself to their will. They growled guttural, incomprehensible orders and made me back up farther and farther. At one point I tripped on some object under my heel and fell to the floor. There I was, sitting just outside the door into the paddy wagon. They picked up my legs and threw me inside, slammed the door and locked it from the outside. I figured I was "done for."

I tried to gather my wits about me. I got up on the bench and reviewed the situation. As absurd as it might seem, I had been arrested for running. It had nothing to do with being a suspect of the Gestapo, but I had been caught. They would question me and put me in prison. My papers were under the name of "Béguet" and stated I was born … who knows where? I would have to lie in order for my new identity to be credible. I had never imagined that I would be arrested for such a stupid reason. The false papers were intended only to avoid having the French authorities, who would recognize my name, turn me over to the Germans. I also needed to have a ration card under the new name.

I decided I could not lie. That would be tempting fate, and sliding down a slippery slope of compromises God had not asked me to make. I would speak the whole truth. "My name is not Béguet. I am Reverend André Trocmé.." This decision soothed my conscience. After all, if God had just caught me, as He had done with Jonas in the Bible, if He had chosen me to be sacrificed, He would not appreciate me balking at telling the truth.

But what about Jacquot? Poor little Jacquot who was anxiously waiting for me, and I would not be coming back. He would not be able to find his way to our friends' house on his own. He would be panicking by now. I had to get a message to him, and get his baggage claim to him so he could get his luggage. Through the bars of the window at the back of the paddy wagon, I shouted to the guard who was watching me. In German, of course: what a stroke of luck to know German!

"Pssst … Hören Sie mal!"

The guard ignored me. I repeated it and he came over to me. "My son, a tall blond boy, twelve years old, is waiting for me with my bags in front of the station. Please have him called. I need to tell him where he has to go, because I have been verhaftet (arrested)."

Skeptical, the soldier called his supervisor over. I repeated my request.

"I'll have to ask the captain," the officer said.

I waited for the captain for a long time. Finally he arrived. I explained the situation to him in detail.

"You're lying," he said bluntly. "Why were you running?"

"I was late for the train to Valence, and I was rushing to get the bags we had checked. Here is my baggage claim; you can see for yourself."

"So you weren't trying to escape the raid?"

"What raid?" I asked naively.

"You didn't notice that the station was surrounded by police?"

"No, I was just worried about the time."

"Are you saying you crossed a police line without knowing it? That hardly seems likely."

"Maybe, but it's the truth."

"Well," he said, "we'll find out the truth right now. Take the prisoner to the front of the station," he ordered the guard. "If it is true that his son is waiting for him, bring them back. If not ..." he looked at me with a threatening expression. "If you are trying to dupe the German police, you should know what to expect. You won't be able to escape; you'll be a dead man."

I was taken out of the paddy wagon. The guard pushed his gun between my shoulder blades.

"Los!" ("Go!") he shouted. I walked like a robot towards the front of the station, hoping that Jacques would still be there. He was, and welcomed me with relief and affection.

"Da ist er," ("That's him,") I told the guard. Seeing the German soldier behind me, Jacquot thought that I had asked him to help me with the bags, as Magda, who was always bolder than I, had done one day in the Valence station. When I had criticized her for doing it, she had just shrugged and said, "They should make themselves useful somehow."

"I've been arrested, Jacquot," I said. His eyes widened when he saw the gun pointed at my back. "Come, we have to go and see the German officer, so I can tell you where to go."

"Papa, Papa, what's going to happen to us?" cried Jacques.

He was as terrified as a child could possibly be. We walked back to the officer. He took one look at the handsome blond child who was beyond himself with fear and sorrow, and his expression changed. He was obviously moved.

"You were telling the truth," he said. "I understand. Come now," he told his guard. "Take this man and his son to the security check. Stay with him until he has gone through; don't let him escape. Go!" And then he saluted me.

"Danke schön," I said.

The guard led us to a long line-up going through in the security area, where our papers would be checked. In the distance, we could see an officer sitting at a table, carefully examining all the documents delivered to him and looking up information in a little book of "suspects." Then he compared the faces of the travellers against a collection of photos.

"We're not out of the woods yet," I thought. "My papers are false. I said that Jacques was my son. The guard is right beside me. Jacques's papers are under the name of Trocmé, a name known to the police, and mine are under the name of Béguet. It will be hard for me to lie. I have to avoid the security check, but how?"

The parade filed slowly ahead. Passengers complained that they would miss their trains. My guard began chatting with some friends who had clustered around him some distance away. Soon he fell behind while we made our way slowly forward.

If only I could put the pillar between myself and the guard, I thought, I would be able to see how the soldiers reacted. I knew that behind the pillar there was an exit used by passengers who got off the train and went out into the street.

"Jacquot," I murmured to my son, "Do exactly what I do. Slowly. Don't run. Be ready. Pick up your bags."

"Yes, Papa."

The guard took his eyes off us for an instant. I took my son out of the line and walked five steps to one side. We were behind the pillar, out of the guard's sight. Jacquot had followed me. There was no reaction from the soldiers.

"Let's walk slowly out of the station in the middle of a crowd," I told Jacquot. That is what we did. Slowly, calmly, with other people who were getting off a train, we walked out of the station. There was no need to worry; the security check was only for people leaving on trains.

We went down the stairs. We climbed onto the number 7 tram. Fifteen minutes later we were in the church that Juliette Paillot went to. I picked up the hymnbook and I sang like I had never sung before. It was Sunday, and I was free. I had come close to death; I had even accepted the idea that I might die. Instead, I was free and had not even had to lie. This might have been the only time in the history of the Gestapo that a prisoner had been arrested, already been put in the paddy wagon, and had left without a single policeman stopping him to ask for his papers. The request would have been the end for me.

Who had saved me? I had been saved by my son, whose tears had touched the heart of the officer. Saved by God, certainly, after a strange set of circumstances that had begun with my late arrival, my thoughtless rush through the station and had now ended in a sanctuary. "God did not want me to die yet," I told myself.

Juliette was astonished to see me there. She welcomed us into her home for a second night. The next day, one of her sons left to scout out the situation at the station. The raid had ended; the coast was clear. That night, we left for Perdyer.

Nonetheless, the epilogue to this story was just as strange. A few years ago, when I was in Geneva, a history professor came to see me. He had worked for the communications department of the government and had resigned to devote himself to studying the history of the Resistance movement during the Second World War. He wanted to interview me about my experiences in order to fill some gaps in his information. I did my best to help him.

"But what about your arrest at the beginning of 1944, at the train station in Lyon?" he asked.

"What? How did you find out about that? No one knows that story."

"Oh, don't kid yourself! I have access to the documents that belonged to the Gestapo. It says they recognized you from your photo, but it was too late: you had already got away. How did you do it?"

I told him about the pillar.

"Ah, I see! You had a bit of nerve, I see! After you escaped, they figured out who you were and the officer who was guarding you was held responsible for your disappearance. According to the documents I have, he was sent to the Russian front. That's where they sent policemen who were negligent in some way, to punish them …"

I hope that my kind, distracted liberator did not die on the Russian front. He did not deserve that. He was a good man, for the face of a child crying was all it took to stir his heart.[8]

Message to the Reformed Church in Le Chambon-sur-Lignon

André wrote this message and read it to his congregation in Le Chambon-sur-Lignon during a Sunday service in June 1944. It was the first talk he had given after being away for ten months.

I cannot put into words the full measure of my joy at being back among you after such a long absence.

When the leaders of the Reformed Church asked me ten months ago to leave for a while and to make myself available to the church should the need and opportunity arise, I had no idea that the few weeks we expected I would be away would become so many long and dreary months […]

Today, the day I awaited with increasing impatience is a reality, and I pray to God that I will be able to stay here permanently.

Many things in our beloved parish have changed since I left: tears of mourning, worries over serious illnesses, and atrocious events like the raids in nearby communities.

At the same time, babies have been born, gifts of God that

remind us that life goes on and God provides for our future. New projects and plans have taken shape in our church. People have once again demonstrated their energy and dedication.

I want to thank all of those, both ministers and laypeople, who have preached the Gospel and who have done God's work [...]

Great trials still lie before us in this country, and perhaps even in this church. We are learning about war in all its forms, and we have now been initiated by fire into its consequences, along with the rest of our nation. However, our problems are nothing compared to those of people who are starving in the big cities, whose homes and communities have been bombed, who live on the front lines of the battles. Great trials reveal the measure of men. Some will slide easily into a selfish existence, thinking only of themselves and of how to benefit from the suffering of their fellow men. Others will be carried away by their passion, their willingness to sacrifice their own desires for others, their devotion.

Followers of Jesus Christ do not hesitate when given these choices. They know they must offer their lives and their money for the benefit of others. But remember that Christ's disciples have a particular kind of devotion. Christians do not seek the kingdom of this world but the Kingdom of God. Christians do not use earthly arms to fight against the forces of evil. Violence, lies and vengeance are not the weapons of Christian people. When I came here, I was very happy to see that you are people of calm and firm character. A spirit of moderation and gentleness must reign among us.

The gift of our lives and calm and trusting natures are not enough, however. We also need to use the weapons of God. They are more humane and more effective than any other arms, but are much more difficult to find. If we fight evil with evil, how can we defeat it? [...]

Remember, a Christian is a person who perseveres. A Christian knows that nothing important can be accomplished in the midst of noise, excitement, and grandeur, followed by panic and depression when danger ensues [...] Brothers and sisters, this is not a short period of crisis. Things will not quickly fall into place afterwards. This is a grand battle between love and hate, light and shadows, truth and lies, Christ on the cross and sin.

After the crisis we are now experiencing is over, other forms of struggle will follow [...] May Christians who have been awakened by the great suffering and injustice in our world and who are now ready to give their lives know their commitment is a commitment to God, a commitment of their entire existence. It is only then, in perseverance and in love, that their sacrifice will be of any use [...]

Without faith, we will risk shaking up clouds of dust only to discover that we have worked in vain. But with faith, we will witness miracles. I am sure of it, and I ask you to share this conviction.[9]

Catastrophes and Courage

In this retrospective account, André Trocmé describes the atmosphere in Le Chambon-sur-Lignon when he returned from hiding. At the same time as impressive numbers of courageous acts were carried out, countless acts of violence had occurred.

The interfaith humanitarian organization CIMADE had organized a sort of underground railway to enable Jews to cross the Swiss border. Young girls escorted them, as well as a few adults and Scouts in uniform. Carrying false papers, families split up and travelled in different cars on the trains that brought them into Switzerland. They were told not to say a word, in case their accents gave them away to those more than willing to denounce them. They spent the night in safe stop-overs: an abbey, a Protestant manse, and a Catholic manse in Douvaine, right at the border. At some point, the priest would push a big cement tube under the barbed wire and the poor refugees would crawl through it. On the other side of the fence was Switzerland.

At the beginning, Swiss authorities often sent the travellers back, because they had no travel papers or visas. When they were turned back, they fell into the hands of the German police and were deported. Fortunately, enough Swiss leaders were of the opinion that they should help that an agreement could be made: people whose names were on a list provided by the Ecumenical Council (it was mainly the former mayor of Le Chambon-sur-Lignon, Mr Guillon, who looked after these lists) would be given the right to stay in special camps in Switzerland. The underground railway was extraordinarily successful. Hundreds of Jewish people were able to escape [...] But one thing was sure: the more Jews who escaped, the better known it became, and the more Jews arrived. While I was gone, Magda, with Simone Mairesse's brave help, kept busy finding places for them to live on neighbouring farms.

Édouard Theis had left Le Chambon-sur-Lignon a few days after me, during the summer of 1943. He did not return until the Liberation. Along with our friend André Philip's wife Mireille, Theis helped with the evacuation of the Jews. He was also involved with some political activity. One day Mireille Philip came back from Switzerland buried under a heap of charcoal in the locomotive. She was amazingly courageous. People who worked as "runners" circulated constantly between France and Switzerland.

Other fugitives used the services of smugglers, farmers and rural people from the area who knew their way around the nooks and crannies of the Alps and charged exorbitant fees to guide them to safety. A young minister by the name of Morel, from a village near Le Chambon-sur-Lignon, was disgusted by the situation and decided to put his expertise in hiking through the Alps to good use as a guide. He did not charge a cent, of course. He had a base in a minister's manse in Annecy. I mention him because of an unusual incident that was at the same time typical of that period.

A Jewish family confided in him. It included an old man whose heart could not survive the effort of crossing the Alps; he had a heart attack and died. They would have to go back down into France, on the wrong side of the border. What happened next was unbelievable. The Jewish family went to the Vichy courts and accused Morel of "negligent homicide." Morel was put in prison. The court had to manoeuvre carefully so that the Gestapo did not find out what kind of trial was going on under its nose. Fortunately, Morel was acquitted. There are some good judges in France! [...]

During those troubled weeks, Darnand's militia and then the German troops were still busy on the plateau.[10] We were threatened by well-organized and powerful German troops from both the east (the Rhone Valley) and the west (southwestern France). The German command could only tolerate the most clever and bold incursions of the Resistance, which managed to interfere with the advances of the troops by road or by rail.

To the east, Darnand's militia, led by a new and harsher commander (the previous one, Robert Bach, had been dismissed by the Vichy regime because he was thought to be "too soft"), energetically organized raids designed to intimidate the Resistance. They seemed intent on paralyzing the opposition through a reign of terror. One of their most repugnant acts horrified the population to such a degree that people thought their senseless cruelty could only be the work of "the Boschs." And yet it was Frenchmen who were to blame. Admittedly, there was a very fine line between the German Gestapo and the Milice, rightly nicknamed "the French Gestapo."

That day, a large and well-armed group of militiamen arrived at a farm in the Lizieux area, in the northwest of France, and demanded to know where the Resistance fighters were.

"There is no Resistance here," replied one of the two old people who lived there. "There's just our two brothers who are out working in the fields. They're not involved in politics. You won't hurt them, will you?"

"No, no, don't worry," said one of them, laughing out loud. "But we're hungry. Give us something to eat."

Believing that they would win their favour by giving them a good meal, the old farmers set out everything they had on the table: sausages, salted pork, butter and cheese ... People in the city had not had that kind of food for so long they had forgotten what it tasted like. The hungry men dug in and stuffed themselves. As soon as they had finished eating, they invited the old people out for a walk – at gunpoint. They did not go far. Just behind the farm were the bodies of the two brothers. The militiamen had seen them working in the fields and had murdered them on the spot, before they even set foot on the farm. The two brothers had never been involved in the Resistance.

Such atrocious crimes could not help but spark increasing hatred among the people in the area towards the "Boschs." At the same time, the Resistance fighters became more numerous and more courageous, unaware of how helpless they really were in the face of the massive power of the German troops.[11]

Worship Services for German Prisoners

In August 1944, a certain number of German soldiers were held prisoner in the Le Chambon-sur-Lignon area. André decided to offer them a spiritual presence. He found himself among these soldiers, preaching peace and serving as a role model of Christian forgiveness and reconciliation. He also made sure that people did not commit acts of vengeance or aggression against them. André spoke German fluently, but had trouble writing it, so he asked August Bohny, who was in charge of the Swiss children's rescue mission, to translate his sermons and act as an interpreter for him.

Understandably, having Mr Bohny at his side was not easily accepted by either the French or the Germans, and everyone sided against André. Nonetheless, he recognized that applying the Gospel to everyday life often presents complications.

History continued its oppressive path, trampling through the little stories that make up human lives, playing games with the lives and deaths of millions of people, sending Jewish children, women and men to the gas chambers, stealing sheep left unprotected by their shepherds, hammering the populations of Hamburg, Dortmund, Dresden with bombs that left their cities burning furnaces. [...] The Germans, caught in the cross-fire, began – calmly, slowly, without any panic, because, in contrast to the Allies in 1940, they were well-disciplined – to leave the south of France. As their grip loosened, the Resistance became bolder.

The one hundred and twenty German soldiers occupying Le Puy, in south-central France, were ordered to move hundreds of kilometres northeast to Saint-Étienne and Lyon. On their way there, they were surrounded by a crowd of Resistance fighters that was much too large for them to resist. A few shots were exchanged [...] and then the Germans surrendered. They were taken to the outskirts of Le Chambon-sur-Lignon and put under the guard of French police officers in an old mansion on the banks of the Lignon River. In a stroke of irony, they were the same guards who, a few days before, were carrying out Vichy's orders. They could tell that the tide was turning and were now guarding prisoners whom they had meekly obeyed a few days earlier. Because the prisoners were in my parish, I automatically became their chaplain.

It was not easy for me. These hundred and twenty Germans were accused of abominable crimes. Public opinion was impossible to reason with. The most corrupt collaborators had become the most uncompromising in their hatred of the Boschs. They were enraged; they insisted on getting revenge, not only for the suffering people had endured but, in an astonishing twist, for the collusions and deceit they themselves were guilty of. In the streets of Saint-Étienne, a few months later, the German prisoners were attacked by a crazed mob, and two of them died after being lynched. In a well in Ardèche, the bodies of forty-five prisoners who had been massacred were found.

Our police officers did their best to resist the exhortations of the most vocal and violent people in town, who would have liked nothing better than to see the one hundred and twenty prisoners executed on the town square. By going to visit them, I helped protect them, but it was obviously not a practice that made me popular. Still, I went. I asked to see the commander, Major Julius Schmähling, and he allowed me to meet the prisoners. They seemed to be utterly demoralized. They were polite, courteous even. They greeted me by clicking their heels and calling me "Herr Pfarrer" (Mister Pastor).

"Our fortunes are going to change soon," they assured me. "Unser Führer has more than one trick up his sleeve. First there is a strategic retreat, and then one of his secret offensives will push everyone into the sea. It will be like Dunkerque! Ha ha!"

They were definitely not humbled by my presence. I offered to come back Sunday afternoon and lead a worship service.

"That's very kind," said Major Schmähling. "I'm Catholic, but I will order everyone to come." Although he too was a prisoner, the other men still looked up to him as their leader.

The following Sunday, when I got to the prison, a guttural order echoed through the camp. Abandoning their activities and running through the yard, the men took their places and filed into the mansion's parlour, four by four, as if they were in the theatre of war. They remained standing.

"In Namen des Vaters, des Sohnes, und des Heiligen Geistes, Amen." ("In the name of the Father, the Son and the Holy Ghost, Amen.") Only then did they sit down on the benches. I had asked Captain Neunkirchen, a very tall, thin man, to read the liturgy instead of me. It was a Lutheran liturgy, with responsive readings and hymns, and I did not know it. He got through it with admirable grace. I discovered later that Neunkirchen had been the commander of the military police and was responsible for the arrests of many Resistance members. I'm sure he would have been happy to arrest me if he had had the chance!

Writing my sermons for the Germans required a lot of work on my part. Instead of writing prolific notes and basing my sermon on them the way I usually did, I had to write out every word of my text and ask Miss Hoefert, an Austrian woman who taught German at the college, to translate it for me [...] And because my visits to the Germans were unpopular in the eyes of the French, especially the Resistance members, I decided to preach the exact same sermon in French on Sunday morning as I did in German in the afternoon.

Never had my sermons received such attention. I remember I wrote a sort of catechism, starting with the Ten Commandments and ending with justice, truth, and non-violence, virtues that we can always practise because God has forgiven us for our sins through the resurrection of Christ. I harshly condemned the war. The Resistance despised my "exaggerations." Since the Germans had left Le Puy, Resistance fighters were everywhere. Squads of them came, their weapons tucked into their suspenders, rather sloppy-looking, to attend the worship service. I had to become angry with them before they would comply with my instructions to leave their revolvers and machine guns outside in the courtyard before they entered the House of God. Obviously, they did not like what I had to say in my sermons.

"Go tell your German friends that," they said when I talked about justice, truth, non-violence, and forgiveness. "The Gospel is a nice theory, but with those guys, brute force is the only thing that matters. Think about Oradour and the gas chambers!"[12]

"You're right," I told them. "This afternoon I am going to give exactly the same sermon to the Germans." They had nothing more to say.

The Germans did not like my sermons any better than they did. "We're not the ones you need to tell this to," they objected. "Preach to your friends, the Communists. They're the ones who have spread the doctrine of violence throughout the world. They claim that the end justifies the means. Germans are honest people, good people, who believe in God. They spill their blood to save Europe from the red scare. You'll see what will happen to you the day we're no longer there to protect you from communism!"

When I talked about Oradour and the gas chambers, they shrugged their shoulders. They did not believe me. "Das is blöde, lügnerische Kriegspropaganda!" ("That is stupid, lying war propaganda!") They pushed away the Allied tracts that I held out to them. The fact is, in times of war, the most horrible crimes are committed by the people on both sides who are the most convinced of their innocence and the unilateral guilt of their adversaries. Their strength of conviction led them to believe that no cruelty was excessive: "With people like that, everything is fair!"

The German prisoners were poorly fed and complained. They did not realize that they had inflicted much harsher deprivations on the countries they occupied. Because of requisitions and rations, butter and meat was reserved for the troops or filled entire trains going to Germany. At the time, we were all rather thin. A photo of Magda taken at the time shows her skeletal silhouette. The large, pink-cheeked Germans protested against the diet they were served, ignoring the fact that it was the diet Hitler had imposed on the civilian population. My reasoning could not quiet the rumbling in their stomachs, though, and I decided to make a token gesture: I asked several people to chip in so we could buy them some grapes – they were shipped from the south of France, and were plentiful at that time (September 1944). Moreover, I managed to drag a few members of the church with me to the prison. Some of them gave a wonderful witness to non-violence. The soldiers marvelled at them. But the donation of grapes made me even more unpopular, and the "tourists" in Le Chambon-sur-Lignon once again started calling me a "Bosch" under their breath.[13]

"Standing Up Against Many Acts of Revenge ..."

Here, Magda Trocmé briefly describes the end of the war and her husband's efforts to calm the hatred and quiet the calls for revenge. Although André was not in a position of power, he was a compelling and influential speaker and was able to inspire dialogue between the two enemies and to resolve several deeply-rooted conflicts.

The major political events that occurred became mixed up in the little stories that were going around in the neighbourhoods and the parish. It was strange: in a way, we were living several lives at the same time. There was the political upheaval between Germany and France, being played out on the battlefields; there were Pétain and De Gaulle, the BBC and the Allies we were waiting for. And then there was the manse, with all its everyday drama: the refugees, the worries, the food to be put on the table. And finally, there were the Resistance fighters, another army, powerful enough to turn trains around. André didn't really like this liberation army, because it was violent. Many of the college students and future theologians were part of the Resistance. Even the gym teacher at the college and the head of the Scouts was a Resistance leader.

Then the Americans landed in the south of France in August 1944. Young people went down through the Rhone Valley and proudly brought back trophies, helmets, souvenirs from the Germans. One day the liberation forces came through Le Chambon-sur-Lignon, in big military trucks. The soldiers tossed out little gifts as the trucks drove through: boxes of Nescafé, candies, caramels, chocolates, little jars of jam. The children rushed into the streets to pick them up. It was the beginning of the end of the war. And that was when the acts of revenge started. It was terrible. André had come back from Perdyer, where he had been hiding for nearly a year. Just as he had been against the war between the Germans and Allies, he was against the partisan battles that were beginning. People wanted to execute "traitors" – anyone who had not helped the Resistance fighters or may have denounced them. Three people in Le Chambon-sur-Lignon received a miniature coffin with a rope in it. André had to stand up for non-violence amidst threats of revenge. In the Chambon area, there were no executions, but in Le Puy, and in the Ardèche Valley, it was terrible.[14]

A drawing of prisoners made by André Trocmé in the internment camp at Saint-Paul D'Eyjeaux.

Édouard Theis, the assistant pastor in Le Chambon,
and his wife Mildred.

In March 1943, André Trocmé and his two colleagues were released. From left: Roger Darcissac, André, Édouard Théis.

Magda (second from left) with a group of young German pacifists in the salon of the Maison de la Réconciliation, Versailles. The couple's great friend Jispa (Alice Reynier) is visible on the far left.

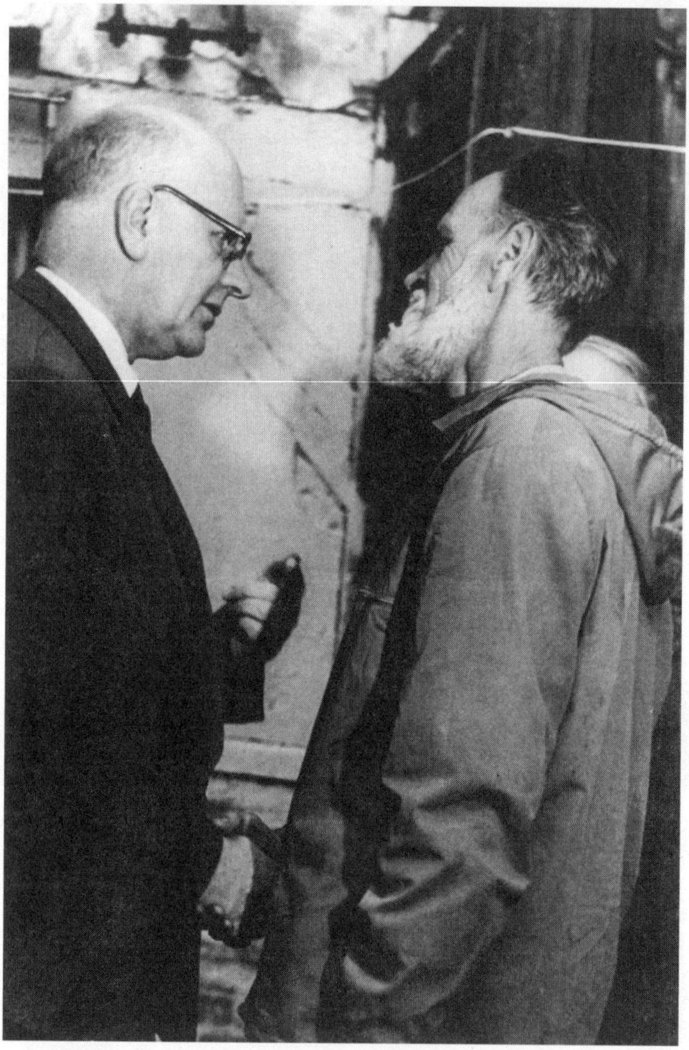

André with Lanza del Vasto, an Italian poet, philosopher, artist, and peace activist.

André and Magda, outside their home in Versailles in about 1960.

A sketch made by a Norwegian artist in 1954 showing the tower at the Maison de la Réconciliation, Versailles.

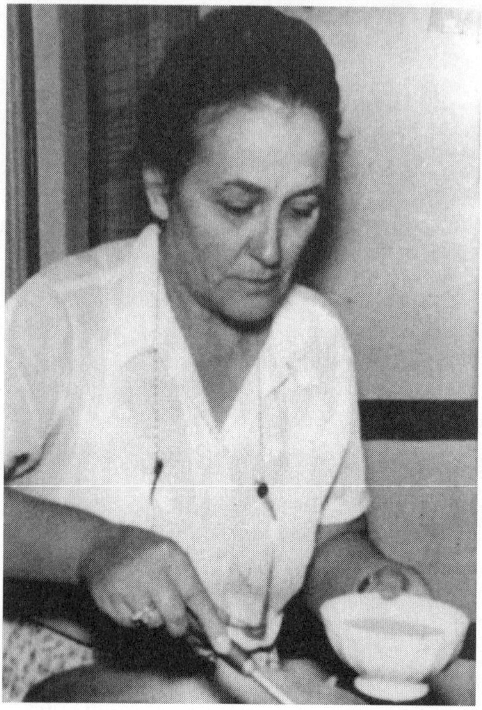

Magda in a typical pose, serving soup in the Maison de la Réconciliation, Versailles, in the 1950s.

André with his godson, Kozo Tanaka Kokutai, a boy from Hiroshima.

Above
Magda attending an international pacifist congress in India, November 1949. From left: an unidentified delegate; Indira Gandhi, a future prime minister of India; Chakravarti Rajagopalachari, the last governor-general of India; Magda.

Left
André and Magda in the study of their Geneva home, 1961. A plaster portrait of his mother is visible on top of a bookcase.

A portrait of Magda, taken in Stockholm, 1974.

A portrait of André from the 1950s.

Magda receiving an honorary degree at Haverford College, Pennsylvania, May 1981. From left: Rosa Parks, civil rights activist; Stephen G. Cary, chairman, American Friends Service Committee; Magda; Barry Commoner, author and environmentalist.

Magda at "Faith in Humankind" conference, Washington, DC, September 1984. From left: Elie Wiesel, novelist and political activist; Magda; Carol Rittner, scholar and Roman Catholic nun; Philip Hallie, author and philosopher.

A plaque at the Yad Vashem Holocaust memorial centre, Jerusalem, in honour of André and Magda Trocmé.

Also from Yad Vashem, a plaque commemorating the people of Le Chambon-sur-Lignon. The Hebrew inscription is from Isaiah 60:21, "Then will all your people be righteous."

7

Reconstruction

As soon as the war was over, Magda and André Trocmé turned their attention to the Mouvement International de la Réconciliation (MIR). The military operations having ended, there was a small window of opportunity in which to reinforce the idea of peace and forgiveness among the nations. The Trocmés accepted countless invitations to serve as observers, conciliators, or speakers at conferences that took them away from the parish in Le Chambon-sur-Lignon on a regular basis.

Between 1946 and 1949, André worked as a minister on a half-time basis. He dedicated most of his energy to pacifist activities. During these transitional years, his trips and lecture tours could last for months at a time. The following excerpts summarize André's travels, which showed him a world left in ruins by the war. He regarded this world with both tenderness and determined hope.

"Happiness … in America?"

This is the title of an article published in *Les Pages du Chambon* in 1946, in which André reports on a four-month mission to the United States for MIR in the fall of 1945. He crossed from Le Havre to Boston on board one of the Liberty Ships used to repatriate American soldiers at the end of the war. Once he landed, André was able to make an insightful comparison between the situation of his congregation in Le Chambon-sur-Lignon and that of the average American.

More than ever, young people in France, as they fall asleep at night, dream of America. America: the land of miracles from which we have been separated by six years of war and poverty. America, which has marched forward with giant steps while we, in France, have slid backwards. America: the home of millionaires and skyscrapers, the airplane and the atomic bomb. America: vast and rich, Hollywood and New York, cowboys and "Negro" blues singers. America: the land of happiness, while we are so unhappy.

Is America really happy? Would we find happiness by crossing the ocean and setting foot on American soil?

Yes, says the weary traveller who has come from Europe. He has barely set foot on the deck of the American ship that will carry him westward before the nightmare begins to disappear. Outside is the miserable sight of what is left of Le Havre, once a prosperous city: ruins, skeletons of buildings and churches, mud, death. A signal is sounded: lunch time in the officers' mess. We go "down below." The table is set with fresh bread, butter, as much milk as you can drink, "real" coffee instead of chicory, meat, fruit, cheese, ice cream. Around the table are the round, well-fed faces of the big American boys, carefree, cheerful, jubilant even because they are going home. The ship is already America. Nerves quiet down, loosen up. The traveller feels more self-assured. He feels young again. All is not lost. Tomorrow shines before him, full of promises.

Three months later the traveller gets back on board in New York to return to France. He still has skyscrapers in his line of vision. He still hears the stimulating buzz of thousands of cars, sees the bright windows, shops crammed with luxurious merchandise in the streets of the city. He remembers the welcoming smiles of his hosts, their comfortable houses, well-lit and warm. He hears a voice and turns around. What a pleasure to hear French again! Unfortunately, the voice is bitter, vindictive. It screeches, "What a mess! Nothing works! I can't get an answer. I've sent three telegraphs to the ministry. Nothing. A bunch of good-for-nothings who are only interested in politics." The traveller lowers his head. He is still in New York but already he is back in France, tense France, chaotic France, perpetually dissatisfied France. He thinks about his wife, overworked, dealing with impossible problems to solve: food, heat, clothes. Does happiness come from material comforts? His Christian, but realistic, soul has to bow down before the evidence. If you took your children to America and raised them there, they would quickly get out of the bad habit of complaining about everything, they wouldn't have to become pale and sickly because of all their chores and homework, they would stop panicking about the next exam, they might even stop thinking about the black market and all the scandals they heard about. They would eat well, do sports, become healthy again. Why do we stubbornly insist on living on the old continent?

And yet ... Are they really happy, living in a land of such prosperity? I have met hundreds of Americans who envy Europeans. Why? Because they sometimes have the feeling that nothing happens in their country.

Have you ever met "rich people's kids" who have everything you can imagine in their rooms and who, because of rather than in spite of this, are bored? Their nanny or governess looks after them. They have electric trains and rocking horses, take car rides, vacation on ski slopes or sea-sides, own cameras, good shoes and beautiful clothes, have records and books, fancy bicycles, and so on. Every little wish that occurs to them comes true. And that is precisely why they are bored: because happiness comes from efforts made to accomplish difficult goals.

Right now, I, André Trocmé, am a happy man. I am dreaming of the Cévenol school which will be nestled at the foot of the Peybrousson mountain. I am happy because I am watching that dream become a reality. Supposing I were Rockefeller: I would just have to say the word and the school would be built. Would I be as happy as I am now?[1]

So Americans, even if they are not all Rockefellers, all suffer a bit from boredom. Magnificent schools? There are hundreds of them all over the country. Hospitals? Likewise. Skyscrapers, planes, washing machines, every kind of machine to cook, to make music, to bathe, to shave, to wax, to clean, to drive, to fly, to play … There is everything you can dream of in every little town. What is left to invent? A steam iron? They have that. A movie theatre for cars? They have drive-ins. A cemetery with central heating? A high-rise church? An automatic restaurant? I am not joking; these things exist already. So what? Well, Americans (like the Swiss) dream of a country where there are still important battles to fight, things to rebuild, to transform, justice and liberty to create. "Give me something useful to do," they sigh. "Let me be part of something bigger than myself. I am tired of my own happiness, my villas with lush green lawns, my perfect fruit, my trips that are so well organized that even adventures and discomforts are planned in advance. Give me adventure, real adventure, not just the fun kind in Hollywood movies." This is why so many young Americans dream of coming to help us create something new and beautiful. But will we, in France, be able to understand and welcome them?

I was told that someone from Le Chambon-sur-Lignon heard about some young Americans who were coming. He shouted, "Great! We'll be able to earn even more money!"

Poor fellow! Did he recognize that if Americans left a few months later, disgusted that they had been exploited, Le Chambon-sur-Lignon would pay for its failure? Le Chambon-sur-Lignon, that is the spirit of those who built Le Chambon-sur-Lignon, who built the first children's house, would no longer exist. In its place would be a corpse, buried under millions of paper bills, a village without adventure, without friends, without a soul, a Côte-d'Azur knockoff with hotels that close down in the winter, and a short season of life. A village that would suck the life out of tourists.

For a long time, the Cévenol school, the Cévenol farm and workshop, the Swiss Rescue would have all fled to less evil places. Will Le Chambon-sur-Lignon be willing to run off with the American boys in search of adventure? Will Le Chambon-sur-Lignon be able to learn how to be happy?[2]

Trip to Germany

André Trocmé was sent by the MIR to Germany; he stayed there from 21 May to 19 June 1947. Despite the horrors inflicted on much of Europe by Nazi Germany, Trocmé was compassionate towards the defeated population who had suffered greatly during the war. A lucid observer of the social and political situation, André offers insightful comments on the complexity of the post-war period, the limits of the occupation by the conquerors, and the uncertain democratization of Germany. His observations were published in the September-October 1947 of *Cahiers de la réconciliation*.

German families, members of the International Fellowship of Reconciliation, always welcomed me warmly into their homes for a meal or to spend the night, although my presence obviously made it even more difficult for them. Their apartments were filled with refugees; it was difficult to find food; there was never enough money. A traveller who is given their hospitality under such circumstances cannot help but feel a little embarrassed. The military authorities will not give him any ration coupons to offer to his hosts as a token contribution. He is not allowed to buy anything […] If he chooses instead to eat at the luxurious mess hall […] reserved for the victors, he must break his solidarity with his German friends, who are not allowed in such establishments. If he crosses that line between victor and vanquished, he will be treated to a delicious meal […] but he will not dare speak of peace the next day to starving Germans living on a few potatoes and red beans. The stupid war continues to prolong its consequences long after it has ended. It sows jealousy and bitterness and paves the path for new explosions of hatred.

The same problem arises with transportation. Allied citizens can travel free of charge in rapid and comfortable military trains. They are nearly empty. But if he were to pay for his ticket in marks in order to converse with Germans on his trips, he would run the risk of being left standing on the platform, unable to board a train already so filled with exhausted passengers and roughly-packed parcels […] that he would not even be able to fit in through the window. And if he did manage to get on the train, he would feel ill at ease, as he would have prevented a German passenger from travelling. Two countries, neighbours but worlds apart, unable to understand each other. The difficulties and failures of occupation always start like this.

I chose to stay with German families. It was not a problem for me, and now that I have penetrated into this world of poverty and distress, I can give you some idea what it is like […]

A man from northern France who, twice in twenty-five years, has seen his homeland, his childhood home, pillaged, who has watched his father flee from an invasion, had family members die in concentration camps, wavers constantly from one extreme to the other. Sometimes he is overcome by a kind of physical repulsion at the sight of authoritarian faces or attitudes that revive painful memories of the brutal humiliation and destruction to which all of Europe has been subjected. Sometimes it is the opposite: he is moved to tears by the inexpressible poetry of certain details of the countryside and village life and by the blond heads of young girls crowned in flowers […]

The spectacle of German cities lying in ruins was certainly pathetic. The gaping holes of empty houses that had been set on fire, the shapeless heaps of bricks and metal in neighbourhoods that had been bombed. Hanover, Hamburg, Cologne, Frankfurt, Stuttgart, Munich, and Nuremberg had all been reduced to a common denominator: soulless, ageless ruins, whirlwinds of dust and debris. But the man from northern France whose homeland had also been disfigured twice by the Germans cannot help but look at it and think to himself: "It's their turn now; they have to see how it feels. They would never understand what they had inflicted on others if they hadn't experienced it themselves. Their pride has finally been defeated. The price they are paying for it is steep, no doubt, but there was no other way for them to understand the horror of the wars they had started.

In 1922–1924, while Reims, Château-Thierry, Soissons and Lens were lodging people in miserable shacks, the Germans were decorating Frankfurt, Stuttgart and Nuremberg with fancy neighbourhoods and ultramodern arenas, and deliberately bankrupting themselves so they wouldn't have to pay for reparations."

However, the endless repetition of the same spectacle of destruction ends up finally undermining the most resolute narrow-mindedness. This kind of language is heard mainly in France. The occupier, whether he is English, American, or French, tires quickly of his inhumanity. He can see, in the midst of the ruins, housewives who are skin and bones, standing in line in the hope of getting a little bit of food, children crammed into schools that are half-destroyed, patients piled up in underground hospitals that served as bomb shelters during the war. Like the Germans, along with the Germans, he too is sickened by the hideous face of war and its consequences.

I am travelling through Hamburg in a car driven by a German friend. He is silent. Suddenly, with a sweep of his hand towards a pile of bricks, he says: "'My father has been under there for three years. We have never been able to get his body out. My sister happened to find my mother on this corner, the morning after that tragic night, but she had gone mad. The first time the English firebombed the city, fifteen thousand people perished. They were living torches. A lot of women and children threw themselves into the canals in the old part of the city, and drowned."

The victor said nothing. The explanation he was about to give was caught in his throat. When horror is all around, whether it is called Auschwitz, Belsen, or Hamburg, there is nothing to do but hang one's head.

In the Ruhr area, I watched a Corpus Christi procession parade through the ruins. White masts decorated with multi-coloured flags had been raised. Makeshift altars flowered in the calcinated facades of buildings. Thousands of children, men and women paraded, singing hymns. The children were too blond, too pale, but they were children all the same. The sturdy men with miners' faces so worn that it was impossible to see if they were starving. In any case, they got double rations! But the women, dressed in black, were pathetic. Their coats, dresses, even their hymns hung off their fleshless frames; their bony hands folded in front of them, walking with identical expressions: hollow eyes, straight noses, thin lips.

The women had evidently been depriving themselves of food for the past two years so that their children could survive. But even there, people could only insist: "We've been through it: now it's their turn!"

Considering the state of misery people are in, there is no point in discussing these attitudes. We feel pity, we want to do something, we cannot do anything, so we listen. We listen to the long laments of the Germans and their increasingly vehement protests: We are starving to death, we cannot go on any longer; even if we are guilty, we should not be forced to die this long and miserable death.

In the English zone, overcrowded with two million refugees from eastern Europe (Prussia and Silesia, which were annexed and emptied of their German populations by the Polish under the pressure of Russia), the situation is hopeless and the bitterness towards the English has become intense. The English officers are polite and nonchalant, drive with their wives and their pet dogs in their modest cars, and reply to the criticism by saying that the situation in England is not much fun either, and that in 1946 British taxpayers paid one hundred and twenty million pounds to feed the Germans. How often have you seen conquerors pay through the nose this way to help the conquered? The anger of the Germans, whipped into a fury by their hunger, is rising with each month that passes, and now expressed unfairly and brutally: "In Auschwitz, from what I have heard, the Gestapo at least killed the Jews quickly and cleanly, so they didn't suffer. The English have decided to murder us slowly and painfully, and that's much more cruel."

In the American zone, the food situation is better and the complaints are different. The Americans are big teenage boys who sometimes feel generous and willing to do the right thing, sometimes naive and determined to re-educate the Germans, and at other times extremely irritable, suspicious, and demanding. The denazification efforts are particularly slow and ineffective in the American zone. Forty-five thousand members of the party – big, medium, and small Führers – are still imprisoned in internment camps and the tribunals in charge of trying them properly lack personnel and are paralysed by the American authorities. The process is so slow that it seems as though the formalities and the internment will never end.

In the French zone, the style of the complaints is different yet: here, the occupation forces cannot agree. Some are responsible for cultural and educational services, and do an intelligent and much-appreciated job of integrating the population. Others try to mitigate the nearly inevitable problems that occupation causes for the Germans, but the contradictory orders from the lower levels of the hierarchy and the police simply make matters worse, leading to red tape, delays, requisitions, and sometimes corruption, which in turn undermine the moral authority of the occupation forces. The population becomes cynical and chides the authorities: "So this is the democracy you promised us?"

Germans of good will who would be willing to shake the hand France is holding out feel helpless and ridiculous, and their influence is diminishing. The bitterness of the Germans, whether it is well-founded and understandable or unreasonable and unfair, penetrates visitors from other countries so deeply that it is hard for them not to get caught up in it as well. The choir of voices, some begging, some threatening, drowns out clear reasoning. Some of the foreign workers who volunteer in Germany end up losing their sense of perspective and complaining just as loudly.

Since I have made a number of trips to European countries, I am in a position to compare situations and to place matters in context. I know that Italy, Spain, and Greece are almost as miserable as Germany, and I have been able to reply to the Germans' complaints about their meagre ration of bread that the ration of the French is no bigger. The moral isolation of the German population, cleverly manipulated by Hitler and maintained by the Allies (for instance, it is still illegal to send printed material from France to Germany!) has engendered a rather odd mentality across the Rhine. Despite the horrors that their armies spread throughout Europe, most Germans focus on their own problems, which they believe they alone are suffering, while the rest of the world is victorious, happy, and prosperous. They are usually stupefied when I tell them about the difficulties other countries are experiencing. When asked if they read the papers, they reply: "Yes, but we thought it was all propaganda."

The reaction is identical when a German audience hears someone describe crimes the Nazis committed. They lower their heads; some of them have tears in their eyes. More than once a presenter has uttered words of repentance or called for a moment of silence. I sometimes ask, "But you must have known the facts. Didn't you follow the Nuremberg trials?" They answer me: "Yes, but we thought it was all propaganda. Now that you have told us what you witnessed we can no longer doubt it is true." The only time that I was aggressively interrupted when I talked about Auschwitz during a lecture was in an internment camp for SA and SS officers. "That's not true!" they shouted. "It's lies! Propaganda!" But afterwards, as I calmly continued to describe the events, they began to bow their heads. The lecture ended in an atmosphere of mutual trust and humility.

In Allied countries, some people have asked whether this humility is really necessary. Would it not be better to wipe away the past? This is how I would respond: the greatest obstacle in any deep and lasting reconciliation with the Germans comes from their naive tendency to trust their leaders. Their cruelty came from their naivety more than anything else. Today, they are open to what we have to say and willing to trust us, as long as we speak to them in a spirit of truth and brotherhood.

Wiping away the horrors of Nazism would not do them any favours. It would not be treating them as equals and as brothers. We must invite them to consider the causes of their own misery and lead them naturally to the parallel consideration of the blame we have accumulated on our side.

Here are some examples of the naivety of the Germans.

I heard a young man cry out in public: "We chose Hitler; why did they take him away from us?" This boy did not know and did not want to see what had been happening for the past ten years. Hitler was his personal dream of happiness, a dream he continues to chase as if he were sleepwalking through his life.

Another example: "We were unified, why do you want to divide us? Is that what democracy is?" This second young man was unaware of the fact that other people had paid dearly for German unity. He had no interest in democracy and freedom, and seemed to have no wish for freedom of thought or action. For him, diversity was division. This state of mind is common in Germany.

We have not yet found a solution for the challenges of re-educating, or rather educating, Germans about democracy and liberty. Furthermore, the efforts made by the Allies to re-educate the Germans have usually been misguided. They have been successful, however, on two or three points. For example, the French have introduced cultural initiatives, and their decision to publish literary magazines [...] has been greatly appreciated.

In the British zone, the officers responsible for youth programs speak perfect German and are very popular. Unfortunately, there are not enough of them. In the American zone, I sometimes felt that communication and understanding was more strained, but that may be a superficial impression. Is America too happy, too carefree to be able to build a relationship with Germany in anything but material ways? Paradoxically, it is the American Quakers who are making the greatest efforts to help the Germans, but it is the American soldiers who give out chocolate and cigarettes who are the most popular – especially with the young German girls. But these superficial contacts are inadequate. Perhaps one must have endured a similar suffering at the hands of the other in order to meet on a deeper level. America represents a different universe. The unending series of successes it has enjoyed since its founding may have given America the idea that human psychology is an easy problem to solve.

Aside from the success of a few cultural initiatives, the Allies' re-education efforts have failed. The only thing that would work would be to be able to invite hundreds of Germans to England, America, and France, to put them in contact with good people in the west who could show them what is possible: "You see, this is what it is like when you live somewhere else. And we are not any unhappier than you are at home."

It would also help to inundate Germany with literature: not propaganda, but real literature. It would help them get to know what democracy is like, to understand Western thought. Alas, any serious effort in that direction would be hampered by unintelligent administrative regulations. Germany must export paper, but does not have the right to receive it or print anything. The books the children are reading have not been "denazified"? Too bad, they say.

It takes a few weeks in Germany and a few contacts with people of good will, on one side or the other, to become deeply discouraged. The situation is changing rapidly, but in the wrong direction. Sympathy for democracy is collapsing from week to the next. Democracy is an enormous process, and millions of people are affected by it. It is difficult to influence the masses when they are hungry. We leave the country resigned to the worst case scenario, convinced that the chaos in Germany is but one of the many signs in Europe that a Third World War is inevitable. It is disappointing to realize that western Europe which, compared to Russia, is lucky indeed, has not been able to win over the soul of Germany. Too many petty public servants take advantage of their opportunities to poke pins into public opinion, so mutual understanding cannot develop. We should add that the German temperament is not easy to deal with. Germans appear to be too meek and obedient; they rarely protest in public; they show courage and civil behaviour. However, they also become violently and unfairly critical when the leader of the day turns his back for a moment.

But let us not end our report without finding a little bit of light in the shadows.

First, we have met many teachers who are determined to completely reinvent teaching methods. The denazification of schools has been energetic, to such an extent, in fact, that there is a real lack of teachers and classes of sixty and seventy students are not uncommon, and the students do not have textbooks to use. But I have spoken to teachers in elementary and high schools who were very cultured and enthusiastic about democratic ideas [...]

Germany, like Italy, has an open-door policy; things will remain this way for a few years or at least a few months more. Germans, especially young people, have such a hunger to learn, such a desire to broaden their horizons that we sometimes travel for six months at a time, going from place to place, being well received everywhere we go and attracting large audiences. A lecture I gave in Bad-Pyrmont, to which young high school students and elementary pupils with no exposure to pacifism were invited, left me with a wonderful memory of their sincere, fresh enthusiasm. Everywhere I go I hear the same thing: despite the demoralizing effect of Nazism, our young people are much better people than we expected. It is true; idealism is not dead, and dedication to a great cause is ready to be reborn. Alas, Protestant churches have only a theological and abstract faith to offer them, and the youth need to hear a radical message. Those of us who share a message of social action are a tiny group.

Will the ecumenical church see that an opportunity to preach the Gospel has been given to it, and rise above the heads of local pastors who are too fearful, too busy with religious ceremonies, too far behind their flocks, too inflated with pride in their administrative functions and so lacking in any sense of initiative that they wear on the patience of young people, who flee from political action or simply wait for the arrival of some new Führer?

I believe this summarizes my impressions of Germany. What we need to do now is immediately send a dozen devoted Christian men of sound judgment and strong pacifist beliefs and, of course, who speak German. They would sow the seeds of a glorious harvest.[3]

A Visit to the Pope

A delegation of the Union of European Federalists which included André Trocmé, attending a conference in Rome from 7 to 10 November 1948, was given an audience with Pope Pius XII in Castelgandolfo on 11 November.[4] André describes the meeting in a letter to Magda thus:

At 11 o'clock, Maria Montessori addressed us. She is an older woman now, but just as refined in her appearance and her feelings.

At 12:30, Abby Pierre, a French priest who had founded a religious order, loaded us into his car and we "were off to see the pope." There were forty of us at the Congress.

We waited before a massive brass door. The door opened. Framed by a long, wide corridor with a monumental stairway at the end of it, the Swiss Guards, dressed in their fabulous uniforms designed by Raphael, stand at attention with their halberds as we walk by. We turned right. We entered a room used as a guard room for soldiers garbed in Restoration shakos. Stairways, more hallways, a new room. This time, grenadiers with Napoleonic bearskin hats, two metres tall and the hat on top! More salons, increasingly Raphaelesque in appearance. Fireman's helmets. The Noble Guard, apparently. Finally, the room where we would have our audience with His Holiness.

A red throne with a dais, valets dressed in red with white stockings. Elegant stewards who bowed courteously. But there were forty instead of the thirty-four they had expected. A bell rang. "Il Santo Padre!" cried a steward nervously. "Non siamo pronti!" ("We are not ready!") There were not enough chairs. Someone was sent to tell the pope to wait a moment and others went off to fetch more chairs, including one for me. Now the pope could enter.

A stentorian voice bellowed: "Il Santo Padre!" Everyone rose. His Holiness arrived in white silk, two fingers of his right hand raised to offer a blessing. He sat on the throne. Everyone sat down. He began the apostolic blessing. Everyone kneeled.

Tension among the Protestants. I remained standing, next to a Dutch pastor, and two or three others followed suit. We were not dismissed from the audience; everything was fine. We sat down again. The pope read a speech in French.

Then the pope made the rounds of the people gathered before him, stretching out his hand to each one so he could kiss his ring. The Catholics fell on their knees or genuflected. The Protestants leaned down the way they do when they are refusing the host or holy water. A Belgian was a bit brash; the pope ignored him and went on to the next man. He asked the Dutch fellow next to me and placed a medallion in my hand.

"Dutch?" he asked. "No, French. A minister of the Reformed Church, and the secretary of an association of Christian conscientious objectors. We have thirty of them in prison, in France, because of their love for Christ." The pope looked surprised and interested.

"I congratulate you on your actions, and ask for the blessing of God to be upon you," he said, and went on to the next person.

When he had finished, Abby Pierre came up to me and said, "The Holy Father gives his consent to be photographed with the delegates, but he would not want to impose upon the Protestants among you the obligation to be photographed with him."

I replied: "On the contrary! It would be an honour to be photographed with one of my brothers in Jesus Christ."

A moment later, Abby Pierre told the pope what I had said. He did not budge. He had therefore agreed to be considered a brother in Christ rather than a Holy Father. Once the photo was taken, he turned and made a gesture of benediction but, as he looked into the eyes of the Protestants he turned the motion into a wave of "ciao, ciao!"

Conclusion: a very well-brought-up man, who knows how to behave. I had not gone to bow down to him, but to tell him something useful. And it was worth it.[5]

Confessing the Unforgivable

Back in Germany in 1949 for another MIR mission, André Trocmé found himself in the area where his maternal grandfather had served as a minister. Four years after the end of the war, tongues were starting to loosen and some Germans dared to admit the unforgivable truth.

It was in Petzen, in the home of a chimney-sweep [...] Reverend Wilhelm Mensching led the discussion.[6] The conversation was open and frank, and eventually turned to a delicate subject: why, oh why, did Germans, and even the Confessional Church, put up so little opposition to Hitler?

"Luther made a distinction between his religious duty and his civic duty. One must serve the prince. His authority is bestowed upon him by God. Therefore, any believer who affirmed his faith in the Gospel should serve the State faithfully as a public servant, as a teacher, as a soldier. It is his duty!"

"But the State was committing crimes! Why did we not protest the concentration camps?"

"We did not know they existed." This response made the atmosphere thick.

"Did we really not know?" asked Mensching.

Silence.

An old man, a farmer, took the floor. He hesitated. He was afraid. "Do not repeat to anyone what I am about to tell you," he said quietly. "Not to anyone. I don't want to get myself in trouble [...] But I had discovered something."

"Nein!" the others cried, incredulous.

"Yes, near the Porta Westphalica (the Weser Gorge). There was a camp. I went there several times to deliver charcoal. I had to go through two checkpoints with my cart. I was searched. In the camp, I saw men with striped uniforms. Their skin was yellowed; they were thin as rails. The guards were rude to them. Mean. One day, I saw twenty of these men carrying big bags full of stones walking around in circles, while an officer barked out orders to them. When one of them fell down, he was kicked until he got up again."

"You never told us that!" the others said.

"No," the old man said slowly. "Before I left the camp they threatened me. They said if I told anyone what I saw there, we'll find out. And we'll come after you and put you in the camp, too."

"What was this place called?" I asked.

"Dora," he answered.

Dora! Daniel Trocmé and so many others had been there. The underground factory where the V.1 and V.2 were being built in secret.[7] The executions by hanging, accompanied by music, which the prisoners were forced to watch under threat of death themselves. I told them what I knew. My German friends were devastated.

A young woman began to speak: "I was a member of the Hitler youth. My friends and I used to spend the night outside in a tent in the woods near Dora. We heard screams, horrible human screams, the howls of people being tortured. When we got home we told our parents about it. They were horrified. They ordered us not to tell anyone else about it."

Now, three years later, the mouths that had been zipped shut were opening up. "We knew something was happening," the adults admitted, looking down at the ground.

If we have any hope of day reaching the point that the term Christian civilization makes any sense, we have to completely rewrite the doctrinal lessons we are teaching: the bastardized interpretation of the Ten Commandments, that reduce sin to a few faults that infringe on personal or family order, must be toppled from their pedestal.

First, we must teach children that conformity and fear are the most serious sins. They are the sins that caused prophets to be stoned, Christ to be crucified, and so-called Christian nations to go to war again and again, to raise up arms without any sense of guilt. Non-compliance for reasons of conscience is the first duty of Christ's followers.

And the second sin is complicity with injustice, the exploitation, and humiliation towards of others, the refusal to speak up about the horrors and shame in society.

When a man is delivered from his fear of "What will people think?" he can become a champion of the voiceless. He has reached the maturity that allows him to practise other Christian virtues: purity, goodness, patience, forgiveness. Woe to him who begins with meek obedience. His journey will end in weakness and cowardice, and he will side-step the liberating path of the Gospel.[8]

8

The Travellers

In 1949, André Trocmé was appointed European Secretary of the Mouvement International de la Réconciliation (MIR) and the Trocmé family left the manse in Le Chambon-sur-Lignon. For nearly a dozen years, Magda and André were invited to speak in countries around the world, from Finland to Vietnam, from the USA to Japan, from the Soviet Union to Algeria. In several places in a world that was suffering and torn apart by conflict, on both sides of the Iron Curtain, they watched, asked questions, listened, and tried to understand the chaos of the time in which they lived. In July 1958, during a trip to Berlin with André, Magda described the worries of the people and the nations she had visited: "And so, travelling from one country to another, we find only peace-loving, hardworking countries frightened by the threats of another country. The other country is always warlike and ready to attack: that's the myth that is repeated in every country. This fear of the other, of people with another ideology, another religion, another civilization, is what causes the tensions and problems and gives rise to war. Every country is convinced that it is peace-loving and possesses the right laws, the truth, the true religion and true civilization." Conscious of and attentive to the misery and the problems of the people they met, they were sometimes able to provide concrete help, as they were in Morocco and Algeria. In 1970, leading worship on the radio in French Switzerland, André challenged his listeners to follow suit: "On your next vacation, instead of lying on a beach and getting a suntan, are you ready to go down into the poorest sections of town, into the most disadvantaged areas of the places you are visiting as a tourist, and spend a few weeks among the people who live there, who are stretching out their hands to you?"

Some of the excerpts that follow exhibit a very personal tone, especially the letters Magda and André exchanged when they were apart. In their travel correspondence they show their true selves, curious and gifted and keenly observant, alternating between moments of criticism and of humour, open and welcoming when they meet people, and intent on gaining a better understanding of the complexity of their situation.

Among Gandhi's Disciples

In 1949, Magda went to India with Reverend Henri Roser, Guy Marchand, and Jérôme Sauerwein to represent France at the World Pacifist Meeting. This meeting, originally set for 1948 by Gandhi, had been postponed for a year due to the Mahatma's assassination. Organized by American Quaker Horace Alexander, the World Pacifist Meeting was chaired by Rajendra Prasad; among its vice-presidents was the poet and Nobel prize-winner Rabindranath Tagore.

Alexander gathered approximately sixty men and women from every part of the world and from several different religions. He followed Gandhi's plan of putting international delegates into contact with people close to Gandhi. Part of the plan was to prepare the participants to face all forms of violence and aggression using only "spiritual and moral" weapons. After a week-long retreat, the delegates travelled in small groups to visit different regions of the subcontinent, including India and Pakistan. This trip, without André, gave Magda the opportunity she had been dreaming of all her life, to walk upon the same ground on which Gandhi had walked.

Delhi. Here I am in the capital of Hindustan, in the palace of the Parliament, where they are about to vote on the

Constitution of India. By November 26, it will be ready. On January 26, it will come into effect and the Republic will be officially proclaimed.

We left the office of the Minister of Information and Radio Communications, Mr R.R. Dywakar. He spent nine years in prison as a follower of Gandhi. Until 1930, prisoners were allowed to have only two books at a time with them, books on philosophy or religion. After 1930, they could have nearly any book they wanted and could write as much as they wished. "If I hadn't been in prison," Mr Dywakar told us, "I wouldn't have had time to think or write. And that is true of Nehru, as well. Meditation in prison was instructive to several of our members of Parliament." The young disciple of Gandhi who was showing us around added with a smile, "Westerners were educated in universities, and Hindus in prison."

We had a discussion with Mr Dywakar about the current ineffectiveness of the UN. "For the UN to have sufficient authority," he declared, "representatives from different countries need to have a clear idea of good and evil and have sufficient moral strength to ensure their decisions are accepted. Even if we have a sense of good and evil, we cannot ensure our ideas are accepted if we lack moral conviction. This is the cause of the UN's weakness. To replace its non-existent moral power, the UN would have to be given an international police force and the member states would have to refuse to co-operate with guilty or belligerent nations. This would be enough to make war an impossibility. Obviously, this isn't pure non-violence, but it is a form of violence that is less destructive than war."

Will India Remain Non-violent?

We were received by the Indian Minister of Health, a woman, a princess: Rajkumari Amri Kaur. She is Christian, Protestant. Like the other ministers, she confessed to us that the government of India is moving away from Gandhi's principles: "It's not that Gandhi's principles are wrong or can't be applied," she explained. "It's because we haven't listened to him closely enough and because no one among us can lead a non-violent government. If Gandhi were here, he would protect us and guide us."

What struck me most was the great sincerity of these Indian politicians. Instead of making excuses or embellishing the imaginary virtues of the constitution they were putting forward, they openly confessed their failures and expressed their hope in the future. They all wore the simple cotton clothes and white handwoven caps that Gandhi wore.

Gandhi's Mausoleum

At five o'clock last night, Friday, 18 November, we went to the place where Gandhi was cremated. He died on a Friday. Every Friday at five o'clock people gather there, without a priest, to chant prayers or sing the hymns that Gandhi liked. The prayers are intended to request that Gandhi, if he is reincarnated, will enjoy a happy life in his new form. The site of the cremation is a large, flat area where a very simple monument is being constructed. It consists only of pools of water on the ground and stairs leading up to a platform where a rectangular slab marks the place his cremation took place. People leave their shoes at the bottom of the stairs and walk up to the enclosure containing the slab. It is covered in leaves and flowers shaped into beautiful designs. In one spot, visitors can burn incense or lay flowers. We brought a little sheaf. Someone had brought a little skein of hand-woven cotton; cotton symbolizes Indian independence.

To the right of the vault is a fairly large space with a carpet. There, sitting cross-legged on the floor, people had gathered for the Friday prayer. They were rich and poor, men and women, children of all ages. While we were there with them, in the middle of the crowd, one of Gandhi's sons, Devadas, arrived with this wife. We were introduced to him and arranged to meet him for supper. Devadas publishes a newspaper, *The Hindustan Times*. His brother Munilal, who has taken over his father's work in South Africa, will come to our meeting. While people chanted quiet prayers, the sun set in a glory of gold light. We were right between New Delhi and Old Delhi. Off in the distance, we could see the factory smoke-stacks near the refugees' shanties. It was superb. We could feel Gandhi's spirit floating above us. A woman crouching on the ground, cradling a baby in her lap, massaged her child's head to the rhythm of the prayers. At the end, during the last chant of "Sita Ram," everyone tapped or clapped to the rhythm. We had heard this chant on the boat; Gandhi always wanted it sung. Then everyone got up calmly. Cars and buses came to pick up the tired worshippers.

[…] Nathuram Godse, the assassin [of Gandhi], and his accomplice, Nayaram Apte, were hanged on November 15. How would Gandhi have felt about that? Everyone knows what Gandhi would have said, but he wasn't there to say it. As soon as we arrived in India, Richard Gregg, the American social philosopher who had developed a theory of non-violence, flew to Delhi. He spoke to the governor-general on our behalf. The governor said he understood our point of view, but the law had to be applied all the same. Couldn't the execution of Gandhi's assassins be a new start? Shouldn't we ask all governments to repeal capital punishment?

The afternoon before we left, we met with Governor-General Chakravarti Rajagopalachari in the magnificent palace the British had used. The Indian governor, a friend of Gandhi's, reserved a great deal of the space in the palace for a national museum and lodging for the refugees. The garden is splendid and the guards continue to wear red uniforms and white and red turbans. At tea-time, I was seated next to the governor […] The governor is not a pacifist and seemed to be trying to corner us. Fortunately, I managed to answer two of his questions: "What did your husband do during the war?" and "What do you think of Pétain's conviction?"

"My husband worked against the Pétain government. He preached that it wasn't a matter of holding a single man guilty, but rather holding the attitude of an entire nation responsible." This response … shut him up!

Crowds in India

We went to visit a school where midwives are trained for community health work. The school is located in a working-class district on the outskirts of town, an Oriental-style area where the streets are lined with eclectic shops that sell every kind of item: fabric, toys, fruit, hazelnuts and nuts of all sorts, incense and icons. Barbers shave men right in the street, other people cut their toe-nails; all of these people are so poor, they sell, buy, and are served by people who are even poorer than they are. The coolies (porters) carry enormous parcels on their heads. We bought fruit in an extraordinary marketplace that was open at all hours. From this central square, merchant's alleys stretched out like spokes on a wheel, overflowing with shops pouring from tiny buildings out onto the street, fruits, fried foods, sweets, every imaginable thing, and lanes filled with people in colourful clothes, veiled women, women in trousers, women carrying pots of water on their backs in buffalo skins, children running around everywhere, tinkers and junk dealers, blind people (there are so many in India!), beggars shouting and showing their eyes, their bellies or their mouths and kneeling on the ground to touch your shoes. Beggars follow you everywhere, into train stations, along the streets, into temples. And cows wander around in the midst of all this.

The Misery of the Refugees

We came to a vacant lot soiled by garbage left there, covered with tents, makeshift clay gurbies, shanties made of twigs, shelters made out of whatever debris people could find. The refugees from Pakistan, chased out of their homes by the Mohammedans, are packed into this little space. Women carry their children on their hips, straddled with one leg on their stomachs and the other on their back. Men carry oddly-shaped packages. All this coming and going, crying, laughing, shouting in the blazing heat of the sun: real human misery crushed by suffering but bearing it and even forgetting it, because they believe that their lives will be better in their next incarnation. Elsewhere, 12,000 refugees are parked in dusty camps: tents, rows of little houses with low roofs and a single tiny room for a whole family, large surfaces that a single roof covers with dividers made of torn rags hanging from the ceiling: a kind of maternity home, made of bricks, with little straw pallets on the ground (others sleep on the ground, where a young woman is lying and wailing, unable to say what is wrong). And children everywhere, children of all ages, clad in rags, clustering together, shouting, waving, swarming around any car that comes through.

In another camp, one of Gandhi's disciples keeps a few women busy carding and spinning cotton, and a few men doing some woodworking. A teacher is paid to give classes with no material: no books, notebooks, benches or desks. The children can't go to real schools because classes cost money. In fact, the tuition is even higher now! For a year, the government handed out food to the refugees, basic raw food that people cooked in little clay ovens or between two stones. Refugees forget what it means to have a job. Without any assistance from the state, they have to figure out how to get by. How, indeed? Surrounded by their children, women cook, wash laundry or, more often, crouch in a corner waiting for their destiny to happen to them. They are wrapped in rags, but wear bracelets on their wrists and ankles, necklaces around their neck, jewellery in their noses or even hanging from some part of their ear. The holes are pierced haphazardly and their earlobes are decorated with fancy ornaments. There are 460,000 refugees in the province of Delhi and they live everywhere: in the city, in the country, in villages, often under a little roof of leaves to shelter them.

An Odd Sadhu

Yesterday we went to a well-known ashram, the Yoga Vedanta Forest University in Anandakuter, Rishikish-Himalayas. The founding saint is still alive, a hefty man named Shri Swanu Sawathanauda. When he laughs, his fat belly shakes. He was waiting for us and buried us in literature [...] He had us come into a room where secretaries, his disciples, work without pay on his magazine, *The Divine Life*, and print his books. The door was open. Beggars and pilgrims watched us while we were served tea, fruit, and biscuits. One of the Sadhu's disciples filmed us and took photos of us from every angle. A gramophone chanted prayers or repeated sermons recorded by our host who, meanwhile, was quickly signing books for us. From the next room came the voice of a lecturer speaking about sacred books. Monkeys danced and ran around the balcony; they hung from trees and eyed our food with envy. Outside the Ganges flowed peacefully and majestically.

We visited the building, a curious mixture of antique and modern objects. On the one hand, records were produced, books published, and photos and films developed there; on the other, we attended a session of "asanas," ascetic exercises a young Sadhu performs to discipline himself and achieve communion with divinity. These movements consisted of extraordinary contortions of the body. The bodies of those who practise yoga regularly can bend as easily as rubber, but the big saint, the chief, didn't take part in these exercises. In a sort of temple, the members of the ashram followed each other in hour-long shifts; each of them sat cross-legged on the floor in front of the icons, repeating continuously the names of gods: "Rama-Krishna, Buddha-Jesus ..."

An image of Jesus and a Catholic Sacred Heart were on the wall with the other idols. As well, in the museum that contained a collection of books on how to reach God, there was an image of St Francis and another of ... St Anthony! In the temple, the idols frightened me. I was offered sections of mandarin oranges and the water of the Ganges accompanied by an unidentifiable herb and an incomprehensible blessing, and someone put some powder on my forehead. The photographer-Sadhu continued to film and photograph us.

Gandhi Wasn't Perfect

In India, Gandhi's personality was often a subject of discussion. What wasn't discussed was his non-violence. Gandhi was one-hundred-percent non-violent, but he may have been too willing to accept the help of Indian capitalism, which he believed was better than British capitalism. This might explain the considerable influence that capitalists had over the current government, and their slightly fascist tendencies. Basically, Indian capitalism had come to Gandhi's aid to help him rid the country of the English. Capitalists used his non-violence as a means to their ends, but they didn't adopt it as a philosophy. Similarly, in France, Communists agreed to encourage conscientious objectors because that could help them reach their goals, rather than because they believed in non-violence as a guiding principle for the future.

The true disciples of Gandhi, the truly non-violent, have never been very numerous in India. This confirms my belief that the masses are not yet ready for non-violence. Non-violence seems to me to be an individual, religious, and prophetic position, taken not in the interest of obtaining immediate and tangible results, but rather in order to lay the groundwork for the future. Our work must be geared to having our governments accept this prophetic position, that is, to obtain the right to conscientious objection. We cannot let ourselves become discouraged simply because Gandhi did not possess every imaginable quality, that he didn't always grasp social problems or because, in spite of abolishing the caste system, he sometimes didn't take the side of the people against capitalism.

If Gandhi had been a saint, a god, none or very few of us would have been able to follow him. But Gandhi set the best example possible: he pushed his faithfulness to an idea, a vocation, that of non-violence, to its furthest possible limit. He died for this idea. It is up to someone else to step forward and continue this work. Despite Gandhi's imperfection, he is quickly being turned into a divinity: his picture is already hanging in temples next to idols and pious images. Yesterday I saw a calendar showing Gandhi in the foreground superimposed over an image of a cross and one of Buddha under that, in transparent layers.

In Pakistan

I was at the women's prison, in the section reserved for Muslim women abducted by Hindus and returned to Pakistan. In the infirmary, the abducted women were kept on one side of the room and the real prisoners on the other. Many of the women had children in their arms, on the bed or on the floor. In India, young children are taken with their mothers into the prisons. A childless woman sat staring into space. She had committed murder. An extremely lengthy trial. Another had a baby in her arms and had been sentenced to a month in prison. She had just wanted to visit her homeland, her parents were on the other side, and she had crossed the border without her papers!

In the "Ganga Ram" hospital, in the bright sunlight on the patio, I saw the Hindu women the Muslims were handing over and who were waiting for the final details to be looked after. I talked to them a little, a few sentences that someone translated. I talked about the world's sympathy for their fate, my wishes for their safe return, the misery of Europe, refugees and displaced persons. They smiled, their eyes lighting up with new hope, and they joined their two hands together in front of their mouths the way Hindus do to greet or thank people.

In this country, where death is accepted as a natural event more than anywhere else in the world, funerals are so much different from each other! Hindus cremate their deceased and scatter their ashes in sacred places. In Calcutta, near the Kali temple, there is a space surrounded by a wall, but the gates are wide open and people come and go, some bringing bodies, others gathering ashes, still others carrying wood. I saw several funeral pyres there, and several bodies waiting their turn. Often the faces of the deceased were uncovered and their eyes were open; they looked like they were waiting the way they had waited patiently and passively when they were alive.

In a corner, near the wall, a young man who was nearly naked was sleeping, his arm folded up over his head. Surprised by the strange choice of a place to sleep, I went up to him. He was sleeping deeply … very deeply, in the last sleep of death! He was a poor man. No one was there to put a necklace of flowers around his neck or to relax his limbs, to lay him out on a bamboo stretcher. In death, he was still in the same position as he was when he was alive. He was lying in sleep or suffering, waiting like the others but without seeming to be waiting for anything in particular. Waiting his turn. He would be the very last one to be attended to. The gentleness and kindness of the Hindu, who performed his duties as my host and described his wife's funeral to this stranger, pleased to be able to talk about his religion, his faith, all the future lives that would bring him closer to God who gives all forms of life.

In Bombay, I saw one of the crematoria on a wide boulevard, behind a wall which, on the side facing the street, was covered with movie posters. I watched the whole ceremony for a Brahman's cremation. The priest hurriedly initiated the closest relative in prayers and mysterious gestures. The poor man could barely keep up and didn't understand anything, yet he obediently did whatever he was asked. He wasn't even suffering; he was performing a rite of passage for his uncle, who was an aged bachelor.

A little farther away, a funeral pyre was being prepared for a woman wrapped in a red sari, symbolic of marriage, and in another corner a family was waiting their turn. gathered around a person who had died in an accident. The wait was a long one. They had gone to ask the employer for money to buy wood. No money, no wood. No wood, no funeral pyre. Behind another wall close to the first one were the Mohammedans' tombs. An insane woman with haggard eyes and unkempt hair scratched the earth over a grave with her fingernails …

In the United States

Magda and André Trocmé had personal ties with the United States, first because they had met there and also because found it easy to make good connections with Americans. Between 1945 and 1960 they took turns travelling there every year to represent the MIR. The lectures that they gave in parishes and universities raised the awareness of the most open-minded members of American society about pacifism and non-violence. Their speaking tours also raised money for the American branch of the International Fellowship of Reconciliation. Magda and André introduced the Cévenol school and the story of the refugees sheltered in Le Chambon-sur-Lignon to their audiences. The appreciation of the Americans who heard them is perhaps best shown by the creation of the American Friends of the Cévenol School by Carl and Florence Sangree. In addition, anyone who visits the United States Holocaust Memorial Museum in Washington, DC will be struck by the importance of the Plateau Vivarais-Lignon, prominently displayed among those honoured by the Righteous Among Nations, in large part because of the Trocmés' work.

The five excerpts below were selected to illustrate the Trocmés' travels and encounters in the USA. The first is an article by André entitled "Unfamiliar Aspects of Rural Life in the USA: Impressions and Memories from a Recent Trip." It describes the underdeveloped and often neglected countryside. Then there are Magda's comments about a trip in the summer of 1954; this piece reflects on the possibility of a real dialogue among religions and cultures. Finally, three of Magda's articles explore the struggle for civil rights by Black Americans.

Rural Life in the USA: Pennsylvania, October 1953

After travelling down a major highway, my guide's car turned left onto a side road; as though it were a time machine, the car drove us into the last century. We came across an odd black carriage, perched high on wobbly wheels and pulled by a sturdy workhouse. "It's an Amish buggy," my guide explains. "You'll see lots more of them around here." Indeed, to our left on a hill leading up to an Amish church, twenty horses were lined up along the wall, waiting patiently for their masters, steam swirling out of their nostrils, beating out an irregular rhythm with their hooves, shaking their bridles and the straps of the little black carriages. And the countryside had cleared out now; the electrical and telephone wires had disappeared, there were no tractors chugging along. The setting was tranquil, idyllic. Once in a long while we passed a farmyard enclosed by a white fence with a spacious farmhouse. We were in Pennsylvania Dutch country, home to ultra-orthodox Mennonites who have cut themselves off from the modern world. Men, women, and children live together in a tight community, refusing to use electricity, combustion engines, artificial fertilizer, insurance companies … and violence. They have given their lives and their futures over to God and hard work, relying on them to care for their large families.

I visited two Amish farms with my guide. I felt as if I was in one of the Darbyist households in our own mountains: the same austere simplicity, the same rough wood, the same cleanliness. The first time, because the master of the house was away, we were welcomed by a tall young woman with calloused hands and arms and a broad smile. At a neighbouring farm, it was the owner, a forty-year-old widower, who was our host. His black felt hat didn't leave his head. He had long hair and a beard but no moustache, just like our forefathers in daguerreotypes from the 1850s. His sons, ranging from five to twelve years old, stared at us with their big eyes. Except for their clean-shaven faces, they were slightly grotesque miniatures of their father, wearing the same long, loose pants, black vests and round hats. Our visit was interrupted by a rather brutal but very usual country event. A livestock dealer arrived (in a motorized truck) and, after a great deal of effort, forced two suspicious and reticent cows into the "paddy wagon" that would cart them off to their slaughter.

Despite their old-fashioned farming methods, the Amish enjoy increasingly prosperous life-styles. Other farms in the area have electricity, television, tractors and chemical fertilizers, but they also have a lady of the house with a fancy hair-do, manicured nails, and a habit of spending more money than her husband makes on trips to town, and they can't compete with the Amish farms. Naturally, life is hard for Amish families as long as their seven or eight children are young. But as soon as they turn twelve, the boys are put to work at their fathers' sides, risking problems with school authorities, and when they are twenty-five their fathers will choose wives for them and give them some land to farm. The first thing the new homeowner does is disconnect the electricity and telephone. We're still waiting for a sociological study [...] which will explain how farming methods from the Middle Ages manage to triumph so effectively over mechanized and industrialized agriculture. Does history sometimes progress in the opposite direction of the one promoted by economists? Does faith in God have something to do with it?

November 1953. The little town of W. (Ohio) lies flat before our eyes; from one end to the other, nothing gets in the way of our view. Our villages are closed in on themselves, as though in little shells. But W. was founded a hundred years ago out of the determination of the government and the invasion of a hoard of settlers. Each newcomer was given a lot in town to build his house and thirty acres in the country to feed his family. To finish this picture of W., there is a little college on one side and a little factory on the other, and in the middle there is a crossing where a train lumbers through twice a day. They call it the "station." Add a string of churches along the main street and you've described the whole town. The Quaker pastor I was visiting told me, "Tonight our meeting is at the Presbyterian church; the Baptists also host us sometimes. All the different denominations have reconciled now. We don't really remember what we fought about in the past." This isn't to say that there aren't any problems in W. The Quaker pastor spreads a map showing the land deeds in the area. "Because of the incredible corn crops we harvest, our township ranks first in the United States for pork production. But the way the land is passed down through the generations is the same as it has been for a hundred years, and it's jeopardizing our prosperity. When a farm ends up being smaller than ten acres, it's no longer viable. Some farmers have been able to reach a hundred acres, but their children, like everyone else's, are drawn to life in the city. Once they've graduated from college, they've lost their taste for the country. Cars have driven them away to the capitals. Our little college has lost its attraction; the young people consider it too small. So our local life-style is gradually dying out."

Florida, December 1953. Florida is a land of pines interrupted by subtropical marshes. Grey-green garlands of "Spanish moss," a kind of stringy lichen that can be used as animal feed, hang from all the trees. Here I am in a rather rustic frame house sheltering a pioneer family that was built in the middle of ragged clearing about forty years ago. Under the roof of the shed, members of the second generation of settlers, the father, the mother, and two sons in their thirties, are busy working around a large pot, their faces and hands red and hot. They are "crushing cane." The juicy sugar cane is pushed between two primitive rollers when a crank is turned, and the juice pressed out of the cane flows into a basin that is later emptied into a big pot to be heated and condensed. The sons tend to the fire while the mother skims the liquid. It is like a picture out of a book on pioneers: the family's rather harsh features, honest blue eyes, and simple biblical moral values; the two sons are conscientious objectors. Why would they want to go to Europe or China to massacre people who have never done anything to them?

After cordial handshakes, my driver takes me to his car. It is a wealthy man's car. After all, didn't a student from France, freshly landed in New York, once say: "People around here are really rich; they all have American cars!" [...] I like Florida, with its astonishing contrasts. The train stops, for no apparent reason, after passing a few "Negro" shacks from which hymns rise up in puffs of blue smoke. The lazy train chugs through the landscape of swamps and sand dunes, perpetually behind schedule, until it gets to a bright little town called Clearwater. While

New York is shivering under gusts of polar snow, Clearwater's children are noisily playing amidst flower gardens and workers are raking the gravel in the sun.

The few days I stayed in Clearwater were a dream-world in a saint's sanctuary. I met a thoughtful Methodist pastor who spends his days visiting his parishioners and collapses with sympathy when one of them becomes ill. He took me to meet a Negro pastor's wife, a big, talkative, kind "mama." She even washed my clothes.

I bet you can picture the pastor. You imagine him looking like one of our clergymen in France, distracted, unkempt, his nose plunged in his Bible. Not at all! This man is dressed in a light-coloured flannel suit and drives an American car (yes, another one!). Every morning, after his prayers, he dashes over to watch his new church being built. The old one is ugly and only has room for five hundred people. It is too small now, because the pastor has doubled the number of people in his congregation. Nearly twice as many people attend Sunday services. A new building was obviously needed, but where could it be built? Where the manse was, naturally, because it was the only place available. So where would the manse go? Across the street, of course. So it was heaved up onto rollers and, with furniture and paintings intact, hauled over to the other side of the street and carefully installed in the other direction. All set!

"I still get confused," the pastor's wife admits. "I come home and head for bedroom when I'm ready to make supper." The new church is nearly finished. One morning, four enormous colonial-style prefab columns arrived from Chicago. The pastor was excited: "Everything is going to be ready for the opening on January 24," he told me. "Outside, beams of light will be projected onto the steeple."

The ironic French smile that was starting to show on my face suddenly disappeared when I thought of the heartbreaking situation of our own rural parishes. Most of them couldn't find enough Christian charity to afford a coat of paint.

Magda in the United States, Summer 1954

I was invited to make a speaking tour of six Quaker Institutes in the United States in June and July. I made the crossing on the *Queen Mary*. I travelled across the vast American continent from the east coast to the midwest, and from the Gulf of Mexico in the south to the Great Lakes of the northern states. I gave talks in schools, universities, churches, and any number of halls, on the radio and on television. Some people came because they were interested in the Cévenol school, others had been in Le Chambon-sur-Lignon, still others were interested in our Mill of Peace where a few people had spent some time. Some people attended because they had heard André Trocmé, appreciated what he had to say, and wanted to meet me, not as Magda Trocmé but as "the wife of André Trocmé." I wasn't insulted; in fact I was quite proud and amused by this idea. However, I was afraid I wouldn't be able to meet their expectations.

On my first evening there I left New York to speak in a Quaker meeting house in Scarsdale. Because the train was running late, I asked an employee what was going on. "It's Saturday, ma'am, and we're waiting for the Sunday papers!" (On Sundays, American newspapers run to 50 pages.) "You'll be happy tomorrow morning," he added. "When you come home from church you'll have your Sunday paper to read."

Tomorrow morning, when I come home from church? It seemed that this man expected that tomorrow morning I would go to church. Maybe he expected that everyone in the car would go to church. In France, he would have said, "Madame, tomorrow morning, after a nice cup of coffee, you'll be happy to read your newspaper." When you compare the two countries, this little detail is very telling.

The next day I was quite moved by the service. I had been asked to enter the sanctuary after the choir, step up to the pulpit to speak and then exit, again in the procession. The pastor had encouraged me, telling me not to be nervous, to be myself, and to speak as though I were in a living room with friends. I did my best to follow his instructions, but when I looked out from the pulpit at the people in the sanctuary and thought of all the other people gathered in other sanctuaries, dressed in their Sunday best, serious and attentive, true believers, I felt my heart in my throat. So many Christians! It was such a surprise for me, coming from a country which was losing its collective Christian faith, and such a responsibility for a wealthy and powerful nation with a predominantly Christian population.

How is it that we can fill church pews on Sunday and prepare for war the rest of the week? I have often raised this question in the United States, where people are so generous, so enthusiastic, so ready to be of service. I have realized that, whether we are in a country where the majority of people are Christian or in a country with a minority of Christians, human love and brotherhood seem to crash up against the borders of countries and party lines. Feelings of fraternity and solidarity don't extend past the borders of allied countries. But allies are allies one day and enemies the next. Alliances change frequently, and even Christians are brainwashed to confuse their religious ideals with their governments' politics.

After my trips to India, Muslim countries and numerous European countries, I may have a clearer idea of the Christian responsibility. We are designed to see the inconsistencies in other people more easily than in ourselves. Here was a flagrant contradiction in America: on the one hand, churches filled to capacity on Sunday mornings, and on the other, a horrific stock of A-bombs and H-bombs piling up, rampant financial imperialism and consumerism, and racial segregation.

What would happen if, tomorrow in Evanston, basing their decision on the message of the Gospels, the World Council of Churches decided to outlaw war and declared that a Christian could not take up arms? The Vatican would probably follow. And then, what would happen? What is war all about? In the United States, I had the feeling that war was an abstract word people were comfortable with, while in Europe it was a horrible word, a scourge to which people had resigned themselves. What is important is not so much working against the war as an abstract notion, but against the concrete causes of war. Outlawing war would mean eliminating the causes of war: patriotic arrogance, the individual or collective profit that drives our actions, competition for vital resources, the oppression and exploitation of one nation by another, racism, and the cult of military glory.

I have been in the homes of church-goers, rich industrialists, modest working people; I've known people on every rung of the social ladder. I've been in small towns where typical American life carries on and in major urban centres like New York, Boston, and Chicago, which are monstrosities.

I have been in little log cabins nestled among the trees and frame houses on green gardens, and I have been in skyscrapers. In Chicago, I was invited by a member of the McCormick family into one of the most modern apartments imaginable, in a high glass tower on the edge of a lake. I may as well have been in an airplane, hanging between sky and water. And, despite these very different environments and fortunes, I heard the same questions everywhere, repeated like clichés. Everywhere there was anguish for the future of America, the conviction that an American had a duty to defend his country and use arms to do so. I couldn't help but think of three experiences I had had …

I was in Italy in 1923 at the dawn of Fascism, in Germany in 1933 shortly after Hitler arrived on the scene, and in France in 1940 at the beginning of the Pétain regime. In spite of my good intentions, I couldn't help but draw a connection between the state of affairs in Europe at those times and the climate I found in the United States during my trip. I did, however, see one important distinction that plays in favour of Americans. In Italy, Germany, and France, people won't tolerate contradictions. In 1954, however, I was able to speak to the Americans I met, express my ideas, and share my experiences. I could compare the situations and provide clarifications, and people didn't refuse to listen or to think about my viewpoint. This is why international exchanges are so important, why lectures and all sorts of contacts between people are urgent priorities.

The word "peace" has a lot to do with it. Alas, it too is an abstract word, like war. It is used too often by people who haven't seriously considered its implications. In fact, it can be used to mean things that are diametrically opposed. On the other hand, "better understanding" is a more practical and useful term. Most of us can gain a better understanding of the world. Don't misunderstand me: this isn't an advertisement for our work and our centre. I left for the United States exhausted and discouraged, doubting the value of the work we were doing in France. I returned full of hope and energy, because I had met people who were eager to accomplish things, even the tiniest actions, and more interested in deeds than words.

A young Catholic woman who was studying at the Institute to get university credits told me, as she shook my hand, "I am really interested in everything you had to say. This is the first time I've ever talked to someone who wasn't born in the United States." Imagine my surprise! Europeans believe that Americans are globe-trotters who fly all around the world. We picture women who wear high heels, spend very little time looking after their homes and their families, go to the country club, get divorced, and have fun! A little trip anywhere in the United States but especially in the midwest, and we see that American women do the housework themselves and raise their children without nannies, do the gardening and the yard work, are homebodies and take their jobs as housewives even a bit *too* seriously.

It's later on, when the children have grown up, that American women can, if they want, start a new life. They can do charity work, get involved in politics, and even travel! Instead of giving into their worries, their age and their fatigue, they try to keep fit and slim, wear young and stylish clothes, and enjoy the second phase of their life. They also try to improve their education and to understand what is happening in the world. Many mature women decide that taking a course at an Institute of Foreign Relations will replace travelling.

What was my general impression of the Quaker Institutes and Reconciliation groups I visited? I found my audiences had a great desire to learn and understand, ideas that were perhaps a bit simplistic about good and evil – a tendency to believe good lay on one side of a divide and evil on the other – and, more than anything, a tendency to have trouble understanding that actions and motivations, in real life, are rarely pure. Our Friends sometimes saw things in black and white terms, ignoring the grey zone so many of our acts and thoughts fall into.

Resistance to Nazism, the Gestapo, the persecutions of the Jews? Magnificent! Splendid! But once I realized there was a misunderstanding, that my audiences had a childlike, rather simplistic admiration for the "heroes" of the resistance movement, a tendency to turn events of human dimensions into legend, I tried to explain, perhaps awkwardly, the problems, conflicts, crises of conscience that had accompanied this "non-violent resistance." I talked about the false identity papers the Jews needed, because using their real names would have been to denounce them to the Gestapo. I said that it was sometimes necessary to hide the truth in order to save a man or a woman from the police, the concentration camps and death. The faces of my listeners darkened; in their eyes, white had suddenly turned black, without even going through grey. Some of them even felt we should have sacrificed the Jews, to keep our souls pure and honest!

Obviously, it would have been easier for us to continue our comfortable lives. We weren't Jewish. We could have avoided lying, left Jews to their fate, like Tolstoy's angel who, according to legend, returned to heaven without helping human beings because she didn't want to soil her white gowns! "God is Truth and Truth is God," Gandhi said. But the truth, the supreme value, lies in the existence of another human being. That is what Love is. If Love and Truth sometimes seem to be in conflict, that is when we need to remind ourselves that the Supreme Truth is to save human beings, our neighbours.

Non-Violent Resistance among Black Americans

When we think about Christmas, we remember the decorated tree and its bright lights from our childhood, the warmth and light in the dark night of winter. We think about snow and cold and forget that on the night Jesus was born the shepherds were outside tending to their sheep … I have been able to experience that kind of Christmas twice in my life, and I have to admit that it was on those two occasions that I truly felt the Christmas message: "Peace on Earth to men of good will." In 1950, in Sevagram, India, in Gandhi's ashram, the stars sparkled in the night, and on Christmas eve, in the stable, the Nativity story was performed by Hindus. Joseph, Mary, the Baby Jesus, the shepherds, the donkey and the ox were all there. Not nativity figures, but real people. Gandhi had died by this time, but his spirit was still alive, and the way the Gospel was felt by a non-Christian filled the stable. The message was a message of peace and non-violence for all men of good will, whether they are from the East or the West.

Another year, I was in Florida. There, too, the stars shone in the sky. Crickets were singing and the trees had all their leaves. Long "beards" of Spanish moss (also called greybeard) hung from their branches. And there, too, I felt the peace of Christmas. There, too, men had brown or black skin and were living spirits of the Gospel.

In Tallahassee, the capital of Florida, people were getting ready for Christmas: one Christmas for whites and one Christmas for blacks. For seven months, the buses had not been running on schedule because Negroes were boycotting them. They were fighting for the right to sit where they wanted, instead of in the back of the bus. They were fighting against discrimination and exclusion. American Negroes now had their prophet: Martin Luther King, from Montgomery, Alabama, a 27-year-old pastor who had discovered that non-violence was the best weapon against segregation and injustice.

On December 23, Reverend Joseph M. Rollins Jr, a Negro pastor, had come to pick me up for a mass meeting, where I was invited to speak. The large church building was packed. Important decisions had to be made. I was the only white there, except for my son Daniel, who was studying at the University of Tallahassee, and a few reporters and cameramen. I was invited to sit on the platform. In front of me was a compact crowd of Negroes in colourful suits. The ceremony was a bit exotic and very touching. The leaders, some prophets, others orators, stood up one after the other, delivering their prayers, hymns, and speeches about justice and equality to the rapt audience.

That night, I understood what Negro spirituals and jazz was all about. The mystical songs, the aspiration to rise and to build a world of justice, far from the sufferings of this world, at the side of a very powerful God. Slow and mournful tunes alternated with rhythmic singing that gradually turned into cries and gestures, the clapping of hands and tapping of feet. Sometimes the people gathered entered into a trance, calling on God, the Holy Spirit, tapping the pews in unison, their bodies swaying in rhythm, and their voices rising to extraordinary scales. Prayers, punctuated by exclamations and invocations, called on God to be their witness. God was there, with them.

And how could God have resisted this crowd, so determined to obtain justice through love and non-violence? From time to time the prayers and speeches stopped and collections were taken. It takes money to obtain freedom and equality. And people got up from their pews, one by one, and paraded up to the altar to give their little offering. Sometimes a high-pitched solo covered the sound of the procession. It was a bit like a crowd lining up to place their ballots in the box, voting for a better world, a better understanding among human beings. During the meeting, one of the leaders of the non-violence movement gave a strong, persuasive speech. He talked about Montgomery, the boycott of the buses that had ended two days before and the relatively calm mood in the city. Should Tallahassee end the strike the way Montgomery had, try to get the buses moving in a democratic way, work for changes in the segregation policy? There was a long silence, and then all the hands went up. But the leader continued: "You agree that our leaders should end the strike non-violently, but are you going to follow them? Are you morally prepared to accept the consequences? A single act of violence would destroy all the efforts we have made during the seven months of the strike. Everyone who is ready for this, raise your hand!"

About half of the people in the room raised their hands. Their heads high, their eyes shining, uttering the name of God, Jesus, the Holy Spirit, they waited, their hands still up in the air. Emotion took over the crows. Mimeographed papers were passed out and one of the pastors read the list of recommendations out loud. The main recommendations were the following:

1 If someone strikes you, turn the other cheek.
2 If someone condemns you, ignore him.
3 If someone pushes you, keep your physical, moral, and spiritual balance.
4 Do not speak unnecessarily.
5 Do not forget that the success of our efforts depends on the way you conduct yourself.
6 The bus company and the drivers will be happy to see you come back, because without us they will be unemployed. No one can harm you, because God is on our side.
7 Read these instructions and pass them on to your friends.

There was more singing, more praying, and then a woman stood up and said, in her unique Southern dialect, "Don't rush to get on the buses tomorrow. You did without them for seven months. Don't give whites the impression you're going to harass them or disturb them. People who have a car should keep on using it for another few days. People who don't need to go out should stay home. Just those people who need to use transit should go and sit on the bus."

One of the pastors got up and said, "Think carefully before you get on the bus tomorrow morning. Pray. Make sure you're calm. Ask God to give you the strength of non-violence. When you go to get up on the bus, if you feel you're not ready, you're not at peace, then get down and walk. If you can, go with someone else on the bus the first few times. Take a friend or two. You will feel stronger and calmer together. If one of you gets hit, insulted, even injured, don't budge, don't say a word, just pray in silence. God will help you. If you rush to help your friend, you'll form a group around him and another group of whites will form automatically. The two groups will turn on each other. If you don't react, if you stay calm and polite, the white man will be ashamed of his action against you. And God is with those who suffer."

A tall, strong man in the audience stood up and asked, in his booming voice: "Why are we assuming the worst will happen? Why are we thinking we will be hit, insulted, injured? Why don't we imagine whites as normal beings? That they don't care? Let's try to think that white people couldn't care less what seat we sit in. Let's remember that all they care about is getting to work on time, with no malice toward anybody. I think that will help."

I couldn't speak that evening. Three long hours had gone by and they announced my talk would be given the following Sunday, in a bigger church. I was asked to talk about our experience with non-violent resistance under Nazism, during the period when Jews were being persecuted. The newspapers announced my speech with the headline: "White Woman to Talk to Negroes."

Some whites had warned me that it could be dangerous. But it wasn't: it was one of the best experiences of my life. The church was full: 700 people, not to mention the ones in the basement connected by the PA system. I spoke as though I was being carried by the crowd. I didn't describe the parallel between the situation of Europe under Nazism and the current situation of Negroes in the USA, but the audience felt it. Every time the parallel seemed more obvious, the volume of the exclamations rose, and God was called to witness: "Yes, Jesus!" "Holy Spirit, come unto us!" "Oh, Lord!" or "Amen!"

Never in my life had I been able to gauge my effect on the audience the way I could that day. What sometimes seemed exaggerated, bizarre, even unhealthy in big rallies had a special quality here. People raised their hands to the sky as if to beg for justice, and humble men asked God to give them the strength to resist without hatred and without violence.

Just as in Le Chambon-sur-Lignon in 1942, when one Sunday in August the municipal councillors were gathered at the town hall and asked to turn over the Jews to the authorities at the very moment when non-violent resistance was being organized in churches, non-violent resistance was being organized in churches in Tallahassee at the very moment that the white Citizens' Council was meeting at the town hall to find a way to break down the resistance and to exempt Florida from the federal law abolishing segregation.

France in 1942, USA in 1957 … Humanity is the same everywhere. It wasn't enough to simply write on public monuments words like Liberty, Equality, Fraternity, or to erect a Statue of Liberty in New York. This didn't mean there would be equality among men or peace on earth to men of good will.

The Difficulty of Being Non-Violent

On Monday, December 24, the bus boycott in Tallahassee came to an end. Starting in the morning, Negroes got on the buses and the situation was relatively calm. Relatively, because there was a feeling that the white Citizens' Council was going to take revenge. Police kept people moving and tried to get rid of the cameramen, wary of sensationalist photos or films. Negroes travelled "democratically" (Negroes refused to sit in the seats set aside for them at the back of the bus), but the leaders did not have a moment of peace.

Reverend Rollins came to see me. "The phone doesn't stop ringing. All day and all night. I am constantly being threatened. My wife is expecting a baby any day now and her nerves are being sorely tested. Sometimes they tell us to get out of the house because it is going to blow up in a few minutes. Then they tell us not to leave the house because they're waiting for us outside, and we'd better watch out! We've tried to disconnect the telephone but we can't block the line too long because of the neighbours.[1] We stacked pillows and cushions on it so we couldn't hear it ring, but that didn't work either because people who were ill or in trouble wouldn't be able to get in touch with us. Being sleep-deprived is horrible, especially when there is so much to do and the situation is so stressful. In Tallahassee and in Montgomery, telephones are used to wear the leaders down."

The night of my lecture on non-violence, in one of the huge Negro churches in Tallahassee, several speakers followed me at the podium. The bus boycott had ended nearly a week before, and one of the women came up to share her experience. "On Monday morning," she said, "I got in the front of the line to get back on the bus for the first time, I felt sure of myself, strong and non-violent. I had promised myself I wouldn't react, wouldn't say anything. I sat down in the front, right behind the driver's seat, and I waited. I was early. The driver came, he looked at me, and he shouted, "Auntie, move on back!" I said nothing. Then the driver took me by the arm and took me to the back of the bus. I lost my composure. I forgot the advice you all had given me. I was red as a beet. I said to him, "I paid my fare and I have the right to sit where I want! If you want to keep me from doing that, then give me back my money and I'll leave!"

"The driver gave me back my money. He was happy to get rid of me. And right then, standing on the sidewalk, I realized I had missed my chance. I'm poor, but I took a taxi and went to another bus stop, where I stood at the front of the line to take another bus, this time "democratically." The story started off the same way. "Auntie, get up and move on back!" I didn't budge. "Auntie, go sit in the back." The driver's voice was getting louder and his face was getting angrier. So I picked up my handbag (and the woman, in front of the altar, looking out at the room, acted out the story by picking up her handbag), and I started hunting for something in my purse. I took out my papers, some money, looked down in the bottom of my purse, and the driver said: "Auntie, go to the back!" So I started going through my pockets. "Auntie, to the back!" I took out my handkerchief and blew my nose, I put it back in my pocket

... I still hadn't said a word. I kept busy looking through my things. And when it was time for the bus to leave, the poor worn-out driver went and sat in his seat, started the engine, and the bus started to move! So that was what it was like for me, to go on the bus democratically for the very first time!"

At the beginning of the second week, the windows of Reverend Steele's house were broken. He was one of the leaders. Then there were gunshots in the windows of his nephew's grocery store. On January 2, the day I was leaving for Montgomery, Alabama, the buses were taken off the roads on an order of the White Citizens' Council.

In Montgomery, I stayed at a little guest house for "coloured people," right next to Reverend Martin Luther King's house. His house was empty and well-lit outside. His family was away. He was sleeping somewhere else. We could see remnants of a bomb on the front porch. The lights were supposed to discourage other attacks on the house. I learned that the Ku Klux Klan burned crosses in front of the houses of Negroes they wanted to attack, and also in front of the houses of white people who supported integration. They were warning signs of violent attacks. I went to see Reverend R.L. Graets, a white pastor from the Negro Lutheran church. Remnants of bombs could be seen in his yard, as well. It was the evening. He was alone, making supper for his three little children. His wife was at the hospital; she had just had their fourth baby. The minister couldn't sleep. The telephone rang constantly at his place, too, the same way as at the Negro leaders' houses. Right after the baby was born, he got several phone calls. Someone asked him, in a nasty tone: "What colour is your baby's skin?" Several days later, I saw Reverend Graets's house on the television. It had been badly damaged by a bomb. The door was blown off and there was a hole in the front wall ...

In Orangeburg, South Carolina, I spent three days in a Negro university. The town was too small to afford buses, but the civil rights movement was focusing on integrated schools. People who had signed a petition in favour of integration had been punished. The pastor's wife, a schoolteacher, had been fired. Business people and merchants had been refused credit.

What would be the point of continuing the list of examples like these? Should Americans be condemned? Let he who is without sin cast the first stone. Instead of condemning and criticizing each other, why don't we try to see the positive on both sides? Martin Luther King isn't afraid of suffering. This is what he wrote recently: "Every time one Negro teacher is fired because of a stand for justice, that must be faced by the fact that five or ten thousand more must be fired. Every time one Negro's home is bombed because he decided to take a courageous stand, they must face the oppressor with the fact that he must bomb the homes of fifty or hundred thousand more. This amazing unity, this profound self-respect, this refusal to hit back, this willingness to suffer will soon cause the oppressor to become ashamed of his own methods. He will be forced to stand before God and the world splattered with the blood and reeking with the stench of his Negro brother.

> There is nothing in the world greater than freedom. It is worth paying for, it is worth losing a job for, it is worth going to jail for.
>
> I would rather be a free pauper than a rich slave.
>
> I would rather die in abject poverty with my convictions than live in inordinate wealth a mental slave.
>
> Once more the Negro must come to the point that he can cry out with his forefathers of old: 'And before I'll be a slave, I'll be buried in my grave, and go home to my Father and be saved.'"[2]

I wish courage and success to Martin Luther King. I am proud to have met you. Thank you for showing the world that non-violence is not only possible in the East, that it is not the monopoly of some so-called Hindu fakir, because it can also be used in the most western nation of the West.

Martin Luther King, Negro Pastor, the Apostle of Non-Violence in the United States[3]

Martin Luther King is 27 years old. He is a small man. He doesn't look like an ascetic monk.

Nor does he look like a saint or a prophet. He is neatly dressed in a light suit and a fedora hat; his face is clean-shaven; he has a boyish smile. He is alert, athletic, and doesn't put on airs. He has a principle and he lives by it. His principle is the same one that Gandhi rediscovered in the Sermon on the Mount and in the sacred texts of India: non-violence. Non-violence, for Martin Luther King as well as for Gandhi, is not the passive acceptance of an unjust situation. It is a struggle, a resistance, as well as the acceptance of the necessity of suffering in order to achieve the goal one has set for oneself. King's goal is the same as the one Gandhi aspired to and achieved, the freedom of an oppressed people.

A few years ago I visited Vinoba Bhave.[4] I sat with him in his ashram, located near Gandhi's. He was a thin man with skin fine and wrinkled as parchment. He continued to eat his white cheese while he answered our questions in monosyllables. He looked the way I imagined reclusive monks must have looked in the Middle Ages.

But Martin Luther King is a "modern saint." Not only does he use modern gadgets and conveniences – planes, cars, radio, television – but he also lives and moves through the world like a fish in water. He lives in this world but does not accept it as it is, and he works for a better world. This is what he says: "Those of us who live in the Twentieth Century are privileged to live in one of the most momentous periods of human history. It is an exciting age filled with hope. It is an age in which a new social order is being born. We stand today between two worlds – the dying old and the emerging new. But there can be no birth and growth without birth and growing pains." Reverend King describes the situation of the Negro in the United States as an "uneasy peace" rather than a "true peace [of] justice, goodwill, and brotherhood." But with the coming of freedom, with the arrival of "this new emerging world," there are new responsibilities: "A new age brings with it new challenges. We must all learn to live together, or we will be forced to die together. Man through his scientific genius has been able to dwarf distance and place time in chains; he has been able to carve highways through the stratosphere. Our world is geographically *one*. Now we are faced with the challenge of making it spiritually *one*."[5]

Whatever topics he is discussing, Martin Luther King always speaks quietly and calmly, as though they are everyday matters. When people ask, "How can we help with the painful birth of this new age?" King gives the answer of non-violence. He reminds us that the dawn of the new age can only come about through understanding and goodwill. The Christian virtues of love, mercy, and forgiveness need to be at the centre of our lives. Those who have been oppressed, exploited, or downtrodden run the risk of entering the new age with hatred and bitterness. If we seek vengeance through our hatred and bitterness, the new world will be shaped by the same social order as the old one.

This is where the danger lies. We need to abolish, to erase the hatred and injustice of the old age and replace them with love and justice. This is why I believe so strongly in non-violence. Violence never resolves problems. It only creates new problems that are even more complicated. If we give in to the temptation to use violence in our struggle for justice, future generations will inherit senseless chaos. Our new motto must be: "Liberty and justice through love." I don't mean a sentimental love ... it would be nonsense to ask men to love their enemies in a sentimental way. I mean an attitude of goodwill, of brotherhood. Not *eros*, not even *philia*, but *agapè*.[6] If we can learn to love our fellow men with *agapè*, we can love them not because we agree with them, accept them or are drawn to them by friendship, but because God loves them. This is the only way that we can learn to love the sinner but hate the sin, to love those who do evil even as we speak out against evil.

The evening I spent in Montgomery with Martin Luther King taught me a great deal. I couldn't help but think back to

Sevagram, to Gandhi's ashram, and imagine the thin silhouette of Vinoba Bhave standing before me. Nonetheless, "it takes all kinds to make a world," according to the old proverb. And Martin Luther King, a man the American public (and even his enemies) have considered the greatest religious teacher of our day, paused a number of times during his speech that evening. Why? To turn on the television set so he wouldn't miss the last baseball game of the series!

This is what a modern saint looks like, especially those who are from the New World, who are preparing for a new world, and who take time to enjoy the pleasures and distractions of the world in which we live.[7]

Jerusalem, Israel

During a mission for the MIR to Israel and Lebanon, André Trocmé wrote to Magda from Jerusalem. The following excerpts are from letters written on 20 April and 2 May 1954.

It is quarter after five in morning. I'm standing at my bedroom window. I've been awake since four thirty and I have before me the most beautiful view of Jerusalem that exists. It is the classic view of the Temple square, with the Omar mosque, the old city walled by ramparts, the black Cedron torrent, the Garden of Gethsemane and the Bethpage hill. If I go out onto the rooftop balcony beside my room I can see, to the east, Bethany, with the sun rising over it, and the deep valley of the Jordan River [...] Everything is intact. There isn't a single modern building, a red roof. Nothing but the stone walls turned gold by time, pines and cypress trees, a few olive trees in the bottom of the valley. This is the contemplative side. The sun casts a golden hue over the city, catching every house and the peak of the ramparts in the background in its light. The mosque is still in the shadows. The view is a painting in two tones, the colours of Tuscany around Siena: the golden stones and the dark cypress trees (the pine trees are almost black here). The sky is clearer and purer than in Tuscany. Even in the distance, the smallest detail can be seen distinctly.

Yesterday and today, I reread the passages in the Gospels (Matthew, Luke, and John) that told of the comings and goings of Jesus in Jerusalem. Everything is in perfect accordance with the city I see before me, down to the most minute detail. Who could believe that the Gospels (which weren't even written in Jerusalem, but from memory) were legends? Idiotic. Except for a few tiny details, I find myself before the Jerusalem of Jesus ... (The sun has arrived at the Mosque of Omar now, bringing its pale green tiles into view and then invading the ramparts. The trees on the Bethpage hill draw silhouettes, casting shadows on each of the towers.) The corner of the Holy Temple, high above the city on Temple Mount, towers over the Cedron Valley.

In the foreground, on this side of the Cedron, a biblical village remains: one-bedroom houses with low domed roofs. Yesterday I watched two people, draped in black and white, crouching and talking intently on a verandah. Jesus and Nicodemus? No! One of them got up and walked down the stairs to the house. By the way the person walked, I could tell it was a woman. Jesus and Mary of Bethany.

Now the valley holds only a blue shadow that seems to have fallen from the sky. I can hear children shouting in the valley. Modernization is prevented from entering the landscape by immense Israeli cemeteries on the hillsides. The Russian church, with its five gilded onion domes, guards Gethsemane and in no way mars the view; it is small and modest and blends easily into the rest of the scene. But trucks are already on their way down to Jericho, their noise jarring the tranquil setting. Is this something we should regret? Life brings people to every place, and Jerusalem – now completely bathed in sunlight – is able to hold onto something stable, enduring, that material destruction can't touch. Jews seek miracles, Greeks, wisdom, modern men, power; but what we look for is the crucified Christ, scandal and madness. However, God's madness is wiser than man's.

[…] I wasn't able to go to Israel on Friday because it was the Arab sabbath, nor on Saturday because it was the Jewish sabbath. Today, because it is the Christian sabbath, I hope I will be able to go […] The day before yesterday, I went over the classic tourist circuit: Bethlehem (0), Bethany (two out of ten), Pilate's pretorium (two out of ten), the Via Dolorosa (medium). The Holy Sepulchre: 1,500 years of accumulated superstitions and ugliness. On the other hand, the Mount of Olives, high up over Jerusalem to the west, and the Dead Sea, twenty kilometres to the east, are both inspiring. The Garden of Gethsemane may be authentic, but the atmosphere and the location, under the high ramparts of the Temple, are impressive. The Siloe Fountain is also authentic. It is the only source of water available in Jerusalem.

Yesterday, though, I was completely mesmerized. The Mosque of Omar, which has replaced the Temple on the immense white terrace built by Solomon, is at once sumptuous and simple, with clear and understated lines. The rock upon which it sits, Mount Moriah, is certainly one of the most ancient sanctuaries in human history. Muslims sit and listen to the teachings of an ulema, a scholar of the law, who is also squatting as he reads and explains the holy texts. I walked around the inside of the walls of the tower. The view of the Cedron, the Mount of Olives, and the village of Siloe is completely intact. I don't know if the letters of Cicero and Piny the Younger would provide such an accurate picture of the setting for visitors in Italy. Can readers of *The Divine Comedy* recognize Dante's Florence as easily as the landmarks of Jerusalem can be identified from the Gospels?

This morning is Sunday and, since six o'clock, the cracked bells of the Russian church on the Mount of Olives have been ringing out streams of music. I listen to the chimes through an open window. Every sound in town comes in by that window: on Friday, at about two o'clock in the morning, strange-toned litanies chanted by a priest, held for inordinate lengths of time, descend from the esplanade of the Temple. Birds chirp, cars honk, a turkey gobbles, children shout, an American, the keeper of a bed and breakfast in the village, speaks in a nasal tone on the terrace while two women argue in Arabic on the roof-tops of Siloe.

Jesus was too great for human beings. He looms over the entire landscape with a melancholy authority. Fortunately, underneath the muddle of superstitions and the ruckus of arguments, there are always pure souls, fine examples of Franciscan nuns, fervent and faithful, and Jerusalem (its children, its orphans, its poor) is immersed in Christian charity. Alas, the result is a people of beggars. But the children are so beautiful! Meanwhile, adults are carried away by the attractions and confusions of the city, or else languish like mummies in the countryside.[8]

On the *Île-de-France*

On board the *Île-de-France* ocean liner in the fall of 1955, André Trocmé was heading for the United States to give a series of lectures for the MIR. During the crossing, he shared his observations on the microcosm of the passengers around him in letters to Magda.

Sunday, 18 September 1955

This morning, I went to Mass and to the Protestant Worship which took place in the auditorium, at 10:00 and 11:00. The service was led by a priest (Canadian, I think) who dressed in front of us, with the help of one of the ship's boys, and performed the Mass with compunction. An ugly altar, a large audience that was rather chic, many with Spanish silhouettes and black hair. Contemplative piano and violin music and utter silence because the priest murmured the entire service. The whole thing lasted thirty-five minutes, including communion (taken by about ten women). There was a single uplifting moment, which was the reading of the Gospel passage: the healing of the man with the withered hand on the Sabbath. However, everything was respectful and religious. For the people attending, it was definitely a special event. As for me, an outsider (just as I am an outsider in the synagogue or the mosque), I "felt" (aesthetically rather than religiously) the miracle of God made flesh.

Then it came to an abrupt and badly planned end. After a quick "*Ite missa est*" and a hurriedly murmured "*Ave Maria*", I suddenly found myself watching a robust and jovial priest without his frock, a boy, really, who had finished serving Mass reverently and was now folding up the altar and the linens with the dexterity of a magician … The musicians fled towards the ballroom in first class with their instruments tucked under their arms.

At eleven o'clock an Anglican priest in a long black robe appeared. With a rather false geniality, he handed out little green hymnbooks printed by the General Transatlantic Steamship Company for the use of American Protestants. Why just for Americans? What about us? Seventy or so people arrived, as many blonds as the dark-haired Catholics for Mass, their fingers bare of red nail polish, heads unadorned by mantillas, more serious and less pious than their predecessors.

The minister uttered some words, rather awkwardly, explaining that he was Anglican and used to leading proper rituals but that, at the insistence of the General Transatlantic Company (and where was God during this?) he had agreed to do this interdenominational service. Anglican prayers murmured as though we were continuing the earlier Mass. Three people left, probably signalling their disenchantment. A Gospel reading that couldn't be heard properly: "Be anxious for nothing." A hymn or two accompanied by a proxy pianist who stumbled over the rhythm. A sermon that started out badly, but gradually improved, about recognizing the beauty of God, the beauty of God in others, the beauty of God within ourselves. Closing words as rushed as in the Catholic Mass, and the priest signed the cross high in the air before hurrying to gather up the hymnbooks … I found myself standing up … beside Mr André Siegfried, who had escaped from first class and was intent on thanking the minister […] for his message![9] Mr Siegfried invited me for tea. He knows Robert, the "Cotton President," as he called him.[10] … We'll see if he comes through.

What shall I conclude about all of this? I can see that divine reality is out of our reach. Taken on with great vigour by Protestants, it remains closed to us, and we have no language to speak of God. Closed into the mysterious confines of the Catholic Mass, it escapes us as well. What remains clearest and most articulate is the silence. But how can we ensure that silence is not filled with our mediocrity?

Monday, 19 September 1955

The sea has been rough since yesterday morning, angrily storming since 6:00 last night. The ship is rocking a little, pitching from side to side. It is pursuing its course at a slow gallop over the waves, but the troughs have begun to rise dramatically and crash with all their might on the ocean. Loud pounding, then the moaning and trembling of the ship which wakened the passengers from their sleep or their quiet daydreaming. The ensuing activity sounded as if a child had hit a bee hive with a stick. As for me, I was frightened. Fear came and settled into my left shoulder (my father often had aches in his left shoulder), a fear that was more physical than emotional, and didn't stop hurting all night. Fear is so strange: a month ago, when the truck taking me to Aix-les-Bains turned over and landed on its roof, I wasn't afraid. I didn't have time to get frightened, and yet there I was, like the vehicle, on my head with my limbs in the air. But being afraid on the open sea is irresistible. It comes from the extraordinary and mysterious force of the ocean which is all around us. What will become of me, all alone, in the throes of the powerful waves, in this immensity? It's a metaphysical fear. The other passengers are there, around me, some turning pale, others laughing nervously. I took refuge in the thought of the clever engineers who designed the ship we were on … but the ship was getting old, the instruments and engines were as well … zzz oooh oooh whoosh whooof … Funnels of water beat against the shutters of the portholes as I read in the lounge, barely a metre away from my ear. The ship nosed up, lurched, shuddered, plunged … What if a machine gave out at that very moment? What if the boat went off course, or if the rudder was damaged? Boooom baaang, the sounds of dishes clattering and crashing, of furniture tumbling to the ground ... What if the winds got even stronger? [...]

And then I get up, get moving, walk around, try to shake off the panic. I meet one of the stewards, chattering nervously in an attempt to be reassuring as well as polite. "How are you, Sir?"

"Fine, thank you. I don't get sea-sick, fortunately."

I return to my cabin. My travel companions are already asleep, or pretending to be. From my tap, I can get the water of wisdom, still and clear, channelled by human beings, hot or cold water, whatever I wanted, while my porthole is darkened by the violence of the waves, wild water, brutal and mindless water that "knows not what it does," water which, like a mad crowds, has me at its mercy.

What is the earth, if not a planetary ship, guided by a few sailors who were tossed onto the vessel by unseen hands? The fear of primitive people, imprisoned in tyrannical and threatening Nature, has dissipated the way the sea is returning to its calm. It continues to blow and whisper around us, but the daylight has chased the nocturnal phantoms away. All it took was for the wind to fall a bit and the vessel became calm, returned to its orderly behaviour, pushed through the water with its majestic prow. The comforting whirring of the machines, their faithful vibrations could be felt once more. The lounge was filled with little useless conversations, a distracted man plunking at the piano, the clinking of glasses of Coca-Cola served by a smiling waiter.

Was I afraid that night while the ocean used the boat as a plaything, my body lying in my berth, while the closet door opened and closed each time the ship tilted this way or that, to the rhythm of the buoys? Was I afraid? No! I was in a normal state, safe and healthy. I forgot what anguish and suffering felt like ... just as I will forget in a moment what it feels like to be safe if fear comes and captures me in a stranglehold once more. Which men are superior? The ones who are hardened to fear, because they lack imagination? Or the anxious ones who have conquered fear? Since I belong to the category of the fearful, I admire the second group. Every thought, every religion, every true faith is based on the idea of overcoming fear. For this reason, I am thrilled to belong to the weak and fearful, so that I can also know humility, inner struggle and true faith.

As I wrote "How can we ensure that silence is not filled with our mediocrity?" I didn't realize that I was so right. One of the fellow-travellers in my cabin, Bourde, a good Catholic, told me this morning, between bursts of laughter, a story about the Canadian priest who led the Mass yesterday morning. He said, "He drank so much Saturday night that when he went to go to bed, he got completely undressed and then couldn't put on his pyjamas. And then he got into the wrong berth! My friend Denis found him stretched out in his bed and had to call the steward to change the priest's sheets, because he had to sleep there! On Sunday morning, the head steward tried discreetly to find out who had served liquor to the priest the night before, but none of the stewards or bartenders had served him. They figured that the priest brings his own supply in his luggage." The priest, who had sobered up in the morning, even celebrated Mass with great dignity, haha! What a great story! [...]

The most scandalous part of it, Mr Bourde, is not that the priest was drunk – what is left to do when you are a priest, always alone, and all around you on the boat there are lovers embracing and old married couples writing letters to their children? No, the scandal is that (ha ha!) you, Mr Bourde, tell this story with such humour and then go to Mass with such a superficial notion of proper appearances. May the ten pious women who took Communion from the hands of this big joker of a priest never learn what happened! The Anglican minister, with his Lenten face, his bourgeois wife and his awkward and sincere sermon, suddenly seemed kinder and closer to my heart, while the "contemplative Mass" with its allusions to "God made flesh" collapsed like a badly constructed theatre set ... I know there are good priests and bad ministers, but what are we to think of a Church in which bad priests only serve to put a smile on the face of parishioners who have seen plenty like them before?

Wednesday, 21 September 1955

11:00 in the morning. This time the sea is wild. I have never seen it like this: the mist settles like fog on the surface, foams like a head on beer and is of a sombre grey colour. Security measures have been taken: chairs have been nailed down, ropes have been installed in the hallways. Since early this morning a damp heat that bodes ill has replaced the cool cabin air. My head feels as though it is clamped in the vice of a storm, as the ship looms up and sinks down again on the waves, making a sound like the crack of a cannon shot and then vibrating in every inch of its hull. The atmosphere has returned to the surrealistic character I wrote about the other day. It is getting hard to think. A little group of children, three metres away from me, continue to draw as though nothing is happening. If they had any fears, they would be completely panicked by the sounds of the waves breaking against the boat, the variations in air pressure when tons of water beat down on us, the detonations of the hull … But since everyone is making an effort to appear as normal as possible, the children are behaving normally. It is an interesting phenomenon. Adults place their trust in the (invisible) captain of the ship but their confidence is limited, because adults have seen or even been in accidents when human beings are overpowered by the brutality of Nature. The captain places his trust in machines and in God; in fact, the idea of a sea-captain being a complete atheist is difficult to believe. When one has two thousand lives in his care, one cannot help but be at least in some sense a believer. Even if he accepts none of the dogma of a church, he must pray to God. (If the storm subsides in a few minutes, the captain may return to his atheism … unless, of course, he is a true believer, that is, someone who believes during the calm as well as during the storm.) But a child can be perfectly calm in the midst of a storm, as long as his mother and other adults are nearby. That is probably what Jesus meant when he spoke about a child's faith.

But let's talk about something else: about Bourde, for example! He has his colleague Denis and two little Americans at his dinner table. The day before yesterday, he asked them to send a written invitation to ... Maurice Chevalier, and to ... Prince Albert of Belgium, who, to their great surprise, accepted! [...] I talked to Bourde about the Cévennes. I mentioned "Le Chambon-sur-Lignon."

"You're familiar with Le Chambon-sur-Lignon?" cried Bourde.

"Well, I should be! I've been the minister there for sixteen years!"

"My young nephew will be attending college there with Mademoiselle Pélenc in October!"

"I am the founder of the college, along with Reverend Theis."

"Do you know Madame Cambessédès?" asked Bourde.

"Of course, she is a close friend of ours."

"I boarded with her, on Rue de Grenelle, for a year!"

[...] What a small world it is!

As I write, the sea is calming down a little, and the "cannon shots" are becoming fewer and further between. At any rate, I am starting to get used to it, and to think that the hull will probably hold out.

And now for André Siegfried.[11] Yesterday, at noon, I found him sitting at the entrance to the passengers' cafeteria. He was waiting for me, after coming to my cabin and setting a time. Only very important persons (such as those recently appointed to the Académie française where he paid tribute to Daniel Rops) would conduct themselves with such elegance. I was quite flustered as I went to the first-class lounge at 2:00 in the afternoon to meet him. He talked about his life, his work, and his distinctions for an hour and a quarter. He had, indeed, received many awards, had been recognized by René Coty and decorated with the Grand Cross of the Legion of Honour.[12] He talked about Daniel Rops, about Edmond Fleg, about his trip to India, about Muslims, and asked me dozens of questions, as if I were more knowledgeable than he was, about North Africa, Islam, Christianity.[13] As for Siegfried himself, he is an old liberal, a monotheist who believes in the possibility of a "monotheistic block" to face Russia. He is not very open to "Moscowteer" ideas.[14] A well-meaning bourgeois, calm and sure of himself. I regret not asking him more questions myself. However, it is hard to grasp the real opinions of a man who has been built up by fifty years of decorations and distinctions ... On the other hand, I actually found him to be more human than Z., less self-conscious, less tense, more comfortable and natural with his celebrity. As evening approached, we headed westward again. The sea was very stormy until three o'clock in the morning. Today its surface is rough, with white crests, but the ship has taken control once more and slides over the waves like a formidable iceberg. Yesterday it seemed so small and fragile.

September 22, 6:00 pm on the Île-de-France

I have just spent the first – and last – sunny afternoon on the deck, reading [...] At the very moment I went to get up because the shadow of the chimney shaded us and it began to get cold, the Nantucket lighthouse appeared on my right. On the calm, dark blue sea, three seagulls flew out to announce our arrival on the continent and an American cruiser came to meet us. Thus, boats give us a chance to steer our feelings and our interests in a new direction, respecting our inner rhythms, while airplanes rush us and throw us into new tensions before we have the time to resolve the problems of yesterday. As always, I am starting to regret not taking advantage of the opportunity to spend more time with my travelling companions. But a choice has to be made between the inner life, contemplation and reading, on the one hand, and conversation, on the other. I chose contemplation, which meant that I read four books on the crossing [...]

All of America arises before me, in the form of cloud banks in the distance. I have never in my life had such a miserable crossing, but the fact that I do not get sea-sick is still a great privilege. I experienced fear, which is useful when one has the time to meditate on its meaning and when everything ends well. Everyone is busy saying their farewells. Young people are stealing kisses in the corners, children are excitedly running around the legs of vivacious adults, as if at a party. An ocean voyage always begins in heaviness and cold, and ends in a rather expansive glee. Apart from the story of the Canadian priest, I had not seen anything scandalous. I was never without a chair to sit on, air to breathe, and enough to live on. For that, I am very grateful.[15]

9

The Nuclear Age

The world entered the nuclear age in 1945. The American bombing of Hiroshima on 6 August and of Nagasaki on 9 August brought about the surrender of Japan and therefore the end of the Second World War, but this massive destruction also plunged people into a lasting state of anxiety about the future. The fact that the United States, the Soviet Union, China, and to a lesser extent Great Britain and France were building nuclear arsenals served only to increase the fear and mutual distrust among these powerful nations. The construction of numerous reactors to produce electricity added to concerns about the safety of nuclear energy. The dangers became all the more obvious when accidents occurred. The arms race was of great concern to André Trocmé who, in 1959, co-founded the Fédération française contre l'armement nucléaire (the French Federation Against Nuclear Arms) with Alfred Kastler, who would win the Nobel Prize for Physics in 1966. Although his work against the proliferation of weapons has been less recognized than his efforts to provide safe havens to Jews, it was one of the major causes he took on while at the head of the European secretariat of the MIR.

During this period, Magda and André lived in Versailles. Although they had certain political affinities, they distanced themselves from political parties in order to avoid mixing causes. They were, however, interested in the work of the new Parti socialiste unifié.[1] Magda participated in the founding of a women's group against atomic war. She also became friends with Marie-Claude Vaillant-Couturier, a Communist member of parliament who was also active in the nuclear disarmament movement.

The Trocmés were frequently called upon to work with politicians and activists. At times it was difficult from them to maintain their position of non-violence, but their commitment to Christian pacifism was irreproachable. It is for this reason that, at the risk of disappointing some of his closest Protestant friends who were also conscientious objectors, André refused to sign the Stockholm Appeal in 1950.[2]

The Marcoule Nuclear Site

In April 1958, Magda and André took part in a protest against the Marcoule nuclear plant, located in a picturesque wine-growing region just north of Avignon. They were among the first citizens to question the wisdom of producing atomic energy, believing that it put human beings at undue risk – an idea that was confirmed by an accident at Marcoule in 1958, when several workers at the plant and residents of the area suffered radiation poisoning during repairs to the facility.

From the floor of the nuclear plant, Magda wrote the following letter to her daughter, Nelly.

There are eighty-two of us here, everyone sitting on the ground in front of one of the buildings of the nuclear plant. We phoned yesterday to announce our arrival, and the engineer in charge of visitors was waiting for us in the watchtower overlooking the plant. We rented a large vehicle and had ten other cars. We brought someone from Radio-Genève with us, a minister (Papa) and a priest. Besides your father, there are well-known journalists and writers heading up the group.

After hearing the explanations from the plant officials, we asked questions about atomic energy in France. The discussion became more and more intense, and finally Papa and others explained who we were and why were there, to protest the production of nuclear arms and to take responsibility for the situation. After that, we got back into our cars and went down the hill to the plant. Going into the complex was like crossing a border; there were guards and a barrier blocking the road.

We parked and walked in, quickly but calmly, and went under the barrier, ignoring the guards who were chasing us or trying to block our way. In a few minutes, we got [...] to the first building [...] and soon the engineer who had met us at the watchtower came. We handed him a written letter of protest and asked to speak to the head of the facility. A moment later the engineer came back and told us the head could not meet with us because we had broken in, and that we had to leave. One of our leaders stated that we were not going to leave, that this was a protest and that we wanted our position brought to the authorities and made public. He said that everyone refuses to accept responsibility for the bomb. Ordinary citizens say it is the fault of the politicians they elect, politicians that it is the government, the government that the country demands it, etc. Scientists have peaceful objectives but once the bombs are made they are available for anyone to use. The people at the plant threatened to call in the police and even threatened us with violence. We sat down on the ground in silence.

The plant is ultramodern, an American spectacle. Three towers. The road in as brightly lit as the highway at the Saint-Cloud bridge exit. Buses loaded with workers – there are four thousand of them in all – go in and out, because the plant operates day and night [...] Papa was sitting beside me [...] in the middle of everything [...] some people were reading. People who had blankets wrapped themselves up. Papa read the Bible, and pointed to Matthew 10:14. "And whosoever shall not receive you, nor hear your words, when ye depart out of that house or city, shake off the dust of your feet." Then verses 18 to 20: "And ye shall be brought before governors and kings for my sake, for a testimony against them and the Gentiles. But when they deliver you up, take no thought how or what ye shall speak: for it shall be given you in that same hour what ye shall speak. For it is not ye that speak, but the Spirit of your Father which speaketh in you." At this point the police surrounded us [...] We made our speech. A man with dark glasses said that he was from the police station and we had to leave; we had broken in, committed a crime, and so on.

At midnight, riot control officers from the national police [...] and some gendarmes joined the police officers from the plant. A large bus was brought in to take us away, and there were also several police cars [...] They ordered us to leave. We said we were not moving; they would have to force us. We did not have any food. It was cold. They were threatening to leave us there all night. The cold became even bitterer. They turned on the lights; there were even lights in the fields, in the scrubland around the plant. Finally, they threatened us with violence and began to take the men by force, carrying them inside. We continued to chant and sing peace songs. The gendarmes became violent, kicked a few people and shouted a bit, and then quieted down and got back to work carrying out the members of our group. But it took a while, with eighty-two people! We allowed ourselves to be carried out, going limp like bags of flour.

More violence. More people calmly carried out. A pregnant woman stood up and allowed herself to be led out by the hand by one of the officers. Two other women agreed to walk out. I was told I should stand up and walk; I am an older woman, and heavy, but I refused to do it. Papa said we had been married for thirty years and I was stubborn. Three police officers lifted me up, one holding my shoulders and the other two holding my legs. My legs were higher than my shoulders and my skirt was hiked up. They put me on the floor inside, up against the wall. I waited to be searched. When it was time for me to be checked, I gave them a letter from Mr Bœgner, a cheque, and a vaccination certificate. I did not have any other papers with me; we had left our passports behind for safekeeping. They threatened to send me to the police station until I could produce proper identification. I told them that Papa had a driver's license. A nice employee went to get Papa. Four men carried him over. They asked me my father's name; they could not spell my mother's name: Wissotzky was too hard.

Finally, seventy-nine persons had been carried in and three had walked in themselves. They sent in our bus and made the women board it. I was worried that they were going to take the men somewhere else, so I went back out, despite the officers getting upset with me, and went over to Papa. A man put a blanket around my shoulders. I told the officers that during the war Papa had been arrested and afterwards he was decorated.[3] They laughed at me. The men got into the bus too, and I went in with Papa. At nine o'clock we left the plant [...] A couple of the members of our group went up to Paris that night to inform the newspapers. The police had confiscated the tapes and photos taken by the Radio-Genève reporter, who was really disappointed.[4]

A Train Ride in Japan

André Trocmé was invited to take part in the World Congress Against A- and H-Bombs in Japan, held in July and August 1958 to commemorate the destruction of Hiroshima and Nagasaki by the atomic bombs dropped in August 1945. Here is a passage from the letter he wrote to Magda on the train that took him from Hiroshima to Nagasaki on 7 August 1958.

We are heading towards the southern tip of Japan, the island of Kiou-Shiou. The train is chugging through steep, wooded hills and bays around capes, like the hills and bays we have seen in Italy, and through rice paddies that are of an astonishingly bright green. Right now, though, we are passing an oil refinery with its harmful fumes; I could do without that! Besides this industrial intrusion, everything is authentically Japanese: neat rows of attractive houses with pointed roofs, fishermen's shacks, islands like little wooded gardens [...]

Yesterday was the biggest day of the commemoration. Not far from the site where the bomb was dropped, in a huge ballroom next to the magnificent hotel where we were staying, a congress against nuclear weapons hosted by the city of

Hiroshima, entirely Japanese in style. They had headsets to translate our speeches. There were many, many speeches. Some were calm, given by dignified survivors of the bombing. Others, by young people, were violently communist and anti-American. To hear them, you would think that Russia did not have any nuclear weapons. I spoke on behalf of the foreign delegation. To help parents understand the situation, I suggested they think about their responsibility to children of other nations, children like theirs who could be killed or harmed by bombs, as a sort of protective adoption. For instance, a grandfather from France like me, with seven grandchildren, could "adopt" seven children in seven different countries and guarantee them safety and life. To demonstrate, I had asked for a Japanese boy the same age as our grandson Jeannot to join me on the podium. A marvellous little boy named Kozo Tanaka came up. He stood on a chair beside me, perfectly still throughout the rest of my speech [....]

Now we can see houses with high thatched roofs, almost Polynesian in appearance, grouped together on pine-covered hillsides which pop up between rice fields. The styles of the landscape and the architecture change as you move from one village to the next, but it is all incredibly beautiful.

I stopped for quite a while on the bridge that crossed the biggest of the seven arms of the delta on which the city was built. There were thousands of lanterns – red, blue, yellow – and each one with name of one of the victims written on it. Following a Buddhist custom, the lanterns floated peacefully out to the sea, into the night, to ease the passage of their souls into the heavens. At the edge of the parapet, one of the war-wounded, his face covered by a cloth to hide some horrible wound, scratched on a strange stringed instrument with the metal grip at the end of his artificial arm. A frightful sight for children, you would have thought, but the young people just ran around, happily playing in the noisy chaos of the religious, the dead, vendors selling lanterns, talismans, orangeade, fragile origami figures and the little plastic objects the Japanese are so fond of.

We were dripping with sweat from the heat that hung over the dust. Impeccable stars guided our human meanderings in search of truth, or life, or at least a path through our foolishness. Somewhere in the middle of the ruins, under artificial light, people were playing baseball. You could hear the enthusiastic exclamations of the invisible crowd. Their shouts alternated with the strange intonations of the priests who, a few steps away from me, were bowing down before the ashes of the two hundred thousand victims.

The day before, we had met the mayor of Hiroshima at the city hall. We also spent a long time at the Red Cross Hospital, visiting the leukemia patients. We ended off our evening with a group of victims who shared their horrifying stories, their descriptions of distraught parents searching for their children and unable to recognize them because their facial skin had melted under the crushing heat of the atomic bomb.

Now the rice fields are descending like stairs towards us and then into narrow gorges. We go in and out of tunnels that end in calm little creeks bordered by fishermen's thatched roof shacks and heavy, square junks with brown nets hanging from their masts to dry. The landscape is as harmonious as Italian lakes must have been before steamships and motorboats disturbed them. The brutal engines of industry and the tedious factory chores are even more painful to watch, as are the neon signs encroaching on the lovely thatched roof cottages.[5]

Nagasaki

André wrote the following theological piece in Nagasaki.[6] His thoughts reveal a deep belief in divine providence and utter obedience to the teachings of non-violence found in the Gospels.

Although preachers in my childhood threatened me occasionally with Hell, I was never fully convinced that it exists. With my tourist guide in my hand, I decided to look for a representation of this fiery chasm in the cellars of Roman churches to prove it did not exist. The flames of Gehenna that can never be quenched, the sun that turns into blood in the Acts of the

Apostles, the stars falling from the sky in Gospel verses, none of these things mattered to me. I told myself that the universe was solid, that humanity had been marching, since the Stone Age, from one landmark of progress to the next.

It was in Nagasaki that the anguish of damnation took hold of me for the first time. For those who were reduced to nothing, for the seventy-two thousand Christians and pagans who did not have time to think before their bodies were ignited by the explosion, for the little Japanese boy whose skull melted to the inside of his glowing steel helmet, there was no problem. It was not their fate that frightened me. They died, as so many whose lives ended during the world wars, as those who die in accidents, landslides, earthquakes. The people I feared for are the living, the ones who dropped the bomb, who made it, who chose this path and accept it even today. And to the right and to the left of the noisy bomb, I saw its hollow-eyed twins: the silent suffocation of concentration camps and the murder of human beings perpetrated by torture.

Here, then, on the banks of this emptiness, this nothingness, I felt as though I was witnessing an attack on God's creation and redemption. When there are no longer any souls to save, God's love will have nothing to sacrifice itself for. The horrible sight was a negation of the Creator; in the solitude of the origins of the world, God does not even have a name. Worst of all, the end of creation and the negation of the Creator were brought about by the most intelligent, if not the most noble, of the Creator's designs: Man.

In a way, Man did not wish for the death of God; he simply thought he could live without a divine presence. He wanted to forget the gates of Hell illustrated in the stories and paintings of the Middle Ages. He wanted to topple the Supreme Judge from his throne because he thought he no longer needed him. The only problem was that in getting rid of the Judge, Man was forced to take his place, because justice needed to be delivered. And because no one feared being struck down by Jehovah's lightning, these flashes had to be replaced by more terrible blows, decisions to put to death masses of citizens, acts of war next to which God's judgement seems mild indeed.

And so Man, of his own free will, opened the gates of Hell we believed had been locked forever. In the name of justice, he wants to push his enemies through them, and they want to condemn him just as harshly. Like the dances of death in ancient cathedrals, aborted lectures on disarmament chant their predictable litanies. Man knows his fateful destiny but can do nothing to stop it from happening. Heads of state are unable to imagine any other salvation for Christians, who seem destined to fall into hells built by others, than to pre-emptively push their enemies into infernal traps set by Christians.

But has it ever been any different? I open my Bible and see that God did not invent Hell. God is salvation and life. It is Man who has turned his back on God and released upon himself the inescapable vengeance of bloodshed that always cries out for more blood. And it will always be like this, until Man discovers that he cannot save himself, that it is because he tried to save himself that he has ended up thinking he must kill others and that he has opened the gates of Hell. Those who understand what is happening cry out to the great beyond they tried to pretend was empty. Their cry is vengeful at first, but then becomes a prayer: "Oh God, if you exist, help us! Deliver your justice on Earth as in Heaven! For the sake of your great design, save your creations from the Hell they have invented."

Jesus of Nazareth was born in an era that was as ignorant as ours. History was at a dead end. As a Jew, he did not know the history of anyone but the people of Israel, God's chosen people. The future of the world was in the hands of Jerusalem, destined to be the capital of all nations. But Jesus knew that Jerusalem was headed toward a suicidal revolt against Rome and knew, in advance, that Jerusalem would be completely destroyed. The destruction of Jerusalem was the end of history, the end of the world as he knew it, the fiery chasm of Hell opened up by the disobedience of the chosen people.

In Nagasaki, it is impossible to ignore or ridicule the prophecies of Jesus. If a third world war broke out, it would bring about not only the destruction of Jerusalem but also, the ultimate act of rebellion against God, the destruction of Paris, Washington or Moscow, the end of Christianity and Communism, the end of the world. The atmosphere would be poisoned by Strontium-90, would eradicate human beings, animals and plants, all of God's creation. In the year 70 AD, the little Christian church could escape from Jerusalem and find refuge in Pella, on the other side of the Jordan River. In the 20th century, however, there will be no Pella, no safe haven where people can protect themselves from the archangel's flaming sword.

The physical and moral salvation of the human race, of its marvellous history and its future, must come, then, from an unexpected act of God, something we cannot foresee, just as Christ's twelve disciplines could not foresee what the Christian church would become in the centuries after they died. God will find a solution for us, we believe that, but what will it be like? We have no idea. What we do know is what the apostles of the Nazarene prophets knew: when the end is near, when Hell is us, the only thing we can do is to wait for God to show us a sign, to reveal his plans, to create an event the likes of which we have never seen, a revolutionary act that will cause His creation to be reborn from its ashes, like a reed that sprouts after a forest fire. But waiting for this deliverance also means no longer believing that Man carries the future of human history in his hands alone, no longer trusting in bigger and bigger bombs to restore justice around the globe, no longer relying on the power of human technology and of accumulated wealth, no longer looking to any of that for salvation but instead looking to God alone.

Those who trust in God have not yet seen the deliverance they hope for. Jesus did not know what miracle God would perform to save creation. Those who want to be faithful to God today no longer see an illuminated future unfold before their eyes. They see only what everyone else sees: machines that reign over human beings, marvellous and anonymous machinery which does not care about their conscientious objections, which is intent on destroying itself and anything in its path, which will soon be reduced to a heap of twisted metal. They cannot see anything else and will probably not survive the Apocalypse. What they do know is that even if science cannot predict the end of the world, they can be sure that God will save His creation and will make use of those who have not capitulated in the face of technology, the pride and foolishness of man's justice, and the monstrosities of violence, this small number of human beings who have dared to trust in God alone.

Jesus has appeared to us poor, disarmed, non-violent, in the middle of a terrible century. He has opened the gates of the future to human beings who were destined for Hell. It is to Jesus that we want to give voice, to Jesus that we want to listen.

Waiting for deliverance means daring to venture down new paths, immediately answering the call of a conscience enlightened by the Gospels, being guided by faith while the majority of men, the masses, and even many of our friends or the Church itself, have decided not to place their trust in God alone.

Portraits of Pacifists

André Trocmé was able to describe the personalities and the faults of those around him succinctly. Here, he paints a humourous and occasionally satirical portrait of some of the delegates at the Japanese congress against the H-bomb. In this excerpt, from a letter to Magda dated 16 August 1958, the names used are fictitious.

The nice ones.

Gerulof is a strident communist of Slavic background. He threatens, he shouts, he insults capitalists, imperialists, militaristic and colonial exploiters, all those who are conspiring to annihilate the human race through torture, the H-Bomb and genocide. After his speech, he comes looking for you, intensely emotionally: "I hurt your feelings, didn't I? I'm violent." "No, no, you are sincere, a friend who never deeply hurts his friends."

Dupont is a crossover from the bourgeoisie. One day he got fed up with the conventions, blind patriotism, and acceptance of the war of members of his class. He is too clever to become a Communist, but his passion pushes him to condemn the society into which he was born. So he travels as a "reservist" with his

Communist friends. He still rails against his government and his homeland, tossing invectives out liberally against them, and probably will do so until his hair is grey. He does not realize that in a satellite country he would be the first to lash out against Khrushchev and to attract enemies: very powerful enemies.

Aboudou is a handsome Black man raised by priests, who speaks French with a beautiful accent, with velvety rolling r's. His conversion to Christianity enlightened him. In France he would be considered anti-clerical; in Africa he is a nationalist, that is, dedicated to the complete independence of his country. His country did not have a written language before the arrival of the missionaries, who were killed for giving its people the alphabet, a Bible, schools and hospitals. Aboudou is a product of these missionaries, but that does not matter. He sees only vice, exploitation, hypocrisy and ambition in those who dragged his father out of the bush. He jumps on priests who preach hatred and have never done anything for him. He seeks revenge for everything good he received and claims that his people are the best on the planet. But he is young and proud, and so naive and idealistic. His white teeth sparkle under the light of the future, his bright eyes do not turn away from those who insult him. All in all, he is a nice fellow, and you cannot help but like him.

The not-so-nice.

Mitchourine is a handsome man with greying hair who speaks more slippery than fluent versions of English, German, and French with a Russian accent. Do not try to make him angry; he will just answer your insults with a smile because he is, after all, a specialist in peace. Russian peace, of course, because he is an unofficial representative of the government in Moscow. But do not try to make him admit it. If you believed what he said, he is a citizen of the most free and open-minded regime on the planet. When he steps up to the podium, the whole audience applauds. He responds with theatrical gestures and begins, in a neutral tone, a speech that is rounded out with generalizations, in which imperialist countries are brought down, trampled on and muddied, while Russia is deserving of universal praise for its sublime initiatives in favour of peace.

Raisin puts on airs of farm-boy simplicity, and comes to us as a protective big brother. "Some day you will join our movement, which is the only one which has ever done anything for the cause of peace. We have the means to succeed. We have thousands of people at our conventions, millions of signatures on our petitions. Your conscientious objectors are laughable. Your platform is an escape mechanism to distract delegates from the only realistic way of ensuring peace. You reproach us for being aligned with the Russian diplomacy? It just looks that way. But I'm not a communist. You want Russians to recognize their part of the blame. I don't understand you. No, really, I don't see what you have to blame them for. But … Budapest?" Raisin has already run off, muttering a response under his breath. A few minutes later, you will find him in a corner, in close conversation with one of the conference leaders. He's already president of the steering committee! But if you ask him about it, he will vehemently deny that his movement has anything to do with the Japanese movement against the H-Bomb. Cordial, tactful, he is impossible to pin down. You can't even look him in the eye for more than a few moments before his gaze wanders.

Richter has not had much luck in life. Because he is Jewish, he was persecuted in Germany. When he sought refuge in France, he had to learn a difficult language; now, unfortunately, he believes he speaks it without an accent. He has lived in the USA and is bitter about Americans because they did not pay him the respect he deserved. When he came back to Germany, he wrote a book about the H-Bomb with ideas so deep and a style so difficult that no one read it. And now the Japanese committee was inviting him to speak and paying for his trip. He is positively glowing with pride, finally receiving the consideration to which he is entitled. He chairs the meetings with excessive elegance, finishes the speeches of speakers. He seems ready to rise in the hierarchy, to climb up a structure in which pacifism is erected on the scaffolds of insults against those who are not there to defend themselves. But as it turns out, he is unable to avoid letting the truth fall from his lip. He is not a good diplomat. He is already seen as unreliable, and will not be invited again.

The simple.

They were invited to join the Mouvement de la paix organization. They were nobodies. They were told they were important figures. They were invited to wear their "national dress." They sit quietly on the benches, listen to all the speeches, always clap. They have never really thought about peace. In fact, they are not very gifted in critical thinking. They were told: "This is what peace is!" They believe it. "That's who's to blame!" They agree. "Here comes the world's great hero!" They are so happy to have found him, and to be in the company of other naive and righteous people. They write postcards to their friends and tell them how polite the Japanese are. Ah, if only there were no Americans, the world would be a peaceful and happy place.

The good-hearted.

Christian was in despair over the hatred in the world. He went to talk to the working people; they insulted him because he was too bourgeois. He went to talk to non-believers; the blamed him for the errors of the church. To Afro-Asians; they read him a list of monstrosities committed by Westerners. To Russians with the Mouvement de la paix; he learned that he belonged to a society of capitalists who were planning to exterminate humanity with nuclear arms. Christian is, as his name suggests, Christian. He knows that his passion is not the fruit of justice and objectivity, but he is too aware of his egoism and his lack of brotherly love to be able to denounce the sins of others. However, he definitely does not want to offend or harm workers, non-believers, Afro-Asians, or Russians. They are all so sure they are innocent. So he confesses, confesses again, and confesses still again the crimes he has not committed. And he recognizes, recognizes again, and recognizes still again that the others are right. You cannot hurt their feelings if you want to convert them to Jesus Christ one day.[7]

The French Federation Against Nuclear Arms

One of many lectures given by André Trocmé to promote the Fédération française contre l'armement atomique, this one, which he gave in Paris on 25 May 1959 at the conference of Learned Societies, addresses the primary issues of nuclear warfare.

Men as famous as Nehru, Bertrand Russell, Albert Schweitzer, Arnold Toynbee, General MacArthur and eighteen Nobel prize-winners have taken the position that all nuclear stocks should be destroyed, and nuclear research and production should be stopped immediately. But we must not forget the warning made by Albert Einstein before he died: "Here, then, is the problem which we present to you, stark and dreadful and inescapable: Shall we put an end to the human race; or shall mankind renounce war?" Humanity, he believed, must abolish war or risk being obliterated itself by the slow torture of radioactive rain and dust.

Answering the call of these men, movements against nuclear warfare have arisen in the United States, Japan, English, Sweden, Germany, Holland, Austria and Switzerland over the past few years. At the same time, countries in the Eastern bloc have become aware of the growing dangers of producing, stockpiling, and experimenting with nuclear weapons.

In France as well, various groups have protested the use of atomic energy, but until now there has been no coordinated action. Some French celebrities who were invited to the European Congress on Nuclear Disarmament held in London on January 17, 1959, were imprisoned for their involvement in the actions of groups such as Campaign for Nuclear Disarmament in England, the Committee Against Atomic Weapons in Germany, and Action Against the Atomic Bomb in Holland. Scientists, scholars, men of letters, clergymen from all denominations, labour unions from all over the world put aside their ideological and political quarrels and came together to alert the public and demand that their governments destroy nuclear weapons, if they have them, or stop preparing for atomic war if they are still at the research stage.

French public opinion could not remain silent for long. The efforts of those who had taken a position on the matter had to be coordinated. Upon on our return from London, Alfred Kastler and I organized the French Federation Against Nuclear Arms.

It is my job here to summarize some of the key statements and the methods that guided our work.

1 We are a federation, which means that we do not have individual members. We have a sponsorship committee made up of celebrities and important figures from all religious, social and political backgrounds. We invite all existing associations who want to add action against nuclear armament to their agenda to become members of the Federation, either as members if they are in full agreement with our campaign, or as observers if they want to encourage us in our effort and give us their opinions.

2 Affiliation with the Federation is, therefore, open to all associations. There is only one condition: they must subscribe to the following declaration, which is part of our constitution: "The French Federation Against Nuclear Arms, as part of a worldwide campaign for nuclear disarmament, is opposed to the manufacturing, stockpiling, and testing of nuclear weapons in all countries of the world."

3 The wording of our declaration should reassure all those who fear that France will become weak in the face of neighbouring powers or that the West will become unarmed while the enemy becomes more dangerous. In reality, the French Federation Against Nuclear Arms seeks only to represent the groups in France who want to be part of a campaign in all countries of the world, in the West and in the East. We are not demanding that France alone give up its nuclear weapons. We are also asking Russia, China, the United States, and England do the same. We do not think that the production, stockpiling, and testing of nuclear arms, whether

in the East or the West, and even when intended for defence, can be justified in any situation. They are a crime against humanity.

4 Nevertheless, as French citizens, it is in France that we must first manifest our resistance. We cannot demand of others what we do not demand of our own government. We consider ourselves privileged because France does not yet possess atomic weapons. We believe that it would be consistent with the best traditions of France to choose, at the very moment that France would be capable of testing nuclear weapons, to suspend its actions. This would serve as an example of a spontaneous and voluntary control of our own reflexes of fear in the face of the nuclear capabilities of neighbouring nations.

5 Practical considerations might also motivate our government to set a reasonable course of action. Whatever efforts France makes to develop atomic weapons, it will never be able to catch up with America or the USSR. It does not have the means to do so. Possessing some atomic weapons would only encourage the more powerful, belligerent nations to bomb France. On the other hand, nuclear disarmament, even with all the risks it implies, might give us a chance of survival.

6 However, our resolution should not be guided by negative thoughts. France, like many other countries, possesses limited resources. If it chooses to allocate them to the nuclear arms race, it will have to sacrifice all else to this effort and forget the rest. But France has another mission to accomplish. It can share its resources, freely and generously, with other nations which are unable to sustain economic growth without the help of wealthier countries. In order to succeed in helping the poorer countries of the world, we must direct all our efforts toward this cause. We cannot divide our energy. France is at a crossroads. It can choose either to rebuild its reputation as humanity's benefactor or to exhaust itself by competing endlessly with its rivals.

We do not ignore the fact that atomic energy has the potential to resolve certain human problems. But to use it for these purposes means to take decisive and courageous action, to overcome our old reflexes of egotism and fear. The French Federation Against Nuclear Arms calls upon French citizens to act upon their consciences and this awareness.[8]

Letter to the President of the Republic of France

On 14 July 1959, in the middle of the Algerian war, André Trocmé and Alfred Kastler wrote a letter of protest to Charles de Gaulle, President of France.

In the last few days, the press has reported on the plans of France to detonate atomic weapons in the Sahara Desert as part of a series of tests. The Fédération française contre l'armement atomique urges you to reconsider this decision.

Our federation is a branch of the European Federation and is supported by men who are well-known and well-respected such as Georges Duhamel, François Mauriac, Jean Rostand, and Albert Schweitzer. The Federation refuses to take part in party politics. It encompasses a diverse group of member organizations and focuses on halting the production and the use of atomic weapons around the world.

As French citizens, the members of our Federation are sensitive to any action that could diminish the reputation of our country. The establishment and development of the Atomic Energy Commission which you introduced in 1945 and the construction of nuclear reactors in Marcoule are accomplishments of great merit, and as a result France ranks among the powerful nations in terms of atomic energy. However, as soon as we possess – and that time is not far off – more than a critical mass of plutonium, the use of this substance for an atomic explosion cannot be considered an achievement. It is a facile and useless experiment. The only technical difficulty related to classic ballistics lies in the speed at which two masses of less than critical quantity come into contact with each other and upon which the explosion depends. A series of test explosions may be required to perfect atomic weapons.

What will be the outcome?

The number of nuclear arms we would be able to manufacture will be very small compared to the thousands that Russia and the United States already have. There is little chance that we would manage to impress these nations with our weapons. On the other hand, we would run the risk of causing more jealousy than respect among other nations, more distrust and hostility than a spirit of alliance. We are thinking particularly of African countries in which France has already tested atomic weapons.

No one today is unaware of the harm atomic explosions cause to the human organism. By choosing Africa as the site of our experiments, we may well give Africans the impression that we accord less importance to their lives than to our own. The psychological effect might be even more serious because certain foreign radio stations would no doubt report on our misguided actions. The long and patient efforts to improve relations between France and Africa would be greatly compromised by this action.

In 1945, President Truman found himself before a difficult choice: whether or not to drop the atomic bomb on Hiroshima. The army and the scientists involved did not agree on the best course of action. In the Franck report, scientists warned that: "If the United States would be the first to release this new means of indiscriminate destruction upon mankind, she would sacrifice public support throughout the world, precipitate the race of armaments, and prejudice the possibility of reaching an international agreement on the future control of such weapons."[9]

President Truman followed the advice of his military advisers, and what the Franck report predicted happened. Hiroshima cast an enormous shadow over human history and set off a worldwide nuclear arms race. We now carry in our minds an apocalyptic vision of the end of human civilization.

Mister President, we have a feeble hope of awakening human beings from this nightmare. Demonstrations of nuclear bombs have been suspended for several months and the experts in Geneva are coming close to an agreement. Today, you are facing a choice similar to President Truman's choice in 1945. The decision is in your hands. If you agree to allow France to test the atomic bomb, you will be surrendering to the terrible fate scientists have predicted.

A few days of renewed belief in the power of France will be won at the cost of the cooperation of the nations of French Africa and a new nuclear arms race: first France, then Sweden, perhaps Switzerland and China after that. How will this benefit our country or the planet we share?

If, on the other hand, you declare that France is now able to manufacture and use bombs but has declined, if, at this conjuncture, you solemnly refuse to make this show of force, you will accomplish an action of global significance. The world's nuclear powers must sign a definitive agreement to prohibit the use of nuclear arms. Confidence and trust will then be restored in the world. You will have eliminated the shadow cast by Hiroshima.

We believe, Mister President, that moral progress alone can succeed in meeting the challenges presented by technical progress. Morality progresses when people make decisions on conscience and refuse to fall victim to the mindless fatality of evil. The powers conferred upon you are such that you can, in the name of an entire nation, make a commitment that will restore to France its proper role: that of a leader among nations, whose strength resides in aspirations to an ideal. The entire world will be grateful to you for this action.

Sincerely,
André Trocmé, Minister, Versailles
Alfred Kastler, Professor, Faculty of Sciences, Paris
Co-Presidents of the Fédération française contre l'armement atomique.[10]

The Four Strokes of Fate

The sermon that follows is based on the Book of Job (3:11–22), the Gospel of Matthew (24:32–35) and the Letter of Paul to the Romans (8:38–39). In it, André offers his thoughts on the Cuban Missile Crisis of October and November 1962, when USSR President Nikita Khrushchev attempted to install nuclear missiles pointed at the USA in Cuba. President Kennedy's firm response led to an agreement of partial disarmament between the two world powers.[11]

The title of the sermon alludes to the first four notes of Beethoven's Fifth Symphony, which were used during the Second World War as the BBC call sign. Radio-Londres (BBC's broadcast to occupied France) also used the notes as a coded message: their "dot-dot-dot-dash" meant V for Victory in Morse code.

Today we all know by experience what it means to have barely escaped from an accident. When I say accident, I do not mean great natural catastrophes like earthquakes or floods. Instead, I mean the unnatural and murderous brutalities caused by men. For instance, any one of us might be that driver who is going a little bit too fast one day or is distracted or miscalculates the distance. He thinks he can safely pass another car and he cannot. He hesitates. Half a second later, an accident. He recognizes his responsibility for that accident, and regrets his actions – for the rest of his life, probably, if there are victims.

Exactly two weeks ago, on Sunday, October 28, we were all travellers in two vehicles. Two extraordinarily powerful and brutal machines. One was driven by the US, one by the USSR. We felt that the two drivers responsible for that historic journey, President Kennedy and President Khrushchev, had lost control of their machines and were headed straight for a crash. An accident was about to happen. And then, at three o'clock in the afternoon, while I sat listening to my radio, the surprising, almost miraculous news was broadcast. President Khrushchev had put on the brakes. The horrible accident that could have destroyed one-third of the earth's population had been avoided.

The pale horse of the Apocalypse had passed us and was riding off. When things like this happen, brothers and sisters, our minds seem to be sharpened by an almost superhuman insight. Our feelings, hopes and fears become so intense that we understand many things that, ordinarily, when things are going well, remain hidden. I would like to talk about the things we realize in times like this.

First feeling: gratitude. The "Te Deum" chant was written after some catastrophes of the war had been avoided, and others were already far away. It is meant to be sung every Remembrance Day until the end of History, to give thanks to God. A thank-you from Man who is still alive, who can still breathe, see the sky, hear the noises of the earth, spend time with loved ones. I hope that gratitude was in your hearts on October 28, when you realized that war had been avoided.

In this situation, we think […] I came close to being in an accident, and now I am going to be a better person. Then we go home. We feel like hugging every person we meet, showing them that we care for them. Because we have come so close to death, we want to be freed from the constraints of our egos. We want to see that pedestrian we almost hit as our brother, and we have a better idea of how precious the wife and children God has given us really are. The impulse that is sparked in us and that makes us feel love for all those around us is always within us. It is this impulse that pushes a young man into his beloved's arms, a young woman towards her fiancé. It is this impulse, as well, that calls men and women to their vocations, to become ministers, priests, missionaries, and deaconesses. And finally, it is this impulse that returns to us after a war has ended, that reinvigorates pacifist movements, that strengthens the resolve to live more peacefully and in better harmony.

This love for mankind that is reborn after each bleak winter […] is never satisfied. A husband learns that his wife is not the infinitely perfect being he believed she was when they first met. She, likewise, discovers his flaws. The children that we have cuddled on our laps, who seemed to be the object and the incarnation of our admiration and our boundless love, separate from us. And the pacifist movements that proclaimed peace and universal harmony can already see clouds on the horizon only days after the war is over. We know that human beings are foolish, that they are unable to love, and so we also know that war will one day overcome peace again.

So we decide to get to work.

Look at all the men and women who are on their way to work, every morning between seven and eight o'clock. Look at the housewives who are cleaning their houses. If you look closely, you will see that their desire to do the right thing, their conscientious dedication to do the work they are asked to do is, deep down, a form of disappointment. "Well then, since I haven't met the perfect man, I will do what my conscience tells me is right. No one will be able to fault me. There won't be a speck of dust on my buffet." Human labour can certain accomplish extraordinary miracles. In the past, it created idols, molochs, temples or pyramids. Today it has produced an astonishing civilization that seems destined to eliminate effort and human suffering. A few years ago, prophets – because good prophets still exist – even declared that Man was about to enter a golden age, that we would be liberated from drudgery and enslavement of every sort. Alas! Today the machines that men have produced behave exactly like the idols of the past. Man believes he is using them, but in reality the machines use men. Look at the way your work has changed, if you work with machines and modern tools. The pace of your work-day becomes faster and faster. To get to work sooner, you buy a motor-car. The traffic gets heavier. The world becomes noisier. And we have not yet seen the worst of it! Soon we will be travelling in airplanes that fly twice as fast as the speed of sound. People will be making trips to the moon or the planet Mars – I have no desire to travel through space – because the great machine of progress insists on it.

In fact, far from resolving the problems of our soul, work is now leading us farther away from our universe, from God. Work, technology, have not helped modern man reconcile with his God. On the contrary. Look at the military technician. He is a courageous and conscientious man. He is sheltered in his concrete building, in front of a keyboard, doing his work. A thousand kilometres away is another man, a surgeon in an operating room. He is operating on a little blue child, performing open-heart surgery, making the blood flow normally through the arteries. He is also conscientious. They are equal in terms of work. The difference is that if the military officer pushes a button, there will be no more surgeons, no more blue children, no children at all. There will be nothing. The idol of destruction, the machine manufactured by Man, will have done its job.

When work is pushed to this extreme, brothers and sisters, it becomes a human idol. It does not bring us closer to God. Many have realized the tragic situation we are in, the impasse towards which our human efforts have led us. They have seen this, and their way of dealing with the problem is to ignore it. They give up trying to give any meaning to life and begin to play. Brothers and sisters, they say that it is children who play, but I say that children do not play, they are very serious with their little cars, they are following their true natures. But I believe that it is adults who play, that you and I play, when we are backed into a corner by things that are unknowable.

Look at what adults do. They drive in their cars, eat in nice restaurants, play sports, enjoy nature, hike up mountains, slide down steep hills on skis, own a nice bungalow, collect stamps, water and weed their gardens, play cards, go to movies. They know very well that none of this is serious. When they play, they can forget serious matters. They erase Kennedy and Khrushchev and all the threats and accidents they can think of from their minds. A few minutes ago they were on the highway, and they passed a crumpled car. They averted their eyes and focused on what they were doing, on their pleasant things, so they would not have to think. They played.

They played when the flood came upon Noah, they played in 1914 when the Great War began, they played in 1939 when the Second World War was announced, they are still playing today. We have just come close to a global catastrophe. Do you think that has changed the mentality of the masses, in any way, shape or form? No! On the contrary, people throw themselves into a collective frenzy more than ever before, into the excitement of sports, the passion of jazz, the contortions of the twist and other dances. They do it to forget.

And sometimes they play with death. They go to Spain to watch the blood-letting of bull-fights. They go to Monza, Italy, or Le Mans, in the hope of witnessing some spectacular accident on the race-track. They run foolish risks by climbing unexplored peaks of the Alps or the Himalayas. In politics, they take what they call calculated risks. It is so interesting for a head of State to venture out to the edge of an abyss, to see if the enemy will take a step back or not. When the enemy backs up, he is happy, triumphant, he tells himself he is a real man, a hero. And at times they play with death to the point of throwing themselves in its face, to prove to the world that they are not cowards. And that is how wars break out.

The only problem is, they have not solved the essential problem, the challenge raised by the Bible, the one with which our destiny confronts us on our own doorsteps. Four knocks at our door. The question is: what lies behind death? What is this strange, morbid fascination I have with death? Why am I bored or frustrated with my life on earth? In the depths of your souls, brothers and sisters, you are now facing this question. If you do not answer, you will never be able to find the meaning of your own life, the way to live properly, to walk next to God. If you have not looked death in the eye, for at least a second, you will not know find your answer.

What destiny is knocking at the door?

The automatic, instinctive answer we have is […] that this destiny is nothingness. As Job wonders, if I did not exist before I was born; why do I not have the right to sleep the slumber of earth, why do I not have the right to not exist? And by giving up my life for some foolish undertaking, I would resolve the problem of my life and death in a cavalier fashion.

No, my friends, the destiny that is not knocking at the door is not death. I think that scientists have discovered things in the last few years that prove that. We have just awarded the Nobel

Prize to two British biologists who have shown that in the smallest particles of our being, in the nucleus of every living cell, there is an acid called DNA. This mysterious acid contains a "program." In other words, in the nucleus of every one of our cells a plan for us is inscribed. Not only does it program us for what we will be, for what we have become, but also, through a series of combinations and marriages and lines of heredity, it contains the program for all of our descendants, our children, our great-grandchildren. All of existence is programmed. Paleontology has also revealed this fact. The discoveries that Father Teilhard de Chardin so brilliantly illustrated and explained proved that from the beginning of time, or at least as far back as we can explore, this program continues its tireless march. What you hear knocking at your door, my dear friends, what wants to come inside, to enter into your being, is not nothingness. It is a program, a plan that is meant to unfold. What began in you at the time of your birth, what God inscribed upon your cells as your destiny, insists on reaching fulfilment.

I want to make an affirmation. These words that I have spoken are not written in the Bible. They have come to me because they make sense, because they are evident to those who would see. Despite all the catastrophes that have afflicted the cosmos, life has always conquered death, and the universe has many long centuries, millions of years, ahead of it. I even think that in God it will not end, or at least that it will only end in God. So, friends, when you come close to having an accident or when humanity is overwhelmed by the terror of its own destruction, you must not tremble. We do not need to be troubled by what happens to us.[12]

10
Algeria

Algeria, which had been a French colony since 1830, fought for independence from the mid-fifties to the early sixties. The Algerian War began on 1 November 1954 (the Toussaint Rouge, or Red All Saints Day) with an insurrection of Muslims in the Aurès Mountain region. It ended on 18 March 1962, when agreements were signed in Évian, France, to grant Algeria independence as of 1 July 1962. Approximately one million French citizens who had supported the French colonialists, including most of the "Pieds-Noirs" (people of European heritage born in Algeria) and "harkis" (Muslim Algerian loyalists, many of whom fought alongside the French forces), left North Africa for Europe in a mass exodus. During the war, incidents of blackmail and torture were carried out by both the Algerians and the French. The repressive policies of the French government as well as numerous political factions gave rise to heated debates both inside and outside the countries involved.

Sent as observers by the MIR, Magda and André Trocmé made a number of trips to Algeria. Among the incidents they witnessed, their experience of the riots of 13 May 1958 stood out. They showed their usual commitment and courage and protested the use of violence. Recognizing the complexity of the Algerian situation, they attempted to analyze the reasons for the war and seek a peaceful resolution. However, they refused to take either the side of the Front de libération nationale, the group that was fighting for Algerian independence, or the supporters of French Algeria. Their neutrality alienated them from most of their friends and attracted the ire of new enemies.

André would look back at this painful period and describe the double bind in which he found himself. "When the Algerian war began, things became even more delicate. I was non-violent. I could not approve of the terrorist acts conducted by the nationalist Algerians, starting on November 1, 1954, nor the repressive actions of the police and then the army ordered by France."[1]

The Church and Politics

It goes without saying that André felt the Church had a duty to become involved in social action on behalf of human beings, and especially the weakest and most disadvantaged among them. Its involvement had to follow particular guidelines and respect ethical and ecclesiastical principles. His "Postulates for the Message of the Church Regarding the Political Systems Which Divide the World," written before the outbreak of the Algerian War, would serve as his guidelines during that horrible conflict which would result in so many deaths.[2]

The Church, which is embodied within a nation, must avoid committing these three errors:

> a) It must refrain from remaining silent out of cowardice or fear that free expression will run the risk of endangering it, or that its words will have no effect. A Church which is silent is no longer doing the work God has called it to do in the world [...]
>
> b) The Church must not abdicate its mission and place it on the State [...] it must not hold any illusions: the order represented by the State is not the same as the order intended by God. The world's order is relative and contains many forms of abuse, exploitation, violence and deceit that are entirely foreign to the Kingdom of God. The inevitable tendency of the State is to use God to ensure domestic order. God's order implies the submission of the State to the common good pre-

> scribed by God. This good may not immediately appear to the State as being consistent with its interests or even its security. To confuse the cause of a political system with the cause of the Kingdom of God is a common mistake in this era. The result is an unavoidable alignment of the Church and the State, and, soon afterwards, in the case of a conflict between diverging political systems, a Church torn between two opposing camps.
>
> c) The Church must not take responsibility for politics. There is no Christian political agenda and no Christian political party. There are no other ways of promoting the Kingdom of God than those which Jesus has given us: faith, obedience, witness, healing, and patience in the face of persecution. Wherever the Church has believed that its triumph as lawmaker or educator meant a victory for God, it has become hierarchical, authoritarian, repressive. It has stood at the side of the powerful and has instigated the revolts of the exploited. Once it is liberated from the temptations of silent resignation, complacent alignment, and theocratic exploitation, the Church will awaken to its own vocation, its duty as a small force working for good in the world [...]

Whenever it is faithfully fulfilling its mission, the Church separates itself from the political regime in which it functions:

> it says no to anti-Semitism,
> no to the government's protection of traffickers of alcohol and women,
> no to shanty-towns and hovels,
> no to war and to the desire to prepare for war,
> no to colonialism,
> no to the enslavement of body and soul by totalitarian methods,
> no to anti-religious persecutions,
> no to arbitrary arrests and to work camps,
> and no to a long list of other horrors.

In this struggle, the Church must not become discouraged. The apparent negativity of this list is, in reality, simply a corollary of its core affirmation: God is Love.

The Situation in Algeria

André went on his first mission to Algeria in the spring of 1955. This trip was followed by several others and motivated the Trocmés to help North Africans by taking part in cooperative projects and other endeavours. An example of one such project was EIRENE (from the Greek word for peace), an international Christian service organization founded by André in 1957 in partnership with Mennonite and Brethren organizations (both offshoots of pacifist churches), which enabled conscientious objectors from Europe to work on assignments in Morocco.

For the past three weeks, I have been living in the lower town of Algiers, right in the middle of the Muslim quarter. What a sad-looking city! While Morocco and Tunisia have retained a good deal of local colour, Algiers, like Cairo, has only grime and rags to show, and even the rags are Western-style clothes.

The attempt by the French to make North African Muslims into French citizens with equal rights has produced a type of people who are no longer good Muslims, because they are influenced by the secular ideology of the French revolution, and who do not really understand democracy, because they do not have the background that ensures men, women, and children are treated equally, one of the basic principles of democracy. Many Algerians are stuck half-way between Islam and the Western world. Two Muslim universities have kept the Arab culture alive in Morocco and in Tunisia, but there is no such institution in Algeria. The number of people who can write in Arabic is very low.

In the cities, almost all North African children go to French schools and mix with French children. There is no segregation in these schools. The most brilliant Algerian teenagers pass their baccalaureate exams. Some of them dream of escaping from North Africa, of living in France and enjoying a French lifestyle. This "brain drain" is considered by Algerian nationalists as a betrayal of their nation, an action of collaborators. The awakening of this sort of nationalism can be seen among young students, but in Algeria, unlike Tunisia and Morocco, the nationalists mainly recruit illiterate and poor people. The Aurès Mountains in the southeast, where the rebellion began, is home to the most backward tribes.

The Fellaghas, Algerians who violently oppose the French colonists, are not very numerous. They manage to disappear as soon as the French police arrive and escape capture. No native Algerian would dare turn them in, because their revenge is horrible, according to the French and their supporters.

Eighty percent of the population is illiterate, and has no understanding of politics. Do they want Algeria to be independent? Definitely. Do they want the French to leave? Certainly they want the French police to leave, because they are synonymous with terror and repression. But the rural population also wants the Fellaghas to leave, because they have become synonymous with terror and repression.

And that gives us a basic picture of the way relations between the two groups have deteriorated, even in the Arab world. Violence has become a topic of debate in Algeria, especially since November 1954.

We could summarize the situation by saying that the French and the Muslims live in fear. Approximately a million Frenchmen settled in Algeria a hundred years ago; they helped modernize the country so that it became quite comparable to continental Europe. In the centre of Algeria, you could forget you were no longer in France. The atmosphere is European, there are more churches than mosques, magnificent cars are driven by Muslim owners whose wives no longer wear the veil [...] But for the solitary French settler, the farmer who owns between twenty-five and two hundred hectares of land and who may be rich or poor depending on the quality of his land, his energy, his hard work and his frugality, fear has become his daily companion, at least in eastern Algeria. Why? Because "bandits" could come at any moment and attack him, his wife and his children, massacre them without any clear reason, burn down their farm. The police always arrive too late, and the Muslim neighbours will not say anything. If they did, they too would be murdered by the bandits.

Yesterday, at a church meeting attended by Protestants scattered over a parish that covers an area three hundred kilometres in length and a hundred and twenty kilometres in width, I told two stories about my experiences the previous week.

In Azazga, a town on the northern coast of Algeria near our mission, a farm had been set on fire three days earlier, the missionary's wife told me. Fortunately, the family that lived there had not been killed, but the farmer was wiped out. He was an honest and peaceful farmer whose grandfather had bought and worked this piece of land. The native Algerians could not explain or excuse the crime. But the night it happened, no one dared to help the farmer, and he could not defend himself. A few kilometres down the road, the bandits destroyed tractors, bulldozers, large ploughs, and other equipment that belonged to a farmers' cooperative. Absurd, isn't it, that they would destroy their own property?

Second story: a forest ranger and his wife told me how their companion and friend, whose job it was to preserve the few forests in Algerian that had not been ravaged by sheep during the Arab period, had been savagely murdered by another group of bandits. He had practically nothing to do with the Muslims and no one could find any motive for the crime. He left behind a twenty-five–year-old wife and two children. It is no surprise that the French, panicking about the danger they face, are convinced that once Algeria becomes independent the Muslims will "throw all the French into the sea." Their fear may be exaggerated, but fear is always irrational and inevitably leads to violence. Some of the French families in Algeria have started to build shelters on their properties. The French authorities have made it illegal, and will not allow everyone to buy a rifle and shoot, because they know this would cause a civil war. But how long are the farmers going to tolerate this level of insecurity?

Fear inevitably leads to violence, I wrote. Tragically, this is true. Fear led the French police to put their machines of terror into motion and plow into Algerian nationalism long before the uprising last November. North Africans speak Arabic or Berber, and in most cases the French have not learned these languages, so the French police cannot get testimony or confessions from North Africans. The police need to know what is happening! They also beat their prisoners, and too often have used torture. Where once they trusted the French justice system more than their own, Muslims are now gripped in fear. "We are helpless at the hands of the French," they say. "If they are looking for someone to blame, they always find someone. When threatened or tortured, any man will denounce anyone else ..." Their fear of the French police was one of the first reasons that the Arabs fled to the mountains and finally revolted in the Aurès last November. "If this is what democracy and justice are like, we refuse to accept it. We will gather resistance forces together and will respond to each act of injustice with our revenge." This is how mutual fear and hatred spreads so quickly. I personally know of one case of serious injustice committed against a Muslim. The man lived peacefully with the French and was innocent. He was turned in, arrested, and condemned to several years of imprisonment by a justice system that flew through the process. Now he is living out his sentence in prison with many other nationalists. Prisons are wonderful schools for revolutionaries. If he is proven to be innocent in the courts, as I hope he will be, what chance is there that he will be anything other than a nationalist when he is released? These are the men who are proud to join the resistance and take up arms to fight for their freedom.

That is my attempt to analyze the situation as quickly as possible. A description of political factors on both sides is another matter; it would require an entire book.

And now, what can we do? What can Christians, what can the reconciliation movement, do to help?

Yesterday, before the group gathered from near and far, I preached (naturally) what I hold as true: we need to start from scratch, to place our faith in the Church, and to bear the cross, rather than inflict suffering upon others. A moment before, I had heard how bitterly some men in the audience were protesting the fact that the government would not allow them to arm and defend themselves against attacks as they saw fit. However, I could see the emotion in the faces of those who heard my words.

A native Algerian, a man from the Kabyle people from the northern part of the country who had converted to Christianity, a French physician who pioneered health care in the mountain villages, and a wealthy farmer who was involved in politics, came to see me after the meeting. "Do you really mean non-violence?"

"Yes, the power of God's love within us, and, as a corollary, the abandonment of violence." They seemed moved.

The doctor said, "Send me dozens and dozens of young doctors and nurses who would be willing to travel into the villages with me."

The Kabyle said, "I am a Christian and I am one of my people. That is the way we treat people at home, the way you said."

Before leaving Algeria, I will have other opportunities to speak to more people, Christians and Muslims alike. Every day I give French lessons to five illiterate men, and I take a lesson in Arabic, using the Laubach method each time. My teacher is an Arab. Through him I have made friends with other Arabs. We need to have disciples of Jesus Christ here to go, in pairs, into the villages. They would not try to convert people, but only to share Christ's love with them and teach them to read and write. A group of five American Mennonites arrived last week and set up a post in Orléansville, where people will work together [...] This summer, we will try a much larger experiment. I am happy to be able to offer our young pacifists a concrete way of serving the cause of peace. It may be dangerous, but isn't a pacifist willing to accept some risks?[3]

About the Algerian War

At a press conference at the end of 1958, André Trocmé pleaded for an international panel to arbitrate in the war between France and Algeria. In his opinion, this would resolve the conflict.

I want to address you as a Protestant minister and simply read an excerpt from the letter of objection against the repressive measures taken in Algeria. The letter was drafted by the council of the Fédération protestante de France last week.[4]

"These abuses," it states, "continue to be rampant. More and more men – ministers, teachers, educators, parents – tell us how distressing it is to think of so many young people who have become discouraged, skeptical, cynical about the teaching they have received and which, for many, is leading to the loss of the very meaning of life. This climate of anxiety and despair was demonstrated by the case of Reverend Mathiot, however the courts may judge him.[5] The council of the Fédération protestante believes that no one in France has the right to lock himself away in convenient and guilty ignorance. It once again urges our public officials to act in a way that befits their authority and the honour of our nation, and to put an end to this behaviour. The actions of France in Algeria will result in incalculable damage to public opinion both in France and throughout the world. In order to make a lasting agreement among the Algerian population and the present and future generations of France, we must break down this prejudice and regain the trust of all involved."

But if we want to end the war in Algeria, it is not enough to protest torture. Torture is a normal consequence of the kind of war being fought in Algeria. Atomic war has its own laws; if it breaks out it will continue until its natural end. It cannot be contained. Guerrilla warfare has its own atrocious laws; nationalists strike in darkness and may attack regular army troops one day and innocent civilians the next. The army responds with similarly random and obscure actions, making arbitrary arrests and trying to find out information in any way possible. Every year, the guerrillas become more corrupt, the hatred intensifies, more blood flows and the hope of reconciliation becomes dimmer. I would like to plead in favour of an immediate halt to hostilities and an agreement to pursue arbitration.

Up to this point, our government has systematically refused

to consider arbitration. They have considered the conflict in Algeria a domestic affair, as if a war in which what is at stake is the pride of the Arab world and its hope of reunification, on the one hand, and on the other the pride of the Western world and its desire to maintain its position of global prestige, could be an internal matter for France.

In luxurious Parisian apartment houses, when certain households come to blows, they make sure windows are closed and explain black eyes the next day by saying they fell and hit their faces on the corner of the stove. But their pitiful attempts to hide the truth do not fool anybody. If the life of one of the spouses is in danger, the neighbours have to call the police. This is what is happening in the fight between France and Algeria. Only our government believes that we can continue to fight as long as we keep the window closed.

You may wonder why I am talking about arbitration. Why can we not negotiate directly with the FLN?

I truly believe we cannot proceed this way. I did believe it at one time, but my contacts with both the French and the Muslims in North Africa have convinced me otherwise. In order to negotiate, there has to be both a degree of common vision and an ability to analyze the situation objectively. Neither North African nationalists nor the French who live in North Africa are capable of such analysis. Why? Because the emotions aroused by every event in North Africa push both camps to subjective interpretation, never arriving at a common point between the two.

To offer you one example: about a year ago, an Arab village in the Mitidja Plain, located in the back country of Algeria, was bombed by French artillery, killing about forty people.

The French explanation: a large group of heavily-armed Fellaghas was found in the village. They were attacking the innocent drivers of the local merchants' trucks.

The Arab explanation: unknown parties had shot at a delivery truck and missed. Without bothering to wait for the results of the investigation, French troops had bombed the nearest village, killing a hundred and fifty innocent people.

Neither facts nor figures are the same; they are the fruits of such deeply-rooted emotions that any investigation by a single person would fail to produce a coherent account.

Besides, neither of the two parties is trying to be objective. Their goal is no longer to seek the truth. Instead, they want their cause to triumph, and in their hands, the truth is only a tool designed to knock down or defeat their enemy. If we look at this situation under a wider lens, we see there are two Algerias: one belongs to the French and a decreasing number of Muslims and one belongs to the majority of Muslims, who are affiliated with the FLN.

It was not so much Arab propaganda that rallied Muslims to the cause of the FLN, but rather violence. When there is violence on both sides, minds are irremediably polarized. Today, in Algeria, the methods used by the French government have pushed the vast majority of the population into the opposite camp; they join the cause of the FLN out of solidarity for their fellow Muslims. To refuse to acknowledge the situation is to ignore the reality of the Algerian people.

On November 1, 1954, Algeria was not a nation. The fight against the French has galvanized Algerians, made them more courageous, better organized, and given them the solidarity of collective action they had lacked. We are now witnessing the formation of a nation, a nation which no longer wants to be French. However, the FLN is intolerant, unjust, and blind. It demands the unconditional surrender of France. Muslims say they can no longer trust our country. This is not the time or place to judge whether they are right; we are simply stating that is useless to hope that negotiations will succeed between two enemies with such extreme positions. That is why I am advocating arbitration.

If we had agreed on arbitration two and a half years ago, at the time when Mr Pinay solemnly left the United Nations, instead of discussing the Algerian problem, we could have reached a compromise that would have saved the prestige of France and the pride of the Arabs. Even a year ago, arbitration would probably have produced good results. If France took the initiative to request the arbitration of the UN or of representatives of neutral nations, today, conditions would be less difficult for us. Since Sakhiet Sidi Youssef, British and American opinion, which was relatively favourable in the past, has turned against us.[6] We cannot count on their firm support to obtain terms that will satisfy our pride. But if we imagine ourselves in the near future, when the Algerian War will be even worse than it is today, when other blood has been shed and the opinion of the rest of the world about us is even more negative, when Nasser's Arabs have gained a groundswell of support, by that time even an arbitration would be disastrous for us .[7]

To conclude, I have offered you my reasons for urging you to abandon the Platonic arguments you have presented defending direct negotiations. I believe negotiations are impossible at this point. I would like to request that you express our desire to put an immediate end to the Algerian War and to waste no time before pressing our government to request arbitration by the UN or another group of neutral nations in Algeria.[8]

"Torture and Contempt of Humanity"

At the moment the war was about to end, André could not remain silent. Once more, he denounced the abomination resulting from the violation of human rights and asserted the need to respect human beings.

Torture consists of inflicting physical or mental suffering on a prisoner who is reduced to helplessness, for the purpose of extracting confessions and information from him. Sometimes people are tortured out of sadistic pleasure, the desire to humiliate or mutilate a victim.

The Pieds-Noirs in Algeria […] refuse to accept that the White race in Algeria has regressed. They reject any sense of collective responsibility that the Whites may have for crimes they might have committed in one hundred and thirty years of occupation. They look for scapegoats, and find them in the "defeatists" from France who put a "knife in the back" of the army when the army tried to control the population. "If the French of France," they say, "had not come and poisoned Muslims with their false ideas, there wouldn't be these problems in Algeria." In fact, in the eyes of certain extremists, we should not treat a traitor as an ordinary man; when dealing with those who are collaborators with a race, a party, a criminal government, we have a right and a duty to assassinate them (hence the plastic bombs and executions). We are also allowed to torture them to make them confess their conspiracies, and can even exterminate them (hence the unexplained disappearance of a large number of Muslims).

One day in 1953, I even heard a Christian lady declare at a church meeting: "The mistake we made was not exterminating them all, when we arrived in this country a hundred years ago, the way the Anglo-Saxons did with the Indians in the USA."

And we must not accuse the Pieds-Noirs of behaving differently from the way we do. Remember the brutal way so-called "patriots" (who were actually nothing of the sort) in France executed the "collabos" in 1944, in order to balance the scales, projecting onto scapegoats their own crimes during the Occupation. It is thanks to this way of transferring guilt to adversaries that men who are usually calm and honest believe they are accomplishing an act of public salvation when they extort confessions from their victims by any means, including torture.

This is exactly what happened when the socialist Lacoste ordered Massu, a Catholic, to put an end to Muslim terrorism in 1957.[9] Massu resolved the crisis by systematically using all available means, including torture, to win the Battle of Algiers. He won, meaning that he succeeded almost as well as the Nazis succeeded with their final solution to the Jewish problem. So Massu won the battle but destroyed the last remnants of affection the Muslims had for France, and any respect the world had for France. As of 1957, Algeria was lost to France.

Those who have witnessed scenes of torture know that the perpetrators exhibit real enjoyment as they watch their victims suffer. They make use of their wildest imagination to invent innovative ways of tormenting them. They have entered into a disturbing world of human sacrifice in which they believe they are delivering salvation. Because they eliminate any sense of remorse they might have had, they attain a total contempt for their victims. This is a masterpiece of the Antichrist.

The results we seek would not punish the powers that be with unnecessary severity. It is true that they were responsible for the use of torture in Algeria for seven years, but it is also true that torture is part of the logic of war. As soon as a government decides to repress terrorism through violent means, it inevitably orders the torture of suspects in order to fight with equal arms against clandestine and fanatical uprisings.

In this way, torture is to clandestine war what the atomic bomb is to war between nations. It is the only defensive weapon that is effective: so effective, in fact, that it abolishes any hope of reconciliation between those who apply it and their victims, who will never forget the unspeakable humiliations to which they were subjected.

The same logical deductions, the same psychological processes, leads those who make war on the battlefield and those who make war in hidden torture chambers to perform their jobs in the most extreme fashion. The most conscientious among them will follow their sense of duty the most closely, venturing into the most remote and dingy crannies of their awful vocation. It is useless to try to humanize war. War has a particular geometry, just as peace has its own.

The postulate of war is that it has to be won. Any means to this primary and ultimate end is derived from this. The postulate of peace is, in all circumstances, at all times, that the value of a human being is worth more than anything else. The geometry of peace rests entirely on this initial affirmation. No rational argument can be found to calculate the value of a human being; Christians know it through God's love for sinners. Unfortunately, the postulate of God's love does not often lead Christians to renounce violence, and therefore war and torture. The weakness of the geometric spirit of Christians is the scandal of our enlightened era. The Holy Spirit takes revenge by occasionally revealing to non-believers the postulate of the value of human beings.

The theoretical struggle for the recognition of human rights is not very important. Real events could not care less for groundless ideologies. While international organizations refine the definitions of "rights," major generals are methodically planning the annihilation of humanity. What matters is applying the postulate of human value to our lives and our institutions, by caring for children, the ill, the infirm, the elderly, through the devotion of surgeons and nurses. This is how we manifest the value of human beings, from the moment they are born until their last breath.

A unique opportunity is being given to you, in this spring of 1962, as the Algerian War is ending. The disgust with terrorism and torture is preparing a new day for France and North Africa. We must take advantage of the momentum to begin new projects like those of Abbé Pierre, the CIMADE, the Service civil international, EIRENE, and the Action civique non violente. But we must be cautious: crowds have short memories. The scabs of their guilt and remorse heal over quickly. In a few months, the window of opportunity will have closed again.

To want to appear generous and humane, while still preparing for war, is ultimately to choose contempt for humanity rather than the value of humanity. Our movement reminds us that opposition to torture leads inevitably to conscientious objection, that is, to the refusal of all war and preparation for war.[10]

The Adventures of a House

On Sunday 10 March 1963, André Trocmé's sermon on the Gospel of Mark was broadcast on Radio Suisse romande. This sermon is an example of the method he used to bring the message of the Bible to life.

They uncovered the roof the house [...][11]

Exactly a week ago, after our worship service, four men who were members and friends of the Saint-Gervais parish from which I am speaking to you right now, left their calm and comfortable houses to go to Algeria, to see with their own eyes and touch with their own hands the unfathomable misery afflicting eighty percent of the population of this unfortunate country.

Last night, these four men had already returned. They were still in a state of shock. They did not know what the outcome of their trip will be, but they could already tell you one thing. I am their messenger when I say that for them, for their families, for their calm and comfortable houses in Geneva, and for the church in Geneva to which they belong, a church which is also a calm and comfortable house, a new adventure has begun.

What adventure? We do not know yet exactly what it will be [...] But I want to address the little houses, the little churches which are isolated in the midst of an indifferent crowd. And I would like to say to these little churches [...] that it is enough if one day they welcome in Jesus Christ, it is enough if one day the power of Jesus Christ heals a sick person under their roof, that is enough to end their solitude.

I will give you an example: the church we just visited, the church in Philippeville, Algeria. On a good day, do you know how many people attend the Sunday service? Twenty-four, the minister told me. And yet, when we arrived at the train station, the minister's name was on the lips of all the little children who gathered around us, chattering, offering to carry our bags or shine our shoes because that was the only way they could make any money. The next morning we went with the minister to distribute food hampers. Nearly eighty percent of the residents of Philippeville are unemployed and live in dreadful poverty. We learned that a church that has twenty-four people at its worship service can be located in the centre of a city of 80,000 inhabitants and that when the mayor or the authorities or the army or the ALN[12] need help, they come to the little evangelical church in Philippeville, Algeria, because that is where the power of Jesus Christ is alive.

[...] Every Christian we met in Algeria – Reformed, Lutheran, Quaker, Mennonite, Catholic, Swiss, French, American, German – was overwhelmed with work. They did not know where to start. They called for help: "Send us more volunteers! We can't afford to pay wages, all we can give is a little stipend, but we really need technicians." And I must say, brothers and sisters, that I am looking for help now, and I believe that I will find what I seek. I'm looking for a mechanic who can teach little boys in Philippeville to repair cars. Any takers? If there is someone listening to the radio who knows anyone, please write to me.

As I said, these men are overwhelmed, and because of that they are remembering how to pray. Jesus, who also did not know where to start, went out in the morning when it was still dark, found a quiet corner, and prayed.

The Church today no longer knows how to pray. We have prayer meetings, but they seem contrived. The Church today is no longer reaching out beyond its walls. It prefers to shut its door and busy itself trying to solve the smaller problems of those inside and trivial domestic matters.

The Church must reach out to human beings again. The Church must take on the problems of the crowds who are starving, who are without God, and then it will be forced to turn to prayer. And to thought, as well, because the theology God came to give to the world is not a theology that was made in a workshop to sit on a bookshelf. The true theology of the Church comes alive on the front lines, not in our study halls but in the places where we are immersed in the problems of real human beings. In these places, we cannot see any human solution to the problems; we see only politicians who look for solutions and find only violence, vengeance, revolutions, and uprisings. We, as Christians, reduced to utter weakness like our Christian brothers in Algeria, we need to be forced to fall on our knees and beg for a miracle. That is the theology God wants for us.

It is at the moment that man is too small, that his knowledge is too meagre, that he cannot act on his own – it is at that moment that we wait for God to intercede. And it was at the moment that Israel was exhausted, close to collapse, consumed by pride and by wealth, threatened with destruction by the Roman Empire – it was at that moment that Jesus Christ appeared. Given to his people, Jesus Christ opened a door that was closed and lifted a roof that was collapsing, that was suffocating a nation, that had lost its way and forgotten its mission.[13]

An Unexpected Encounter

The call for a mechanic in André's sermon did not go unanswered. Immediately, an engineer named Willy Engel offered his services. André had been working on a cooperative project between Switzerland and Algeria to maintain and repair the agricultural equipment that was indispensable for Algerians. His plans became a reality on 1 April 1964, through a partnership between Saint-Gervais parish in Geneva and the city of Skikda (formerly Philippeville) in Algeria, where a school for diesel mechanics was founded with the help of funds from Switzerland.

Revolutions make for unexpected encounters between groups of people who, up until then, have seemed to be irremediably separated by political, religious, and social barriers.

Last April 1st [...] in Skikda, something happened that until recently we would have never thought possible. Algerians and Europeans, Muslims and Christians, stood side by side as they opened a school for mechanics.

This happened in Algeria, a country of painful and exalting contrasts, in a garage that had been declared vacant property and that the municipality of Skikda, with the help of the Department of Social Affairs (Adult Training), has transformed into an auto mechanics shop. Eleven young men were there, clean-shaven and fit; some were from the Sahara. After a very competitive selection from a group of two hundred and fifty applicants, these men received scholarships from the Algerian government to study here. They are experienced mechanics who have signed a five-year contract with the State; after their training is done, they will work as instructors in training centres for automobile mechanics.

The Saint-Gervais Church hopes that, with this project in Philippeville, it can help reduce the crisis in mechanized agriculture in Algeria. French mechanics who were specialists in those diesel motors with which heavy equipment and tractors are equipped have left Algeria, and their departure has crippled the country's economy. By training thirty instructors who will, in turn, train young diesel mechanics, the Saint-Gervais initiative may, in a period of two years, manage to overcome one of the obstacles to feeding a population of twelve million people. The machines in the Skikda centre were manufactured in Germany, and are instructional models. Using them, the students can practise adjusting and repairing the injection devices of the electrical and hydraulic instruments found in diesel motors. A large German company provided them at a very low cost. It also offered a complete training program, free of cost, to the engineer who is the head of the school. The transport company that sent the machines to Algeria, also free of charge, is Swiss. The engineer, his wife, and the young mechanic who will assist them are also Swiss. Mr and Mrs Engel were not looking for a job. Each of them had a lucrative profession that ensured they were free of material worries, but no one knows in which direction the Spirit will blow, and the Spirit carried them to Algeria where, for two and a half years, they will teach technical courses for a small sum collected by the members of the Saint-Gervais congregation and their friends, the members of the American Church in Geneva, and the members of the Saint-Gervais-Philippeville association.

It is on this basis that the opening of the centre on the first of April can be considered an amazing act of Christian faith. One of the speeches at the opening ceremony was given by the Muslim mayor. The Europeans could not understand him because his speech was in Arabic. A former member of the liberation movement, he addressed an audience partially composed of Frenchmen; only a few years ago, he would have considered it his patriotic duty to exterminate them. The Protestant minister who followed him was from France. He spoke a language that the mayor could not understand and spoke on behalf of the congregation in Geneva and the representative of the American Church in Geneva who were taking part in the ceremony. The French minister in Philippeville, whose call had launched the whole adventure, and the vice-consul of Switzerland in Bône, a fervent Catholic representing the Swiss Embassy in Algiers, were also invited, because the department responsible for cooperative projects in the federal government in Berne had contributed fifty percent of the cost of the undertaking.

But where were the good people of Geneva? Where were the ordinary men and women of Saint-Gervais who had saved five or ten francs a month from their pension or their meagre salaries [...] to ensure that Algerians did not starve? They were there as well: a seamstress [...] who was over eighty years old, but spry, keen and friendly. She was keeping a journal of the expedition and, along with the minister of Saint-Gervais and his wife, had the privilege of being one of the guests of honour of the Algerian government (they travelled by air and then in an official car) and the charmed guests of Algerian families who received us for one couscous after another. Christian sensibility had found a serious rival in Muslim hospitality! Thus, a miniature revolution of good will had risen up in the midst of the great upheavals in Algeria.

"What good will it do?" the pessimist might wonder. "A little drop in the ocean."

"Water in the mill of communism," the skeptic might respond.

Such criticism is simply a way of protecting oneself against the temptation of true generosity. I have a statement of fact, an example and a legend to offer these doubters.

The economic, demographic and social conjuncture in a country like Algeria and a city like Skikda is catastrophic when the economy faces a deficit, the birthrate is exploding and the morale of the population is dismally low. The economic support offered by these two Protestant congregations is infinitesimal, but the moral support is considerable. While activity in the port of Skikda is dying out, a new school is opening on the docks. It lights a lamp of hope in dark times. Hope invites people to look forward to a better future and to work to make it happen. The very presence of our three volunteers, in a little town where word gets around quickly, can contribute to turning on the ignitions first of the psychological engine and then the economic engine On one point, at least, the situation can be turned around. A victory on one point can lead to others.

Now for the example. Shortly after Morocco became independent, the author of this sermon had a conversation with a highly-placed civil servant from the Department of Agriculture, in Rabat. "What assets have forty years of French rule given to you?" I asked. "Highways? Telephones and telecommunications? Railways? Hospitals? Schools?"

The civil servant made a face. "All of that, we could have had without being occupied."

"So we have brought you nothing?"

"Sure you have," he replied. "When I was young, I was a Scout in a Catholic parish. I learned from my leaders what it meant to be dedicated to a common cause, to be unselfish, and to be of service, things that our civilization didn't know about before."

The exceptional characters of our Swiss volunteers in Philippeville and the faith inspired from the Gospels are, therefore, even more important than their technical and pedagogical skills. The Saint-Gervais-Philippeville association has been privileged to find people of such great value. We must not allow them to become discouraged. We must give them our support [...]

And finally, a Chinese legend. A Buddhist monk sat on the banks of the Yellow River and watched with astonishment the flight of a dove who repeatedly dipped her feathers in the river and then hurried away again towards the horizon. He asked her: "Why are you going back and forth like that?"

The dove answered: "Don't you see the smoke on the horizon? It's a forest fire. I am trying to put it out."

The monk burst out laughing. "Do you really think that will help anything?"

"I don't know if it will help," answered the dove, "but I know that I must do it."[14]

11

In the Parish, a Time to Reflect

In 1960, after ten years with Magda at his side at the helm of the European secretariat of the MIR Algeria, André Trocmé returned to serving a parish. Still at odds with the authorities of the Reformed Church in France over his pacifism, he decided it would be better to accept a position in Switzerland, at the Saint-Gervais Church in Geneva. He remained there until he retired in 1970.

Although his return to parish life meant he had a great deal of work to look after every day, this did not prevent André from being involved in social justice activities or commitments to the community. In fact, in the last phase of his career, pastoral ministry gave him a chance to revisit the meaning of his vocation and the concrete ways he could spread the Gospel. At that point, he was no longer so busy with the whirlwind of international encounters and projects. Instead, he was dealing with tangible problems in the daily lives of members of his congregation. No longer a matter of "dreaming of revolutions, changes, transformations"[1] on a large scale; this was a time for André to take on the responsibilities of a single individual, which was an important contribution in itself, and to honour the dignity of each person he met.

Another Credo

This confession of faith was written in 1956, while André was hospitalized in Lyon. It gives us insight into the spiritual perspective he had when he began his ministry in Geneva shortly afterwards.

I believe in the eternal truth.

I believe that this truth must pass through many struggles and difficulties before it triumphs. And essentially, this is what I call the Christ: sometimes it is seeds scattered on the ground; sometimes it is the slow growth associated with our material nature that inspires and transforms; sometimes it is the inevitable revenge of truth upon falsehood; sometimes it is the truth that is crucified, denied, dying or even dead; sometimes total and eternal light that nothing can dim, because it has passed through all the trials, because it has undertaken and accomplished all its commitments and carried with it all those whom it has loved [...]

In the end, it is not as important to know if we will live on after death, but to "be with Christ" in all circumstances, living or dead, victorious or defeated.

Faith consists of understanding that we do not carry the passion of the world on our shoulders, but that we are willing to play a part in it, even a small part.

This means no longer passively trusting, being anaesthetized against the realities of a suffering world.

It means walking with Christ, awakened, alert, and aware.[2]

A Retrospective at Fifty-Seven Years of Age

On 7 April 1958, on his fifty-seventh birthday, André wrote a letter to his children. It is clear that he was looking back over his life, but this retrospective also helped guide him as he shifted directions, in terms of taking on a new ministry and in reflecting on the meaning of his existence.

At one o'clock this morning I turned fifty-seven. It is not a round number, but it is an important birthday for me because, for the first time in many years, Maman and I are together to celebrate it. I wanted to take the opportunity to write something fitting and a little serious.

I have no illusions about the significance of an event as unimportant as my birth in the course of history that has carried human generations along for thousands of years. I have often had to pinch myself to remind myself that it was true, I really exist. My temperament makes me philosophize endlessly about life, death, people and things, and I tend to generalize and analyze everything. It is a great pleasure and a temptation for me. Fortunately I married a woman who is firmly rooted in the present, in life and in the lives of others, and she draws me out of my meditations, which can become stagnant and selfish [...]

Five years old. No coherent memory: maids, a mother, a father, trips to Saint-Gobain in the car.

Fifteen years old. The Great War. A world like Davy Crockett's. I made up imaginary characters, all heroes in the war, and I got mediocre marks at the lycée because I did not work hard enough.

At sixteen years of age, I found God, the greatest event in my life. "Finding you, I found so much more besides." As I began to look at the world as God sees it, I started to get interested in something besides the film of my inner life; but the Christian dream was more powerful than my sense of reality.

Twenty-five years old. I got married that year. I had to push myself to decide to get married. The risks seemed so huge! I was unsure of myself, even though I was deeply in love. My engagement occurred in the middle of a strange year I spent in New York, in a room at Union Seminary where, away from my usual surroundings, I felt more than ever that I was daydreaming. Maman had her feet firmly on the ground, and the first favour she did for me was to say: "Hey! I'm here! I exist! Wake up!" I took a few years to wake up, and it was sometimes difficult, because the presence of someone else can be disturbing. Another person's demands, their character (which we always judge worse than our own), can interrupt the magnificent monologue we like to carry on with ourselves like a broken record.

1936, thirty-five years old. Five people took over my life, demanded my time, my substance, my life. I was in Chambon, and a gang of people in my congregation was attacking me. This time I was fully awake. I really put up a fight [...] I fought to adjust my Christian dream, which I refused to give up, to turn to real, flesh-and-blood people named Magda, Nelly, Jean-Pierre, Jacquot, and Daniel. I finally made a real discovery: that each other human being exists as wholly as I do, that everyone else is as important a person as I am. I now knew what it meant to love. It meant looking at another as attentively as we look at ourselves, to put ourselves in the place of others instead of dreaming that we love, being of service to them as well. I realized that Maman, despite sounding strict, had always been more loving and therefore more Christian than I. As for Jispa, who would soon be moving in with us ... no comment.

1946, forty-five years old. Strangely, the war had brought us something we had been missing: by trying to save a few lives, we had finally reconciled the dream and the reality. The truth of God is in the Other, the other human being, the Jew we are hiding, taking some of the risk ourselves in his place. People became so precious to me, especially my children, my wife, to whom I became attached with an immense respect ... I watched my children grow and blossom. Nelly, almost seventeen, so beautiful and alive! Jean-Pierre, fourteen, philosophical and imaginative. Jacquot, twelve, pious and enthusiastic. Daniel, ten and a half, cheerful and energetic. In 1945, because I had taken my children too seriously, I became a tree that lost its top, leafy, growing branches to a strike of lightning. Jean-Pierre died. Maman rushed around, keeping herself busy so she would not cry. Jacquot and Daniel began a difficult adolescence, muttering with exasperation when they had to do their homework. My children play so many tricks on themselves! [...] I could not console myself, as others could, with an inner dream that could replace reality. A man was born, grew up, was about to begin his adult life. A man died. He would never get a chance to live, my Jean-Pierre.

1956, fifty-five years old. Ten years of struggle have changed the shape of my ministry. It was less deep, less mystical, farther away from the individual man and his egocentric worries, closer to the social man charged with concrete responsibilities, and in a sense disinterested. Versailles, a beautiful setting, friends coming to visit, a lot of excitement, interesting encounters. The "contemplative" home I had dreamed of in my pacifist dreams never came to be. Instead, it was a whirlwind. My children disappeared, swept away, carried off to the west. They were […] at the age where people begin, through the eyes of their own children, to discover others. They cannot remain egocentric teenagers forever; they have to play their lives for all they are worth, delve into marriage and family life, put themselves aside.

I am fifty-seven years old, with a few successes to show for myself, failures too (all due to flaws in my own nature). Time is running out to finish everything I have to do on earth. I have not done very much. I may have helped broaden the narrow-mindedness of French Protestantism […] I would like my children to carry on, in their own ways, some of these struggles […] that inhabited my childhood as a sort of dream, that became concrete when I discovered the importance of the Other, that have stood up to the test of suffering, to weariness, to experiences … I would like them to believe in God. I love them as I love Magda.[3]

Christ, Our Hope

At Saint-Gervais Church in Geneva, André Trocmé gave a series of sermons on Christian hope. The following passages from one of these sermons include a commentary on Isaiah 40:25–31, Matthew 24:52, Peter II 3:8–14, and Timothy 1:1.

The best is yet to come: the Kingdom of God. The yeast is hidden in the dough; Jesus is at work in humanity.

Some people will say: "Your faith is blind. Open your eyes and see!"

Faith is blind? Come now. It's quite the opposite: it sees very clearly. Its eyes are open wide and see our social corruption, our infected political system. Its eyes search the depths of the abysses of death and annihilation towards which humanity seems to be marching like sleepwalkers.

But while economists are wearing themselves out calculating gigantic sums, while moralists are uttering curses like powerless witches who cast spells with the venom from their hearts, while the skilful take advantage of the majority's foolishness, faith brightens the night with its pure light. It can see through the torrent the rock that shall serve as a stepping stone, through the wall that is about to be ruined the stone that shall serve as a foundation, through the diseased man the fibre that has not been affected.

And just as the astronomer connects the distant stars into constellations, faith brings the sparse signs of the Kingdom of God together and finds – in the black sky – the illuminated letters of God's providence through history: Abraham and Isaiah, Saint Augustine and Saint Francis of Assisi, Luther and Calvin, Jean Henri Dunant and the Red Cross, and so many other stars that glow in the heavens of humanity.

There is immense human misery that cries out and the misery that cannot even moan.

There is the diabolical deceit of peace that hides the preparations for war.

There are, even so, men who want to pray together for the schoolchildren and the babies in nursery cradles.

There are incurable cancers and hunger that consumes half of the world's people.

There are tricks and superstitions and the fears they are used to create.

There is alcohol that kills, publicly, under our noses, more people in France than cancer does.

And everywhere there is gold, the great tyrant who is cruel and secretive.

There is, even so, every day and everywhere in the world, the silent companionship of those who search, sometimes putting their lives in jeopardy, the scientists with their eyes pressed up against their microscopes who chase evil and disease into their remotest hiding places. People like Doctor Schweitzer are more numerous than we think.

There is the mystery torturer of men who speaks out of both sides of his mouth, who has the face of a false angel and also the face of a demon.

There are those who refuse to serve others, who repay goodness with ingratitude, who commit little obscure crimes of aspersion and revenge in the shadows of mean-spiritedness.

There are, all the same, temptations that are resisted, dedication that is not proclaimed.

There are acts of forgiveness from family to family, awakenings of conscience and restorations of justice.

There is all the dirt, all the obscene books, dishonoured lives, the ineffable stains on the spirit.

But there are also vows of faithfulness that are never broken, the stars of Christmas that shine above each cradle.

There are crimes and scandals on the front pages of the papers.

But there is also so much good will, so much true solidarity, at work in our villages.

The yeast, according to Jesus's word, is hidden in the three portions of flour. The fisherman's net does not know what it carries to the shore, but once the net has been cast into the water the fish are hidden in its folds.

And who among men can say, without lying, what stage of our journey to the Kingdom of God we have reached? The first Christians, in their zeal, believed that they would not all die until the great Apocalypse. They did not eat and sold their belongings. The impending arrival of the year 100 caused great panic. People were frightened, acted charitably in order to save themselves. Every year some sect, informed by a direct communication from Heaven, sets another date for the return of the King of Glory. We are living in the age of the atomic bomb and imagining our earthly landscapes transformed into lunar deserts. Are we approaching the end of time, living in the last years before the Apocalypse? But who knows if we are at the beginning or the end of history? The earth has existed for one thousand, five hundred millions of years. Human history dates back only four thousand years. Who were the first Christians? Perhaps they are us. Perhaps, on the scale of history, we are primitive men. It is easy to believe it when we look around us. The coming of the Kingdom is a mystery which hangs over every age, every hour. When it comes, it will be a surprise to us.

What do we really know about the history of the Kingdom of God, except that it revealed Jesus Christ to us? God is coming …

Like the familiar footsteps of a friend, we can hear Him coming. While we are waiting, let us work as though He might arrive tomorrow, or even today.[4]

The Church and Inequalities

This sermon, broadcast on Radio Suisse romande, is a good illustration of André Trocmé's mastery of the art of homily, and his ability to reject those convenient illusions that prevent people from struggling against alienating mystification.

There is nothing more pleasant than inequality, as long as you are on the right side of the fence. Nothing is more beautiful than to be young among the old; nothing is more comfortable than to be healthy among the sick. We take flowers to the sick to ask forgiveness for our health, but we are happy to find ourselves once again walking with other healthy people. Nothing is more exhilarating than to be surrounded by mediocre students when you are a brilliant scholar who passes exams with flying colours. Nothing is more marvellous than to be a successful businessman or architect and to watch foreign construction workers who are almost illiterate work long days on construction sites in Geneva. Nothing is more enjoyable than to be a

European in Algiers or Casablanca. Nothing is more joyful today than to be white in South Africa or Alabama. Nothing increases our sense of self-worth as much as doing good things for people who have not had the same good fortune as we have. It soothes our guilty conscience and makes us believe we have filled the cruel chasm of inequality.

On the contrary, brothers and sisters, there is nothing more humiliating than inequality when you are on the wrong side of the fence. The ill, the old become bitter, the mediocre, the worker, the North African, the "Negro" revolts. He pushes away the hand that reaches out to him. What he wants is not a handout but equality.

The cry that I want to hear this morning is the cry of all the Blacks on the earth, the cry of the underprivileged all around the world: "Give us equality! Now! Right away!" Alas, history teaches us that the privileged will never voluntarily give away their riches and their advantages. The poor must rise up, their revolt must be spurred on by revolutionary ideas: "Unite! Stand united! Bring down the rich! If you can't get equality through passive resistance, take it through violence!" This is what we hear in the world today.

Yesterday I opened an American magazine and read an article by one of my friends, a Black American, notoriously nonviolent. He wrote: "From now on, we can no longer disavow Blacks who use violence to obtain their rights. We have been patient long enough." This is why [...] the Church of Christ cannot have any illusions! It is not because the problem of civil rights is about to be resolved in our country that the problem has been solved around the world. Repeating that "everything is for the best in the best of all possible worlds" would be like burying our heads in the sand. Christ's Church cannot get away with so little. It cannot be content with doing its good work and seeking the support of the privileged. Actually, it will be betraying the cause of the poor and will be rejected by them if it does not become an active force of social transformation very quickly. Christians know how men can become equal. All it takes is to apply the eternal law of God's will. The Bible tells us: "God makes no exceptions; He treats the rich and the poor, the weak and the strong, the same way." When Jesus tells us: "God rains on the just and the unjust," he is saying the same thing. The principle is that once equality is given, it will grow and ferment in the Christian world.

I would like to remind you [...] what outcomes we have already produced in the Western world when we applied the biblical principle of equality. One example is the French Revolution, which abolished the privileges of nobility and gave to all what we now call human rights. "Men are born and remain free and equal in rights." This is an expression of civil equality. Another example is the Russian Revolution which, by eliminating the private ownership of the tools of production, instituted what we might call State capitalism. In the socialist world where everyone is a civil servant, working for the State, people must be satisfied with their salary, because the most egregious differences of social status have been levelled. This is the beginning of economic equality. Now, here is an example that I call a "family revolution," a transformation taking place without violence in the nations of the West. By establishing a mandatory social security program, all citizens, young and old, healthy and weak, are given equal protection against the risks of aging, illness, accidents, and unemployment. They are also given a family allowance, which is what we could call "family equality." Finally, there is the example of anti-colonialist revolution, which is abolishing racial differences between people of colour and Whites. This is racial equality.

Seeing all of this, brothers and sisters, we have cause to celebrate. God has put the ferment in the world. But alas, good legislation has not yet eliminated inequality. Far from it. Nature itself is not egalitarian. When I go into my garden, what do I see? I see that the shadow of the tall tree is stifling the flowers I have planted. When I look at my family, what do I see? I see that the more gifted child triumphs over the less gifted one; he humiliates and discourages him.

In modern society, we have wanted to equalize everything by instituting a matriculation exam that will be the same for everyone. What has this accomplished? We have created a hierarchy of intelligence. We have privileged those who have above-average intellectual capacities, and relegated those who are less gifted to a second-class status. Certainly, better laws would prevent the most obvious inequalities, but they will not prevent inequality. I will share a cruel truth with you, in a quotation from Balzac: "Laws are spider webs through which the big flies pass and in which the little ones get caught."

[...] When Jesus declares in Luke, chapter 13, verse 5 that "ye shall all likewise perish," he was proclaiming a principle of equality before death. It is a powerful statement. I can even confess that as a pastor who has to lead funeral services, alas, this equality before death is a triumph for the Church. Think about Bossuet, preaching at the court of Versailles on the occasion of the death of Princess Henrietta of England and saying: "You, Princes, are but dust. You are nothing but poor wretches." What a triumph for the Christian pulpit! But do you think that Bossuet's sermon would have made a single rich man change his habits? I am afraid it would do the opposite. I can imagine the wealthy leaving and saying to themselves, "Since I am going to die in a few years and my condition will be the same as the most miserable of men, I may as well enjoy what I have while I am still on earth. After that, we'll see."

As for poor Lazarus, who listened for centuries as people preached resignation and told him: "Don't worry, in the next world you will be compensated for your suffering here on earth," the Church did him a disservice. By distorting the parable of the rich man and poor Lazarus, the Church prolonged his misery and encouraged the pride of the rich. We must now search deeper in the Scriptures to find the roots of equality [...]

God is not fundamentally egalitarian. If it pleases God to favour Jacob and to disfavour Esau, the Bible tells us, you who are only one of God's creatures and who are not equal to God, you have no right to judge or condemn your Creator. If it pleases God to destroy all humanity with a flood and to save only one man and his family, you have nothing to say about it, for God is wise and all-powerful. If it pleases God to choose Abraham alone among all the pagans, to make him the father of the chosen people upon whom God will heap His blessings, while the non-Jewish people will be left to fend for themselves, you should not protest.

And if we go to the New Testament, what do we find? This: God decides to call among all men (who are incapable of doing good) only one man, Jesus Christ, and declare: "This is my beloved Son, with whom I am well pleased." I, who am only a man like everyone else, can do nothing but bow down before him. The first act, the fundamental act which would one day allow me to uncover the secret of my human condition, is to recognize my deep inequality with Jesus Christ, and my equality with other men, in my inability to do good. This is the act that Jesus calls a change of spirit, and causes men to convert or repent. This is the act that will open the gates of eternal life.

It is obvious that repentance, presented this way, is rather repugnant. Geneva is paved with ancient communicants who could not swallow what I just said. They did not accept that there was a single chosen person and that it was not them. They were scandalized at the thought. Jesus was for them an opportunity to fall. The parable Jesus told about the barren fig tree withering away was designed to show people like this what repentance really means. "Repent, or ye shall likewise all perish." It is not only equality before death, but also equality before repentance [...] Repentance does not mean hitting one's chest in vain remorse, it is essentially a change of attitude [...] You know that what encumbers a man is his past, his accumulated errors, the pride that fears a fall. Repentance liberates us from this slavery. It makes us capable of imagination, of invention, like those scholars who, when they put aside their biases, suddenly make marvellous discoveries in the laboratory. The man who repents is a liberated man. This liberation is the same for the brilliant architect as it is for the illiterate workman. It is even easier, Jesus tells us, for the illiterate workman, because the brilliant intellectual is so inflated with his own importance that he cannot fit through the eye of the needle.

Repentance also liberates man from the yoke of human laws. It is not that we are allowed to break these laws. No, repentance liberates us from above; that is, it allows us to be better than the law. By repenting, we move beyond the literal meaning of the Ten Commandments. And it is not only the letter of the law that we are able to move beyond, it is also the civil law [...] The freedom given to us when we repent, given to Christ's Church, places the Church in exactly the same situation as Jesus himself: it makes it take stock of the distance between God's law and laws made by men.

Look at what is happening in the United States: you have heard about civil rights volunteers, Blacks and Whites together, who are educated and sent into the southern states of the USA. Why? To break racist laws in these states. Break them in the name of what? In the name of the federal law of the United States, which is anti-racist. The volunteers will go to prison in the southern states for obeying a divine law higher than the laws of men. That is exactly what the Church needs to do to break down the walls between the races, to put an end to the atomic destruction that human laws are leading to, so that all differences among peoples, nations are abolished, so that every man, weak or strong, is respected as a child of God. [...] "When there is no equality," a Christian author once wrote, "It is time for fraternity."[5]

"As We Get Older"

The following text presents excerpts of a letter André wrote to his daughter Nelly on 2 August 1967, when she turned forty. In a few lines of reflection on a common subject, he reveals a wealth of experience.

As we get older we must learn to be indulgent, or we will become isolated and bitter towards other people.

We must learn to laugh at ourselves, at the faults we are beginning to see in ourselves, at our own faces which are beginning to wrinkle, at our limitations that make it impossible to be something other than who we have become. We must learn to smile at others again, to look at our spouse, our children, our partners with the indulgence they need to accept us. And especially, we must live for others, voluntarily, deliberately, for there is no future for those who retain in maturity the instinctive egotism of their youth.

Knowing these limits, remembering to fuel ourselves by listening to others and by always finding in their words, their courage and their faith an example to follow. It is crazy to want to draw only on one's own strengths.[6]

New Theses for A New Church

André and Magda Trocmé travelled to Le Chambon-sur-Lignon in October 1967, on the 450th anniversary of the posting of Martin Luther's "Ninety-five Theses" against indulgences.[7] On this occasion, André proposed twelve theses that would allow the Church to remain faithful to the mission which was conferred upon it by Christ.

In the manner of Martin Luther. 31 October 1517.
450 years after the 95 Theses Against Indulgences.
October 1967.

----

1 We do not want any of the old fights between Christians to continue. We do not want a "civil war" between believers for we all worship the same Lord.

2 Neither do we want an ecumenical attitude which is satisfied with assembling all Christians who are no longer "with the times." We do not want a marriage of old people; we want a true union to accomplish something new.

3 We want a truly universal Church, without nationalism, racism, borders. We do not want little parishes hiding behind their fences, but churches that open their doors to the world

and where time and space are made for prayer and intercession.

4 We want a Church where people do not believe they are better than "unbelievers," a Church where we are brothers and sisters of all people, for Jesus Christ gave his life for us. We want a real fraternity among Christians. We do not want them to argue amongst themselves; we want them to forgive each other. We want the Last Supper to have its rightful place at the centre of our worship and the meaning that Jesus gave Communion to be honoured.

5 We want a Church that is humble and poor like Jesus Christ, a Church without ornamentation or pageantry, a Church that is not aligned with the rich and powerful but on the side of the ordinary man, a Church without titles and honours, that cannot be confused with civil, military, or religious authorities.

6 We want a Church where we are in service to others not in our words but in our deeds.

7 We want a Church where we do not always talk about money, but where we know how to give and share it.

8 We want a Church that will not be towed behind political, philosophical, or moral theories, which will not belong to an era, a party, or a country. But we want a Church that is engaged, that "jumps in," that takes risks for justice and for peace.

9 We want worship services where we are not amorphous spectators, services where there is no distance between us and a remote "clergyman" high in his pulpit and in his robes, two metres above contradiction. We want services where the liturgy is not a repetition of the same ideas, where music and hymns are not always the ones Grandfather listened to.

10 We want short, clear, living sermons; we do not want a solemn or sorrowful tone. We want a "how-to manual" to help us understand and live the words of the Gospel.

11 We do not want to be "catechised" like babies. We want to seek, discuss, understand, and discover for ourselves. We

want to learn how to be a faith community, and how to reflect on religious and other questions together. We do not want "confirmation" and "first communion" (which often turns out to be the last one we attend) to be required of us or to be led to the altar as a "herd."

12 In short, we believe that the Gospel of Jesus Christ is true and is forever young. We do not want to dress in second-hand garments.

NB Those who oppose these theses are welcome to burn them on the town square or, better yet, to discuss them.[8]

The After-Life

Below are some comments made by André when his sister-in-law, Madeleine, died.

I am less and less tempted to picture the after-life as a visit to a place outside the earth, which is so beautiful. It is more like a different reality which we glimpse in a moment of revelation. Our feeling that our loved ones are far away from us comes from the fact that we continue temporarily to live in time and that, as long as the earth keeps on turning, the loved ones we have lost no longer travel with us. They seem to have stayed behind somewhere in the past.

We think of the previous generations – our grandparents, parents – as downtrodden, crushed by hardships we have forgotten today, and who survived, who left us their principles and instructions as a legacy, people who were generous and courageous. I hope I will leave those I love the memory of a man like that.

Never would I be able to explain to my grandchildren the rivers I have crossed, the Red Sea and the Jordan, but I can leave them the picture of a grandfather at peace, a man whose faith could be shaken by nothing, not even death.

And here are some admirable words from my friend Jules

Isaac: "Before the separation of the flesh. No vain sorrow. The acceptance of hearts. Forgiveness. Memory, comforting memory. May whatever was pure in me survive in you. Farewell. Return to your lives, without me and yet with me at your side"[9]

"The Time Is Fulfilled, and the Kingdom of God Is at Hand."

During Advent in 1969, André Trocmé expressed, with great conviction, the hope that humanity will be transformed, a hope with which the Gospels filled him.

Beware! God can coexist with evil, with society as we know it, with ego and the self as they exist right now.

Advent is therefore a terrible season. As soon as God appears, all the false claims, the lies and half-truths, the vanities that wealth, power, domination, brutality procure, collapse and are trampled on the ground. Even the pride of knowledge and science is humbled and falls to its knees, for God's reign cannot allow the houses of straw, the theatre sets in which men perform the comedy of human glory, to stand. This is, I think, one of the things that Jesus meant when he proclaimed: "The kingdom of God is at hand."

We ourselves felt that God's kingdom was at hand when a humble disciple of Christ named Gandhi appeared. He was the apostle of gentleness, but when he appeared, an empire greater than that of ancient Rome collapsed before the presence of this man and the power of the truth he represented.

We witnessed another collapse when Martin Luther King appeared before an unarmed crowd that sang hymns. King led the crowd as they attacked the mountain of racial prejudice that dishonoured America, a country that believed itself to be Christian but was not.

Do you not know – yes, I know you do – that everything in you that is boastful, prideful, which claims it is innocent, and everything in this world that presents itself in flashy advertisements or narrow-minded propaganda, that every military parade or religious procession, every coat stained with blood, all wealth, all this is of another time than God's, and must perish the night that Jesus, the man and the son of God, is born? My brothers and sisters, have you thought about the real reason, deep inside you, that you tremble as Christmas approaches? Have you thought about the secret thoughts which drive men to avoid Christmas, to escape the change it is meant to bring them?

There are those who have replaced the true Christmas with a liturgical ceremony mindlessly repeated each year, an imitation of pagan celebrations that mark the longer days and the eventual return of spring. Or shall we do as did Jonah, the most reluctant of the prophets, hide in a cabin and criticize God for not having consumed the entire earth by fire two thousand years ago, as had been prophesied?

[…] Because old institutions are crumbling to the ground, will you, too, be dragged down by the defeatism of our era? Will you let yourself be overcome by the chaos in which our churches find themselves? It is true that our churches, despite the lessons of the two world wars, have not yet resolved to be united in Christ. They continue to condone wars and to profit from wealth, even though they know that in Christ all power is reduced to nothing and all problems will be solved.

If some of us begin to believe in Christ in this very moment, in Christ alone, all revolutions will become possible, and old things will become new.[10]

Moses and Mazes

On 1 November 1970, André Trocmé gave one of his last sermons in Le Chambon-sur-Lignon, where he was invited by the congregation he had served several decades before. The passage we include here was transcribed from an audio recording by Roger Darcissac. The Bible passages are Psalms 123 and 124, Deuteronomy (chapter 4) and Hebrews 11:10.

I am sure you know that I am deeply moved to be standing in this pulpit after so many years. After sixteen years in this parish, I left behind people that I loved, and I lost those I can call my brothers and sisters, those men and women who, many years ago, sat where you are now, and with whom I had so much in common and shared magnificent times but also very painful ones. And I will indulge my sentiments only briefly to mention those figures who are no longer with us, and to talk about the shut-ins I was able to visit yesterday, some of them old friends or comrades in the struggle for a common cause; I found they had aged, but I, too, am at an age when my wrinkles are getting deeper. And yet our hearts still beat for the same joys, our faith is as fervent, and we realized that between the dead and the living, the old and the young who are taking their places in the world, there is not much difference at all.

But I did not come here to make a show of emotion. That is not my role among you. I came here to proclaim the Gospel, to show you that even when a pastor is retired he is not really retired. We do not retire from the Gospel the way we give up a job or a duty. We remain, until the end of our days, men with a calling. And that is what I am doing this morning, preaching the Gospel. I hope what I say will be helpful for the old and the young, and for the middle-aged people who, as usual, seem to predominate in the congregation I see before me.

Before I proclaim the Gospel, I want to read it to you. We will start with a Psalm from the Old Testament. It is a psalm about liberation. You know that I am someone who is enamoured of freedom; since I was young, I have always been detached from the prisons that enclosed me, including the winds and fog that sometimes imprisoned me in Chambon-sur-Lignon winters [...]

The freedom we look for is not only just our own. We also try to ensure that others are free. You know that the world has not improved since our childhood, that there are millions of slaves on the earth today who do not have enough to eat. If we speak of freedom today, we cannot only talk only about inner freedom, we need to think about the freedom of those who are oppressed. And there is also freedom from evil. And yes, I do believe that we can be liberated from evil. That is the subject of my sermon today.

To better understand the theme of liberation, the liberation of a nation, the liberation of a human being, we are going to perform a rather strange exercise. We are going to compare a Bible story that you know very well with a pagan tale.

The Bible story [...] is about the way Moses, the great liberator, seized his people's freedom from the Pharaoh, Ramses II. How he led them out of slavery, down the Suez Canal (which is what the Red Sea is called today) towards Sinai, where they could live in freedom.

The other story is about Daedalus in Knossos, on the island of Crete. Daedalus was an architect, a builder. He had built a famous palace called the Labyrinth for King Minos, to hold a mythical creature called the Minotaur. But that is not what I want to focus on today. You all know the Greek myth about the Greek hero Theseus, who killed the Minotaur, and who was the first human being able to leave the palace. The labyrinth had been designed by Daedalus in such a way that once a person entered the palace, he could never leave. Theseus asked his fiancée Ariadne to give him a skein of thread that he could use to find his way out. Because of Ariadne's thread, Theseus was able to leave, a victorious hero, for Athens. But that is not our story either.

Our story is one that not very many people know. It is that Minos was furious with Daedalus because his Labyrinth was not a tricky enough maze. Minos locked Daedalus in the centre of the Labyrinth with his son Icarus for eternity. And poor Daedalus was a victim of his own invention. I chose to talk about Daedalus because he is a fitting image of modern man. We have only to travel to Paris or elsewhere to realize that modern man has invented a maze from which we cannot escape. He has invented streets, capitals with six or seven million inhabitants, cars, and fumes that are quite poisonous. Now we cannot circulate freely, we are caught, stuck in the traffic of our own making. Because we wanted to go faster and faster, sometimes we cannot move at all. Like Daedalus, we are the prisoners of our own inventions.

What did Daedalus do? To get rid of the invention that imprisoned him, he invented something better: aviation. He made two pairs of wings out of chicken feathers and beeswax, one pair for himself and one for his son Icarus. One fine morning, Daedalus and Icarus flew out of the Labyrinth. They were free! Wonder of wonders!

On the one hand, we have the story of the freedom of Moses, and on the other that of Daedalus. Now, let us compare these two events. We will be surprised by many things as we compare the work of Daedalus, the architect, and Moses, the prophet. Today, when we think of Moses, even though we know he possessed the sophisticated knowledge of the ancient Egyptian civilization, we cannot help but think of him as "preacherly" ... Moses, Jesus, the disciples, they are all so far back in time. When we think of Daedalus, an engineer, an architect, we are impressed. He seems much closer to the men of our age. But when we think more carefully, we find that the story of Daedalus has some surprises.

The first surprise is that Daedalus, modern man, was thinking only of his own salvation and that of his son. The fate of the people of Crete did not even occur to him. He escaped from his Labyrinth, and once he had escaped he was happy. He was free. And you know that today, the people of our generation are also pursuing their own liberty, but mainly for themselves. Even believers say: "I am happy! I have been saved! The Lord has saved me!" And then they forget about everyone else. Once they have been saved, they think that is great, everything is fine, and they can enjoy life on earth and then eternal life as one of the chosen among all others around them. That is exactly what Daedalus was like.

Moses, on the other hand, was truly free. He had already saved himself. He was in the home of his father-in-law, Jethro, and he returned to the land of slavery. He came back with a willingness to endure all the trials, all the tribulations. He became the leader of a people that was difficult to lead, "stiff-necked" or stubborn. He began to discuss the situation with the Pharaoh, and spent months trying to convince him. Then Moses led these lamentable souls, who complained about everything they had to leave behind in Egypt, onions and garlic, the pleasant sedentary life they had led. He led them across the Red Sea, he rebuked them, he counselled them, he gave them the Ten Commandments. He thought always of others rather than himself. And as you know, the story of Moses ends with his death outside of the Land of Canaan, where his successors would finally find a home.

The second surprise is that Daedalus, the engineer, escaped vertically. I know many people, even in Geneva, who want to rise up out of their situation. "Oh, why I am stuck down here, in this awful town? If only I could fly away!" Daedalus left the horrible Labyrinth below him, while Moses, the religious man, escaped horizontally [...] Moses is, therefore, the earthly being, the practical man with his feet on the ground. Daedalus, the engineer, is the aerial man, the type of person who goes to the moon or through outer space [...] But the populist, the man who thinks of humanity, who takes responsibility for his people, is Moses, the man of life.

Third surprise: Daedalus used technical means to escape. His skills had already surpassed him; he had been imprisoned in the Labyrinth. So to overcome one technological disaster he used superior technology, inventing aviation [...] We have now gone farther than Daedalus, because we can really fly. We can even fly at ultrasonic speeds, beyond the speed of sound. We can already go to the moon. Moses, the religious man, did not rely on technical skill, although he possessed it. He relied solely on the invisible power of God. He did not have confidence in his own skill, he had confidence in God. And his trust in God would manifest itself in difficult times, leading to surprising deliverances [...] Moses was a humble man. He did not use technological means, he used religious means.

Of the two men, who succeeded? At first glance it seems to be Daedalus: his winged flight was so splendid, so magnificent! However, Daedalus followed his son. Icarus committed a monumental error: he looked at the sun above his head. The sun is a sign of God, Apollo the god of the sun. So, confident in the power of his wings, Icarus decided to fly up to see God. He was like the man of today who says he does not need religion, he does not need to confess his sins, he does not need to beat his chest. "I can fly on my own wings! I can rise higher and higher!" And that is what Icarus believed, until he got so close to the sun that it melted the wax on his wings and the proud Icarus plunged into the sea, where he died. The adventure of Daedalus ended in tragedy.

What about Moses? Would we say that Moses had a successful career? Forty years in the desert, the arrival in Canaan. He had told his people that whenever they placed their trust in God they would be free, but if they turned their backs on God and his commandments they would return to slavery. And they continually fell back into slavery [...]

To leave home, to travel the world, can be problematic for us too. The modern world has so many temptations, so many obstacles to trip us up. We are told to follow two commandments that seem impossible to obey: "Thou shalt not lie" and "Thou shalt not kill." Living this way is an act that can seem beyond our means, beyond our faith. Deep down, I understand the Israelites, who felt that Moses was leading them to a dead end. They found a comfortable compromise, telling little white lies. They were reassured by the idea of the golden calf, which reminds me a great deal of our situation today. We believe in God, but there is a golden calf somewhere.

So the story of Moses has its ups and downs, successes that alternate with defeats. We live not two thousand years but three thousand, two hundred and fifty years after Moses. And Christians who have come after the Israelites also go from miraculous deliverances to catastrophes that are caused by their disobedience. Even today, do you not worry about Israel?

I am very worried about Israel, because they have entered Jerusalem. They returned, as God had promised them they would, in 1948. And already today, we can see that they are placing their trust not in God but in airplanes, bombs and missiles. We wonder what will happen to them. But we do not need a great prophet to tell us; God's chosen people cannot afford to turn their back on God's commandments in any way. I say this with great conviction, not because I want to condemn Israel, but because the same words that apply to Israel also apply to the people of God which is called the Church […]

Technology will not repent. It will always go further. An atomic technician who has made an atomic bomb cannot resolve or attempt to resolve the atomic crisis in any way but with a hydrogen bomb. And after that, we may have ray guns, laser weapons, who knows. Technology will pursue its own path. It will progress, and may even rise to what it believes is the sun. All that it will lead to is catastrophe. Pride comes before a fall. What about the liberation of Moses, though? There is always a moment when man is at his most lamentable, his most disobedient. But at that moment there is always a possibility: the return to God. Repent, God says, and you will see that I am still here, that I have not moved and that all the promises of freedom that I made to you are as valid today as they were in the time of Moses.

The only difference is that we Christians have been given something the Jews did not have: Jesus. Moses said: "My friend, you see that you are in misery. It is because you have turned away from God. Repent and you will see that you will be delivered." And the Jew experiences something he knows well; he repents, he returns to God, and then two days later he turns away again. That is human nature.

I wish I had an itinerary. It would be nice to paint our own itineraries on the wall. Today, in Chambon-sur-Lignon, there are no longer Bible passages on the walls the way there used to be. To the left of the pulpit the words: "The Master is here" were painted, and to the right: "He calleth to thee." What if we were to paint the itinerary of the parish or the college? Wouldn't it be glorious? There would be such movement, a beginning ... a return! A zigzag, like the stock market in Paris [...]

Well, the Jewish itinerary zigzags because man is not master of his will. He may have good will, but that is not enough. God gave us Jesus Christ; he gave us an opportunity of eternal freedom. If, armed with my own free will, I try to conquer my liberty and give it to my brothers – whether they are downtrodden or broken-hearted – I am like a fool who is trying to get out of the mud by pulling on his own hair. But God is in Jesus Christ who hears us. He tells us: "I am not asking you to climb out of the mud yourself. You will never be able to do it. I only ask that you make room inside you. I ask you to put your own will out the door, to get rid of your ego, so that there will be room for my Holy Spirit. Then, if you leave, there will be an empty space. And in this empty space, the spirit of Christ, the person of Christ will come and take his place in the empty room. And you will be free for the rest of time" [...]

And do not try to use technological means or inventions, that is to say your own will, your character, your skills, your intelligence, your pride, all that which gives each of us his little knowledge and ability.

If you only knew how many tricks I have up my sleeve, now that I am sixty-nine years old. If you only knew how hard I would be on my parishioners if I were to return to this church as minister, what I would do to keep them in line! Human inventions are not worth anything. Zero. The only thing that matters is what God gave us in Christ, that is to say a return to freedom which can be possible when we make a place for Jesus Christ to enter and inhabit us [...] Come out of the camp, the Labyrinth, the maze in which you are lost; come unto Jesus by taking upon us his dishonour, for in this place we have no home to call our own. We can only seek the city that will appear before us one day.[11]

From One Ill Man to Another

In the regional hospital in Geneva, a worship service was celebrated every Sunday in a large room with big windows on the top floor of the building. Among the patients who took part in this worship service was André Trocmé. This is how he came to read a passage of great compassion and humanity only a few days before his death.

I speak to my brother in misery to share some of my experiences. I speak in sincerity and humility. A pastor who is ill is no different from any other man who is ill. He is a body who is suffering: accident, surgery, sudden illness, and all of our plans are destroyed in a few instants. In their place I discover a wild forest full of rocks, giant obstacles, pain that is sometimes so atrocious I do not even have the strength to get through it. Sometimes the connection with reality is cut, anaesthetized, and all that I can feel is the love of others. However, I never lose God's reassurance for a single moment. It is the God of Moses, who says: "I am who I am." Even if the hospital or the entire universe were to crumble right now, God is. All is well. All is calm. Luminous eternity enfolds us.

The pain after surgery is another matter. It is aggressive, brutal. The body awakens in the form of cramps in the side, sharp pains, headaches, nausea. Then it is the hour of Jesus Christ: the hands of the doctors and the nurses have been for me the instruments of Jesus Christ. Once when I was lying on the gurney I called out, for the first time in my life, as though Jesus had just walked by: "Lord, come to my aid!" Paralyzed, I begged, "Please make me walk again." I did not say it in the hope of an immediate miracle, but calmly. And in the faces of those who came to my aid, I could always see Jesus. Only a few had fallen into routine and did not show God's mercy; they were the exceptions.

I think that the needles that give us modern painkillers, anaesthesia, surgery and medicine have come directly from the spirit of Jesus, by way of research. But they will never replace the kind face of a doctor, a nurse, an orderly or a nurse's aide.

For me, the most beautiful face in the regional hospital belongs to a woman who is forty years old and who works on the night shift. Her life is very hard. She hardly sleeps, because she is raising four children. For me, looking at her face and her hands are the closest thing to seeing Jesus. I was a minister for forty-six years. I remember thinking that I was not good at hospital visits. Now I think I would know how to do them properly, because I am sick myself and I am learning from those who care for me the most beautiful evangelical lessons of my life.

Thank you, God. Courage to you, my companions in suffering.[12]

The Face of God on Earth

Dictated by André Trocmé on 4 June, 1971, the evening before he died at the regional hospital in Geneva, his last text was published in Geneva in the publication *La Vie protestante*, 16 July 1971.

I am among those who have cried out to my God: "Save yourself and us along with you." I do not say this as a taunt or a dare, as the robbers next to Jesus did, but because if God is vanquished by hatred, agony and death, than we must despair of man's future. Everything has been tried, everything has failed, nothing means anything: evil and death triumph.

A few weeks ago I was in Florence, Italy, in a workshop where masterpieces of the Renaissance which were damaged by a flood three years ago are being repaired. There, on a work bench, I saw and even touched one of the great masterpieces: the *Crucifixion* painted by Cimabue, a great Italian painter, circa 1240–1302. It used to be in the Santa Croce church; the water had almost completely destroyed it. An old plaster coating that the artist had used to make the paint stick to the wood had been washed away. All that was left of the face of Jesus was an eye, a mournful eye, dead, the eyelids swollen by defeat.

Devastated, I turned to the conservator in charge of the repairs and told her, "You are going to restore this painting." She replied, rather indignantly, "Sir, one does not restore a masterpiece like this."

I will not hide from you the fact that I detest representations of the resurrected Jesus. That robe with its little pleats, the look on the face of Jesus who seems to have forgotten everything already – they horrify me. But I love the face of Jesus on the cross. Oh! I can't recognize his face very often in the sculptures and paintings of artists who are trying to create a masterpiece. Sometimes I see it, though, in the work of someone who loves the face of my Lord with all his heart, with all his soul, with all his might, and with all his thought.

As for me, I rarely see the face of God. I have caught a glimpse of it a few times in the last few weeks, when I have awoken painfully from anaesthesia, between two nightmares. I see his face when the nurse tells me, with tender emotion, that the little Portuguese man who has been agonizing in a coma for five weeks in the room next to mine is going to die.

Oh, the authentic face of God! I see you in the depths of my soul and I am moved. Sometimes I cannot help but cry, when I contemplate the fact that, through your death, you have healed forever all of those who have cried out to you, and not only those who have found you, but also the weak and sinful. "Today shalt thou be with me in paradise."[13]

And not only the malefactors who have finally seen you, but also the ignorant, the imbeciles who laughed as they pierced your hands and feet with nails. "Father, forgive them; for they know not what they do."[14]

The face of God on the Earth, you are identical, you are the image of the face of God in Heaven. Thank you.

Magda's Testament

It seems appropriate to give the last word to Magda Trocmé and close with a "spiritual testament" she copied onto cards for her children and grandchildren.

Religion may be a cause for joy, confidence, and peace, or a cause for torment. For me, it was a cause of torment for many long years, but also a quest I believe was genuine and honest. It never caused me to be detached [...]

Later, André told me that my experience with Catholicism made me unable to simply believe. I replied that Protestantism also taught things I could not subscribe to, even if André taught them differently. André tried to "free" me, but he respected my "religion," which he called "Magda's religion," as though no one else believed the same things as I did. Perhaps he was right. In any case, I worked with my husband mainly on social issues.

We each had our own area of interest. I often meet people who were helped greatly by André and also "a little" by me, as well as I could, without feeling obligated to say things I do not believe.

The fact that I have only taken communion two or three times in my life as a minister's wife did not scare away the people in our congregation. In my opinion, perhaps because of my Catholic years, I feel that the Reform did not allow the symbolic ritual of communion to be spiritual enough, to reveal its original meaning. In the first few centuries of Christianity, the Last Supper was really a meal. Admittedly, the early Christians indulged in overly copious meals, but it should be possible to transform "things of the spirit into things of the flesh" without becoming greedy, and avoiding excess is not a good reason to stop sharing a common meal in the symbolic ritual of the Last Supper.

Would we invite everyone who takes communion in our churches to our table, to our home? This is a question I often ask myself. Obviously, there would be too many guests to invite at once. But I am not talking about the number. I am talking about race, nationality, social class, friendly or unfriendly, nice or not so nice.

The meal that one shares in a church is different from the one shared in our own homes, at our own tables.

My children have often thought I was not a believer, but this is not true. We should have talked about all of this as a family. But our life, as useful and interesting as it was, was rather gruelling and overwhelming, which did not make it easy to have intimate spiritual conversations together. And besides, it is complicated being the wife or children of a pastor!

My children, grandchildren, brothers and sisters, I leave you these last thoughts as my testament.

Two things seem obvious to me.

We would not have, deeply rooted within us, ideals, hope, a need for justice, truth and love, things that we all possess, whatever religion we believe in or however civilized we are, if there were not, somewhere, a source of hope, justice, truth and love. It is this source that I call God.

Is Jesus Christ the son of God? Is the New Testament always the expression of Truth, without a trace of mythology, error, or legend, without a trace of some need we might have had to express in stories something we felt strongly inside us? It does not matter. There are enough beautiful teachings in the philosophy presented to us by Jesus that we could transform the world and make it a kind of "Kingdom of God," if we put into practice only half of what Jesus taught us.

André used to say that the value of Christ's teaching was that it was relevant to all the ages, at whatever historical, moral or spiritual stage of evolution man had reached. I believe that the teachings of the Gospel remain the same, but their interpretation changes because progress will not come to a halt with our generation.

The teachings of Jesus will continue to be relevant, evolve, and be able to be applied in the future to various problems that we have not yet been able to solve, because we have lived for too long in the Middle Ages.[15]

Notes

CHAPTER 1

1 *Mémoires* (André Trocmé), 1. References in the notes are to several of André's and Magda's autobiographical writings. According to Richard Unsworth, in his biography of the Trocmés (*A Portrait of Pacifists: Le Chambon, the Holocaust, and the Lives of André and Magda Trocmé*, Syracuse: Syracuse University Press, 2012), "Both André's and Magda's memoirs were prepared over many years. They were intended only for their children and grandchildren, and they were added to in rather haphazard fashion whenever time allowed" (Author's Note).

André's memoirs, cited here as *Mémoires*, include handwritten pages which he wrote in a bound notebook starting in 1944 and loose pages written in the 1950s and occasionally later. After his death, Magda Trocmé and a friend of hers put André's autobiographical writings in chronological order, typed them, and collected them in a volume intended for her family under the title *Autobiographie d'André Trocmé*. For her part, Magda kept sporadic notes and later, at the request of her daughter Nelly, recorded the narrative of the couple's life up to 1946. The tapes were transcribed. These pieces form what is referred to here as *Autobiographie* (*Souvenirs autobiographiques de Magda Trocmé Grilli di Cortona, fille d'Oscar Grilli di Cortona et de Nelly Grilli Wissotsky*). The record of the Trocmés' life and work also includes an impressive number of unindexed documents (Trocmé *Archives*). All the documents cited in the notes can be found in the archives of the Peace Collection at the Swarthmore College library, Swarthmore, PA.

2 *Mémoires,* 538.

3 Ibid., 252.

4 *Autobiographie* (Magda Trocmé), 11–12

5 All of the documents mentioned here, unless otherwise specified, can be consulted at the Swarthmore College library.

6 *Mémoires*, 5–7

7 A biblical reference to Rahab in Joshua, chapter 2.

8 Trocmé *Archives*, Swarthmore College Peace Collection.

9 *Autobiographie*, 53.

10 Ibid., 53–6.

11 Ibid.

12 Letter from Magda to her children, May 1976.

13 *Mémoires*, 94–7.

14 The UCJG, active in Protestant parishes of France after the middle of the nineteenth century, is the French branch of the YMCA/YWCA.

15 Refers to the Fédération française des associations chrétiennes d'étudiants (the French federation of Christian students' associations), an open-minded group of university students and graduates founded in 1898. André took on a progressively active role in this movement.

16 The decision-making bodies which consist of clergymen and elected lay delegates.

17 Reference to the Book of Revelation in the Bible, in which the city of Babylon is synonymous with corruption and sin.

18 A campground and summer camp that belonged to the Federation of Christian (Protestant) students, located on the northeast coast of the Île d'Oléron, a little island off the Atlantic coast due west of Rochefort.

19 Established in 1877 to train Lutheran and Reformed Church ministers, the Faculty of Protestant Theology in Paris and another one in Montpellier make up the Institut protestant de théologie today.

20 Final grades in France are given out of 20, so 18 is a very high mark, equivalent to an A.

21 Charles de Foucauld or, as he had come to call himself, Little Brother Charles of Jesus, was a missionary priest who served among the Muslim Tuareg tribesmen. He was murdered in 1916. In 2009, the Catholic Church declared him to be among her *venerabili*, a Servant of God worthy of the veneration of the Catholic faithful.

22 Trocmé *Archives*.

CHAPTER 2

1 It is interesting to note that after Trocmé studied at Union, another French student, Jean Lasserre, went there and met Dietrich Bonhoeffer in New York during the 1930–31 academic year. In his biography of Bonhoeffer, the famous German theologian executed by the Nazis on 9 April 1945, Eberhard Bethge comments on the influence Lasserre's pacifism had on the man. See *Dietrich Bonhoeffer: A Biography* (revised edition, Minneapolis: Fortress Press, 2000).
2 From its beginnings, the Collège Cévenol provided an innovative education based on a curriculum of peace, justice, and non-violence. A good example of the tradition of resistance to all forms of oppression in the region, the school also enabled students to pursue their studies in their home region. Today it continues to exist as a private establishment called The Collège Lycée International Cévenol.
3 The School later became the Columbia University School of Social Work.
4 *Autobiographie*, 107.
5 *Mémoires*, 236.
6 *Autobiographie*, 126–7 and 134–5.
7 *Mémoires*, 253.
8 Ibid.
9 *Autobiographie*, 152–4 and 159–60.
10 Matthew 22:39: "And the second is like unto it, Thou shalt love thy neighbour as thyself."
11 Trocmé *Archives*.
12 André Trocmé was very active in the Mouvement International de la Réconciliation (MIR), the French branch of the International Fellowship of Reconciliation, and was the secretary for the European part of the organization for several years. A non-governmental organization founded in 1914 in response to the horrors of the First World War, the IFOR now has seventy branches, groups and affiliates around the world and is coordinated by a secretariat in the Netherlands. IFOR members promote nonviolence, human rights, and reconciliation through public education efforts, training programs, and campaigns.
13 Quakers, or Friends, belong to a pacifist and philanthropic religious movement founded by George Fox in England in the seventeenth century.

14 A group of German revolutionary and anti-militarist socialists. The suppression of the workers' uprising in 1919, also known as the "January uprising," is thought to mark the end of the German revolution.

15 W. Monod and S. Schultze were nonetheless leaders and pioneers among the Protestants of these two nations who had been at war, and were forerunners of the movement to reconcile France and Germany.

16 Gerhard Halle's apology to the townspeople had serious consequences for him; he lost his job as a direct result of his talk.

17 The preceding stories are excerpted from André's *Mémoires*, 284 ff.

18 *Cahiers de la réconciliation* (March 1930), 4–5.

19 This is how André would remember it much later: "Magda insisted that I leave her in Saint-Gobain. She didn't want me to miss such an important opportunity. How many times, since then, did she sacrifice her happiness for mine or the children's? How many times did she kick me out of the nest, forcing me, once and for all this time, to break my habit of confusing duty with the weight of tradition" (*Mémoires*, 258).

20 The Sturm Abteilung (literally "storm section") or SA, also known as Stormtroopers or Brownshirts, were members of Hitler's private army, formed to protect him from attacks and to control political opposition to the Nazis.

21 This passage is from *Mémoires*, 289–91. It should be remembered that much of André's autobiography was written decades after the actual events described. His comments in the last sentence suggest that he was, at the time of writing, moved and angered by the racial conflicts in the USA, where he and Magda lectured on pacifism and civil rights.

22 This excerpt is from her *Autobiographie*, 184–5.

CHAPTER 3

1 In the early twentieth century, the Reformed Church in France consisted of four groups: the Evangelical Reformed Churches (*Églises réformées évangéliques*), the United Reformed Churches (*Églises réformées unies*), the Free Reformed Churches (*les Églises réformées libres*) and the Methodist Church (*Église méthodiste*), as well as the closely-related Lutheran Church. The groups have moved closer to-

gether throughout the twentieth and twenty-first centuries, and the Reformed Church of France and the Evangelical Lutheran Church of France are now planning to unite as the United Protestant Church of France (*Église Protestante unie de France*).

2 *Mémoires*, 305–7.

3 This town of approximately 2,500 people was first called Le Chambon, then Le Chambon-de-Tence, and as of 1923, Le Chambon-sur-Lignon. Located in the Auvergne region in south-central France, the town had a strong Protestant history, having been settled by Huguenots in the sixteenth century.

4 *Mémoires*, 308–9.

5 In addition, in Le Chambon-sur-Lignon, a large number of children had reached the end of their elementary education. The nearest secondary schools were Catholic, and the closest public high schools were a long distance away.

6 *Mémoires*, 464.

7 After refusing Henri Roser's request for conscientious objection to be condoned by the authorities, the Synod of Evangelical Reformed Churches of France decided, in June 1933, to declare conscientious objection to the military incompatible with the fulfillment of pastoral duties.

8 Protestant charity group fighting alcoholism.

9 *Autobiographie*, 208.

10 In 1952, Carl and Florence Sangree founded The American Friends of the Collège Cévenol (AFCC). The AFCC helped raise funds (from the Quaker American Friends Service Committee, among others), and organized summer camps where volunteers cleared roads and fields, and built classrooms and dormitories.

11 *Autobiographie*, 223–4.

12 The Cévenol school could not purchase land and construct a campus until shortly after the war.

13 Magda is referring to a preparatory school for students wishing to study theology in Batignolles, a neighbourhood of Paris.

14 The same is true, for example, in the February 1943 edition of the newspaper *Pages de Chambon*. In an article headlined "Au Chambon: terre d'asile" (In Le Chambon, a land of refuge), there is a fairly exhaustive description of the places refugees could live, and although the words "Jew" or "Jewish" never appear, the author refers to "children from central Europe whose parents have been

deported or are in an internment camp." This document, in its entirety, is included in *Le Plateau Vivarais-Lignon, Accueil et Résistance 1939–1944* (P. Bolle, ed.) Actes du Colloque du Chambon-sur-Lignon, Société d'histoire de la Montagne, 1992.

CHAPTER 4

1 The lecture, entitled "Le chrétien et les haines politiques" (Christians and Political Hatreds), was published as a booklet in 1938 by the Mouvement International de la Réconciliation and can be found in the Trocmé *Archives*.

2 André Trocmé always carried a letter in his wallet that his father, Paul Trocmé, a pacifist, had written to Reverend Ernest Nyegaard on 21 November 1870. In it, he wrote: "[the war] that has forced you to have feelings contrary to all the Christian virtues, is itself a sin, and to take part voluntarily in it, whether in defence or in offence, would be to do evil [...] I will always strive to not carry a rifle, I will even be a nurse [...] I will refuse to hold any military rank." Paul Trocmé was made a Knight in the Legion of Honour after the war of 1914–18.

3 The "Bekenntniskirsche" (Confessional or Confessing Church) arose in the early 1930s in opposition to the German government's attempt to control and "nazify" Protestant churches (by removing the Old Testament from the Bible, presenting an Aryan depiction of Jesus, etc.). Martin Niemöller, famous for his poem which begins "First they came for the communists, and I didn't speak out because I wasn't a communist" was among the leaders of the movement to separate church and state and to protect the "confessional freedom" of the church.

4 Robert Trocmé, André's half-brother, is remembered first and foremost for his heroism. Suffering from a chest injury received in the Battle of the Somme, assumed dead by the Germans who had taken him prisoner, abandoned on the battlefield, he managed to get to the French lines where he was rescued and saved. In 1918, he was among the first French officers to enter the liberated city of Brussels.

5 Trocmé *Archives*.

6 As noted by Trocmé in his letter, the parish did not accept his resignation, and he continued to serve as its minister.

7 Trocmé *Archives*.

8 The original letter was in English and is found in the Trocmé archives. It was translated into French by Pierre Boismorand and is paraphrased here.
9 Trocmé *Archives*.

CHAPTER 5

1 Issued on 3 October 1940, the Statute prohibited Jews from exercising public functions or engaging in political activities. For instance, with few exceptions, Jews could no longer work for the government, teach in public schools, serve in or work for the military, or be employed by businesses which held public contracts.
2 Roger Darcissac was the principal of the Cévenol school, the chairman of the Protestant Parish Council, the choir director, and the regional reporter for Saint-Étienne's newspaper: in short, one of the most important community figures in Le Chambon-sur-Lignon.
3 *Mémoires*, 345.
4 In 1940, Reverend Marc Bœgner served both as the president of the French National Council of the Reformed Church and the president of the Council of the Protestant Federation of France.
5 After weeks of bombing of British cities, it was widely expected that the Nazis would invade.
6 Trocmé *Archives*.
7 Charles Guillon, pastor of the church in Le Chambon-sur-Lignon from 1921 to 1927, served as mayor from 10 May 1931 to 23 June 1940, when he resigned, and then again from 1945 to his death in 1959. During the war he was the Secretary-General of the international federation of Unions chrétiennes de jeunes gens, the YMCA in French-speaking countries. Although he was only in Le Chambon-sur-Lignon on an occasional basis, he carried out his former duties as mayor of the town until Vichy named a new mayor, Benjamin Grand, on 2 May 1941. Charles Guillon was honoured posthumously with the Medal of the Righteous of Yad Vashem.
8 Œuvre (juive) de secours aux enfants (OSE), a humanitarian organization known in English as the Society for Rescuing Children. Starting in 1939, the OSE rescued hundreds of children, many of whose parents were killed during the Holocaust, and cared for them in orphanages throughout France. In 1941, transports brought close to two hundred children from the OSE homes to the US.

9 Mireille Philip was the wife of André Philip, a Protestant activist, resistance worker, and French socialist. She was among those awarded the Righteous Among the Nations medal.

10 The Croix-Bleue (the Blue Cross in English), was the name given to several Protestant temperance unions including the Société suisse de tempérance and the Ligue national contre l'alcoolisme. It became the leading temperance organization in Europe.

11 *Autobiographie*, 225–6.

12 The idea of a "city of refuge" comes from the laws of ancient Israel described in Numbers 35, 9-34, in which six cities are designated as refuges for those who have involuntarily committed murder.

13 These are the figures given by Michel Fabreguet in *Le Plateau Vivarais-Lignon, Accueil et Résistance 1939–1944*, P. Bolle, ed., (Actes du Colloque du Le Chambon-sur-Lignon-sur-Lignon, Société d'histoire de la Montagne, 1992).

14 Protestant theologian Madeleine Barot had been the secretary-general of the CIMADE (the Comité Inter-Mouvements auprès des Evacués), a multi-faith humanitarian group, since August 1940.

15 At the time, deportations were still presented as "Zwangsarbeit", or mandatory work service, in Germany.

16 The American chapter of the International Fellowship of Reconciliation (FOR-USA) is the largest, oldest, interfaith peace organization in the United States. Founded in 1915, it has carried out projects in the areas of peace, justice, non-violence, and the rights of conscience.

17 Congregational churches in the US are Protestant churches not unlike the Reformed Church in France. One of their basic principles is congregational governance, meaning that each congregation is independent and runs its own affairs. Congregationalism arose out of the Nonconformist movement.

18 *Mémoires*, 351.

19 Bœgner wrote a famous letter to the Chief Rabbi, Isaiah Schwartz, on 16 March 1941. The letter expressed the pastor's strong feelings about the racist legislation and the humiliating treatment suffered by French Jews. In addition, his "Message from the Reformed Church to our Believers," written on 22 September 1942 and read in Reformed Church parishes on Sunday, 4 October 1942, expresses opposition to the Vichy regime. See *Les Carnets du pasteur Bœgner* (Paris: Fayard, 1992).

20 Trocmé worked with pastors in Marseille, in the Cévennes, and

throughout France, including Reverend de Pury in Lyon and Reverend A.N. Bertrand in Paris.

21 *Mémoires*, 392.

22 Darbyists are followers of John Darby, an Anglican priest in Ireland, who came to believe that the established Church of English had forsaken biblical ideas. He left to form a new church with other disillusioned Christians. They called themselves "Brethren" (and later "Plymouth Brethren," because they gathered in that city) and believed in the letter of biblical texts, rejected clergy and denominationalism, and prepared themselves for the end of the world and the Second Coming of Jesus.

23 *Mémoires*, 349–50.

24 A prefect is the officer in charge of the prefecture, the administration of a regional "département" in which various services, including the police, are offered by the Ministry of the Interior. The prefect is therefore the chief of police for that region.

25 This New Testament verse advises Christians to "be subject to the higher powers" who are "ordained of God."

26 The incident to which the students referred took place on 16 and 17 July 1942. Thirteen hundred Jews were taken first to the Vélodrome d'Hiver in Paris and then transferred to Drancy before being deported.

27 *Mémoires*, 358–9.

28 In 1938, the French national association of pastors had assigned to Antoinette Butte (1898–1986) the role of managing a retreat and meeting centre located in Pomeyrol, in Saint-Étienne-du-Grès, in the Bouches-du-Rhone region. The small community had first attempted to form a Protestant sisterhood in a house near Paris which was requisitioned at the outbreak of the war. They relocated to a retreat house purchased by the pastors' association, but were again forced from their home by German troops in February 1944. In 1951, Sister Antoinette Butte established the Pomeyrol Community, a Protestant religious order for women, in the house, which had been returned to the order in 1946. The Sisters of Pomeyrol describe themselves as "Sentinels of Prayer." Their form of spirituality integrates elements from the Quakers and other similar groups, as well as from Catholicism, and continues today.

29 André and Magda Trocmé's daughter.

30 Gilbert Chabrut.

31 Mondays are traditionally the minister's day off.
32 Trocmé *Archives*.
33 It is difficult to determine the exact number of refugees who were sheltered in Le Chambon-sur-Lignon and the surrounding area, and different numbers are given in this and other documents. Most researchers estimate that there were five thousand or more.
34 A flowering plant belonging to the legume family, vetch is related to the broad bean. It is very tough and commonly used for forage.
35 We now know that several people had come forward to ask for the three prisoners to be released, among them Reverend Albert Chaudier, from Limoges, Dr Roger LeForestier, and Daniel Trocmé, who went to Vichy to try to secure their release, as well as Reverend Marc Bœgner, who wrote about his efforts in his *Carnets*.
36 *Autobiographie*, 230–2.
37 Trocmé *Archives*.

CHAPTER 6

1 Daniel Trocmé was deported and died in the concentration camp in Majdanek in 1944.
2 This residence was located approximately two kilometres from Le Chambon-sur-Lignon. It had previously been a hotel; in 1942 it became the Foyer universitaire des Roches and at one time housed up to thirty young, mainly Jewish men studying in Le Chambon-sur-Lignon. Starting the next year, when pressure was already increasing, Daniel Trocmé was in charge of the residence. Of the eighteen students living in Des Roches at the time, four died in concentration camps, six were listed as missing and the others returned to the area. For more information, see Patrick Henry, *We Only Know Men: The Rescue of Jews in France During the Holocaust* (Washington, DC: Catholic University of America Press, 2007).
3 *Mémoires*, 415.
4 Jean-Pierre Trocmé's death, at the age of fourteen, was sudden and tragic. Jean-Pierre had been reciting a poem about hanged men by a famous French poet, François Villon, and accidentally strangled himself. An actor by the name of Jean Deschamps had recently recited the same poem at a performance in Le Chambon-sur-Lignon.
5 André Trocmé, *Oser croire*. Unpublished manuscript, 1944. Trocmé *Archives*.

6 See G. Bollon, "Contribution à l'histoire du Chambon-sur-Lignon: le foyer universitaire des Roches et la rafle de 1943" (*Cahiers de la Haute-Loire*, 1996), 407–8, as well as P. Bolle (ed.), *Le Plateau Vivarais-Lignon, Accueil et Résistance 1939–1944* (Chambon-sur-Lignon. Soc. d'histoire de la Montagne, 1992), 635–8.
7 *Autobiographie*, 233–7.
8 *Mémoires*, 406.
9 Trocmé *Archives.*
10 Joseph Darnand (1897–1945) was a decorated soldier who became a notorious collaborator. In 1940 he founded the Service d'ordre légionnaire (SOL) that supported Philippe Pétain and Vichy France. In 1943, he transformed the organization into the Milice and became its de facto leader. The Milice was often considered more dangerous than the SS or the Gestapo, and was known to use torture to extract information, as well as to carry out summary executions of the Jews and Resistance fighters it rounded up.
11 *Mémoires*, 415.
12 The Nazis attacked the martyr town of Oradour-sur-Glane, near Limoges, on 10 June, 1944. The horrific massacre resulted in the death of six hundred and forty-two men, women, and children. No clear reason has ever been given for the attack.
13 *Mémoires*, 448–9.
14 *Autobiographie*, 242.

CHAPTER 7

1 In 1946 and 1947, the Cévenol school was under construction and facing setbacks and hardships.
2 Trocmé *Archives.*
3 Ibid.
4 The Union of European Federalists is considered part of the World Federalist Movement, a precursor to the United Nations. Pope Pius XII expressed his support for the Federalist Movement, praising its efforts towards understanding among nations. Nonetheless, he hesitated to involve the Church directly in political action, and emphasized the need for distance from the events of the war before embarking on the road to a European union capable of building a lasting peace. He argued that, if Europe were to avoid the grim effects of the war, there was no time to lose. His address is published

(in French) in *Fédération. Revue de l'ordre vivant;* no 47 (December 1948).

5 Trocmé *Archives.*

6 A leader in the pacifist and conscientious objection movement in Germany and friend of the Trocmés. His name was put forward a number of times for the Nobel peace prize.

7 Dora, later called Mittelwerk 2, was part of a complex of factories, storage depots, and concentration camps, some underground, that were used to manufacture and test the V-1 flying bomb and the V-2 rocket. The main V-2 assembly line was located in an underground factory called Mittelwerk that was excavated beneath Kohnstein Mountain.

8 *Mémoires*, 534.

CHAPTER 8

1 The Rollins family belonged to a party line to which several other phone lines were connected.

2 Excerpted from "Facing the Challenge of a New Age," Address Delivered at NAACP Emancipation Day Rally by Martin Luther King, 1 January 1957, Atlanta, Georgia. © Martin Luther King Estate.

3 17 March 1957, when she returned from her trip to the USA.

4 A Hindu guru who worked closely with Gandhi.

5 Excerpts in this paragraph are from "Facing the Challenge of a New Age."

6 In the Greek of the New Testament, *eros* means sexual or carnal love, *philia* friendship and liking, and *agapè* Christian compassion and charity, the love of one's fellow man.

7 Trocmé *Archives.*

8 Ibid.

9 A professor, economist, and sociologist, André Siegfried was born in 1875 and died in 1959.

10 André's half-brother, Robert, was the president of the Syndicat général de l'industrie cotonnière, the French cotton-workers' union.

11 A French Catholic writer who was born in 1901 and died in 1965.

12 French statesman and president of the republic from 1954 to 1958.

13 The author of *Why I Am a Jew* (translated from the French by Louise Waterman Wise, New York: Bloch Publishing Company, New York, 1933), poet, essayist, and dramatist Edmond Fleg

(1874–1963) founded a series of Jewish-Christian friendship centres in France.

14 A play on "Musketeer" and Moscow, "Moscoutaire" was a pejorative term describing proponents of Soviet communism, who were considered to be fanatical in the pursuit of their cause and in following the orders of the USSR.

15 Trocmé *Archives*.

CHAPTER 9

1 This party was founded in 1960 as a fusion of the Mouvement républicain populaire – consisting largely of Christians inspired by social, humanist and democratic ideals – and non-Communist socialists. The party took a strong anti-military position. Although agreeing with certain positions taken by the more established socialist parties, it supported the student riots in 1968.

2 The petition protested the American plan to build a hydrogen bomb, and was supported by the Soviet Union as well as the World Peace Congress (which emerged from the Soviet policy to promote peace and oppose the warmongering of the USA). The text of the petition read: "We demand the outlawing of atomic weapons as instruments of intimidation and mass murder of peoples. We demand strict international control to enforce this measure. We believe that any government which first uses atomic weapons against any other country whatsoever will be committing a crime against humanity and should be dealt with as a war criminal. We call on all men and women of good will throughout the world to sign this appeal." André Trocmé and his MIR colleague Henri Roser refused to sign a petition drafted by fervently pro-Soviet voices and which did not include a plan for progressive and universal disarmament.

3 Magda is referring to a medal André received for his work in the Resistance movement.

4 Trocmé *Archives*.

5 Ibid.

6 It was published in the winter 1978 issue of *Viens et voir*, the Saint-Étienne Protestant Family Association's newsletter.

7 Trocmé *Archives*.

8 Ibid.

9 Named for James Franck, the chair of a committee of prominent

nuclear physicists that met in a top-secret environment. The report itself, released in June 1945, was mainly drafted by Eugene Rabinovitch. It recommended that the United States refrain from using the atomic bomb to force the surrender of Japan and cautioned against a nuclear arms race. The report suggested that a demonstration of the nuclear bomb be made in an isolated area; it was made public after the bombing at the urging of Rabinovitch, who wanted the American population to know that crucial issues concerning nuclear arms had been discussed by the committee. The version released at that time (which André Trocmé read) contained many official deletions.

10 Trocmé *Archives*.

11 In October 1962, the USSR sought to install medium-range nuclear missiles in Cuba, not far from the US coast, and pointed in its direction. Fidel Castro was initially reluctant to agree to this plan and warned Khrushchev that he should not attempt to transport the missiles in secret. As Castro expected, President Kennedy was informed that medium-range missile sites had been seen by U-2 pilots flying over Cuba. Kennedy considered using diplomatic channels but eventually decided to make a public announcement. On 22 October, he announced the US blockade in response to the presence of missiles in Cuba. Khrushchev had been told ahead of time that Kennedy would be making a speech but did not know what he would say. Fearing an American invasion of Cuba, he ordered Soviet forces in Cuba to use all weapons available, except atomic weapons, in the case of an attack. By 27 October, still unclear about Kennedy's full intentions, Khrushchev decided to withdraw the missiles and offered Kennedy terms, including a promise that the US would not invade Cuba and would remove its own nuclear missiles from Turkey.

12 André Trocmé delivered this sermon at the Saint-Gervais church on 11 November 1962. It was broadcast by the French-language Swiss radio network, Radio Suisse romande. Trocmé *Archives*.

CHAPTER 10

1 *Mémoires*, 515.

2 This text was published in the *Cahiers de la réconciliation* (July–August 1954).

3 This article was published in *Cahiers de la réconciliation* (May 1955).

4 The letter was sent by the Fédération protestante de France on 23 November 1958.

5 Reverend Étienne Mathiot was tried in March 1958 and sentenced to eight months in prison for giving refuge to one of the French leaders of the FLN (an Algerian nationalist organization) in his home and then smuggling him into Switzerland.

6 French troops bombed the village of Sakhiet Sidi Youssef, in Tunisia, on 8 February 1958. The bombing is commemorated in Tunisia and Algeria every year.

7 Gamal Abdel Nasser was the second president of Egypt from 1956 until his death in 1970. He was one of the leaders of the Egyptian Revolution of 1952, which overthrew the monarchy of Egypt and Sudan and introduced a period of reform, modernization, and pan-Arab nationalism.

8 Trocmé *Archives*.

9 As resident minister and governor-general, Robert Lacoste (1898–1989) represented the French government in Algeria from 1956 to 1958 before returning to politics in France in 1962. Jacques Massu (1908–2002) was the brigadier-general who led the troops in the Battle of Algiers. He was promoted after the victory of France.

10 André Trocmé published this article in the *Cahiers de la réconciliation* (May 1962).

11 Mark 2:3–4: And they come unto him, bringing one sick of the palsy, which was borne of four. And when they could not come nigh unto him for the press, they uncovered the roof where he was: and when they had broken it up, they let down the bed wherein the sick of the palsy lay.

12 The Armée de libération nationale, an Algerian independence group.

13 Trocmé *Archives*.

14 Ibid.

CHAPTER 11

1 In a sermon entitled "What I have, I give to you," at his church in Saint-Gervais on 15 February 1970, André said: "What you are asked to do is not to carry the entire world on your shoulders, but to carry one person. After all, you are only a person. A person can only carry a single person. No one has the strength to do more than that. Each of us is just one individual. We cannot dream of revolutions, changes, transformations. If we are aware of our own responsibili-

ties, we are able to take charge of the life of one individual. But in that case, let us make sure we are truly taking charge of that one person." Trocmé *Archives*.

2 Trocmé *Archives*.

3 Ibid.

4 Ibid.

5 This sermon was given at the Saint-Gervais Church in Geneva on 26 July 1964. It is based on Genesis 32: 7–14 and Luke 13: 1–17. Trocmé *Archives*.

6 Trocmé *Archives*.

7 On 31 October 1517, the Augustinian monk Martin Luther posted on the door of the chapel of the Wittenberg Castle his "Disputation on the Power and Efficacy of Indulgences," commonly known as the "95 Theses." This protest marked the beginning of the Protestant Reformation. In some Protestant churches it is traditional to commemorate "Reformation Day" on the Sunday closest to 31 October.

8 Trocmé *Archives*.

9 Jules Isaac (1877–1963) was a university professor and a school inspector. He founded, with Edmond Fleg, the Amitié judéo-chrétienne. He wrote several books and made a significant contribution to dialogue between Jews and Christians and to the struggle against anti-Semitism. On 3 May 1964, André Trocmé was invited by the mayor of Florence to take part in a posthumous tribute to Jules Isaac, at which he shared his deep admiration for Isaac's unfailing commitment to education and to understanding.

10 André Trocmé delivered this sermon at the Saint-Gervais Church on 7 December 1969. References are to Mark 1:15, Isaiah 2: 1–4 and Galatians 4:4–7. Trocmé *Archives*.

11 Trocmé *Archives*.

12 This text was later published in the *Bulletin de la communauté protestante de l'hôpital*, a hospital newsletter, in May of 1977.

13 The words of Jesus on the cross, addressed to one of the two malefactors crucified at the same time. (Luke 23:43).

14 Luke 23:34.

15 *Autobiographie*, 53, 56, and 57. This passage is dated 23 May 1976.

Index